THE POLITICS (AND RECONCIL SOUTH AFRICA

Legitimizing the Post-Apartheid State

The South African Truth and Reconciliation Commission (TRC) was set up to deal with the human rights violations of apartheid during the years 1960–1994. However, as Wilson shows, the TRC's restorative justice approach to healing the nation did not always serve the needs of communities at a local level. Based on extended anthropological fieldwork, this book illustrates the impact of the TRC in urban African communities in the Johannesburg area. While a religious constituency largely embraced the Commission's religious-redemptive language of reconciliation, Wilson argues that the TRC had little effect on popular ideas of justice as retribution. This provocative study deepens our understanding of post-apartheid South Africa and the use of human rights discourse. It ends on a call for more cautious and realistic expectations about what human rights institutions can achieve in democratizing countries.

RICHARD A. WILSON is a Senior Lecturer in Social Anthropology at the University of Sussex. He has written numerous articles on political violence and human rights and is editor of the journal *Anthropological Theory*. He is also the author of *Maya Resurgence in Guatemala* (1995), and editor of *Human Rights, Culture and Context* (1997) and *Culture and Rights* (Cambridge University Press, 2001).

CAMBRIDGE STUDIES IN LAW AND SOCIETY

The broad area of law and society has become a remarkably rich and dynamic field of study. At the same time, the social sciences have increasingly engaged with questions of law. In this process, the borders between legal scholarship and the social, political and cultural sciences have been transcended, and the result is a time of fundamental rethinking both within and about law. In this vital period, Cambridge Studies in Law and Society provides a significant new book series with an international focus and a concern with the global transformation of the legal arena. The series aims to publish the best scholarly work on legal discourse and practice in social context, combining theoretical insights and empirical research.

Already published:

Anthony Woodiwiss *Globalisation, Human Rights and Labour Law in Pacific Asia*
0 521 62144 5 hardback 0 521 62883 0 paperback
Mariana Valverde *Diseases of the Will: Alcoholism and the Dilemmas of Freedom*
0 521 62300 6 hardback 0 521 64469 0 paperback
Alan Hunt *Governing Morals: A Social History of Moral Regulation*
0 521 64071 7 hardback 0 521 64689 8 paperback
Ronen Shamir *The Colonies of Law: Colonialism, Zionism and Law in Early Mandate Palestine*
0 521 63183 1 hardback
John Torpey *The Invention of the Passport: Surveillance, Citizenship and the State*
0 521 63249 8 hardback 0 521 63493 8 paperback
William Walters *Unemployment and Government: Genealogies of the Social*
0 521 64333 3 hardback
Christopher Arup *The New World Trade Organization Agreements: Globalizing Law Through Services and Intellectual Property*
0 521 77355 5 hardback
Heinz Klug *Constituting Democracy: Law, Globalism and South Africa's Political Reconstruction*
0 521 78113 2 hardback 0 521 78643 6 paperback
Yash Ghai (ed.) *Autonomy and Ethnicity: Negotiating Competing Claims in Multi-ethnic States*
0 521 78112 4 hardback 0 521 78642 8 paperback
Eric Feldman *The Ritual of Rights in Japan: Law, Society, and Health Policy*
0 521 77040 8 hardback 0 521 77964 2 paperback
Peter Fitzpatrick *Modernism and the Grounds of Law*
0 521 80222 9 hardback 0 521 00253 2 paperback

To Thomas, born in the middle of it all.

THE POLITICS OF TRUTH AND RECONCILIATION IN SOUTH AFRICA

Legitimizing the Post-Apartheid State

Richard A. Wilson
University of Sussex

CAMBRIDGE
UNIVERSITY PRESS

PUBLISHED BY THE PRESS SYNDICATE OF THE UNIVERSITY OF CAMBRIDGE
The Pitt Building, Trumpington Street, Cambridge, United Kingdom

CAMBRIDGE UNIVERSITY PRESS
The Edinburgh Building, Cambridge CB2 2RU, UK
40 West 20th Street, New York, NY 10011–4211, USA
477 Williamstown Road, Port Melbourne, Victoria 3207, Australia
Ruiz de Alarcón 13, 28014, Madrid, Spain
Dock House, The Waterfront, Cape Town 8001, South Africa

http://www.cambridge.org

First published 2001
Reprinted 2002

Printed in China by Everbest Printing Co.

Typeface New Baskerville (*Adobe*) 10/12 pt. *System* QuarkXPress® [BC]

A catalogue record for this book is available from the British Library

National Library of Australia Cataloguing in Publication data
Wilson, Richard A., 1964– .
The politics of truth and reconciliation in South Africa:
legitimizing the post-apartheid state.
Bibliography.
Includes index.
ISBN 0 521 00194 3 (pbk.).
ISBN 0 521 80219 9.
1. South Africa. Truth and Reconciliation Commission.
2. Political violence – South Africa. 3. South Africa –
Politics and government. 4. South Africa – Race relations.
I. Title.
968.065

ISBN 0 521 80219 9 hardback
ISBN 0 521 00194 3 paperback

CONTENTS

ACRONYMS AND GLOSSARY

AC	Amnesty Committee of the TRC
ANC	African National Congress
ANCYL	ANC Youth League
AWB	Afrikaner Weerstandsbeweging (Afrikaner Resistance Movement)
AZAPO	Azanian People's Organization
BRAC	Boipatong Residents Against Crime
CODESA	Convention for a Democratic South Africa
COSATU	Congress of South African Trade Unions
CPF	Community Policing Forum
DP	Democratic Party
GNU	Government of National Unity
HRVC	Human Rights Violations Committee of the TRC
HRV Hearings	Human Rights Violations hearings of the TRC
ICC	International Criminal Court
IFP	Inkatha Freedom Party
Imbizo	Meeting or court (Zulu)
Infocomm	Information Management System of the TRC
ISCOR	Iron and Steel Corporation (Vaal)
IU	Investigative Unit of the TRC
Kgotla	Meeting or court (Sesotho); plural *lekgotla*
Khulumani	'Speak out' Survivor's support group
MDM	Mass Democratic Movement
MK	Umkhonto we Sizwe (ANC armed wing)
MP	Member of Parliament
NCPS	National Crime Prevention Strategy
NGO	Non-governmental organization
NP	National Party
NSMS	National Security Management System
NPA	National Peace Accord
NUMSA	National Union of Mineworkers of South Africa
NURA	National Unity and Reconciliation Act (1995)
PAC	Pan Africanist Congress
PAGAD	People Against Gangsterism and Drugs

RRC	Reparation and Rehabilitation Committee of the TRC
SAIRR	South African Institute of Race Relations
SABC	South African Broadcasting Company
SACC	South African Council of Churches
SACP	South African Communist Party
SADF	South African Defense Force (apartheid)
SANCO	South African National Civics Organization
SANDF	South African National Defense Force (post-apartheid)
SAP	South African Police (apartheid)
SAPS	South African Police Service (post-apartheid)
SDU	Special Defence Unit (ANC)
SPU	Special Protection Unit (IFP)
SSC	State Security Council
STRATCOM	Strategic Communications
TRC	Truth and Reconciliation Commission
Ubuntu	Humanity, personhood, mutuality
UDF	United Democratic Front
ZCC	Zionist Christian Church

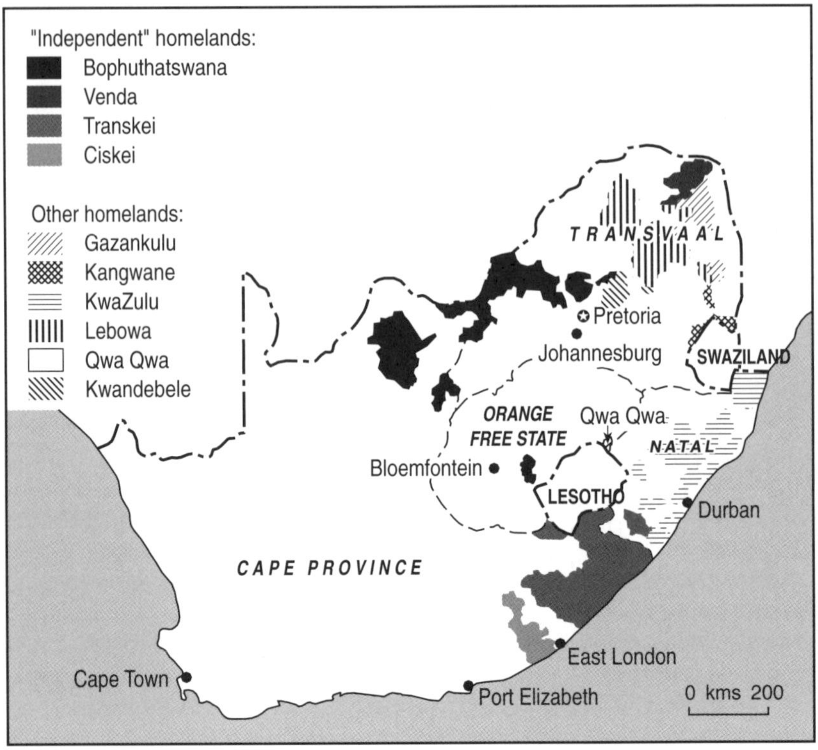

Map 1 Pre-1994 South Africa: The homelands

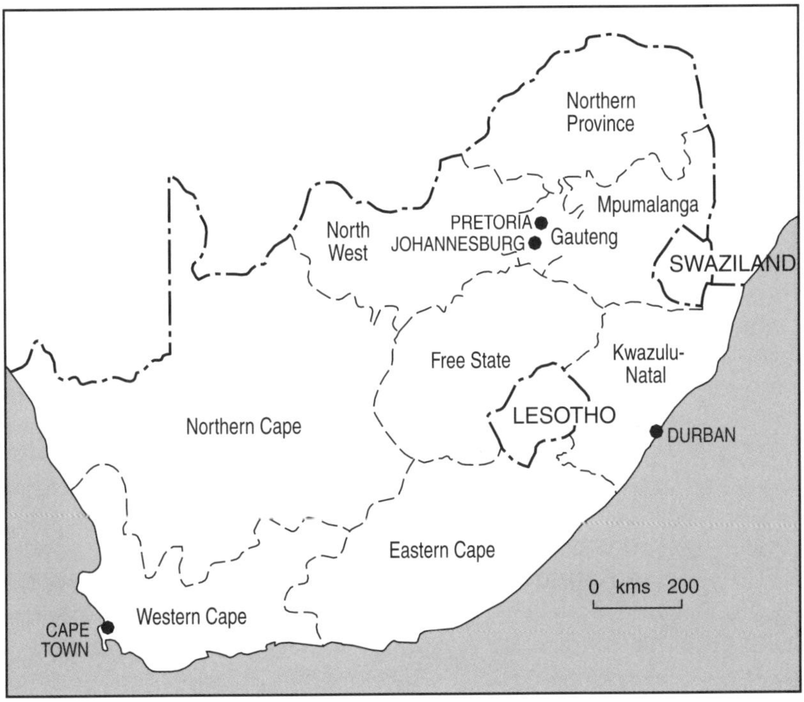

Map 2 Post-1994 South Africa: Provinces of the Republic

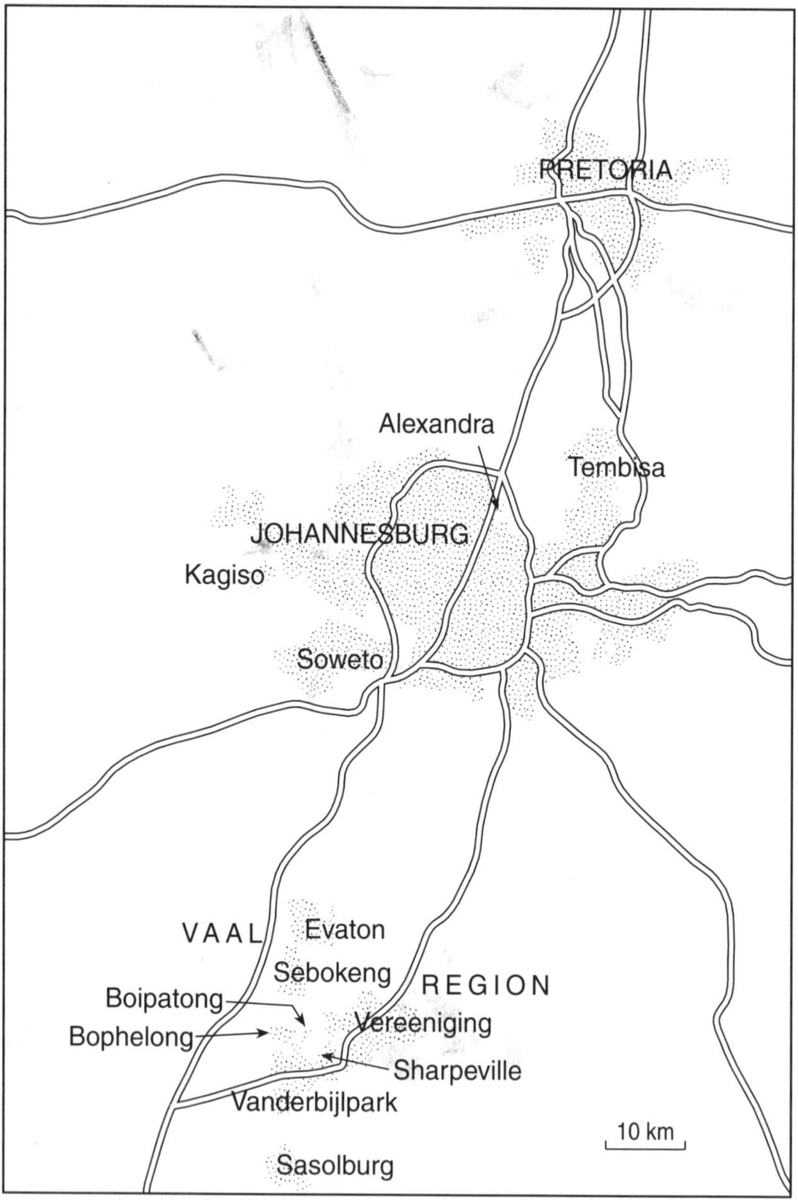

Map 3 Johannesburg and the Vaal Region

PREFACE AND ACKNOWLEDGEMENTS

In democratizing countries of Latin America from the mid-1980s and Eastern Europe from 1989, the language of human rights emerged as a universal panacea to authoritarianism. Human rights were demanded by ordinary citizens massed in the squares of Leipzig or on the streets of Bisho, and they became symptomatic of the kind of 'procedural' liberalism established in post-authoritarian states.[1] Human rights based legislation became a central component in the transformation of repressive institutions and in the establishing of the rule of law after the distortions of authoritarian legality. Each society had to face the question of how to deal with the gross human rights violations of the past, and new institutions and commissions were set up to reaffirm human dignity and to ensure that violations would not occur again. Increasingly, human rights talk was detached from its strictly legal foundations and became a generalized moral and political discourse to speak about power relations between individuals, social groups and states. This broad extension of human rights talk was exacerbated as democratizing regimes with crumbling economies and fractured social orders grasped for unifying metaphors, and human rights talk seemed to provide an ideological adhesive through terms such as 'truth' and 'reconciliation'.

By the 1990s, it was time to take stock and to evaluate critically the role of human rights ideas and institutions in democratic transitions. It became possible to move on from simply extolling human rights to examining what happened when human rights institutions were established in complicated contexts of political compromise, where neither opposing side in a civil war had won an outright military victory, where key perpetrators of the era of repression (from Vice-President F W de Klerk in South Africa to Senator Augusto Pinochet in Chile) still occupied positions of political power and where the former bureaucracies of death (especially the criminal justice system and security forces) were still staffed by personnel from the authoritarian era.

In the literature on democratization, liberal visions of 'democratic consolidation' often adopted a model-building and technicist tone.[2] 'Transitology' attempts to isolate the variables that reinforce or undermine democratic consolidation and build universal mechanistic models that treat democratization as if it were a matter of correctly arranging pieces of a puzzle. Transition theory in mainstream political science often accepted a minimalist liberal understanding of democracy as indicated by constitutions enshrining individual civil rights, political party competition and periodic elections.

The establishing of a bare functioning minimum is not to be lightly dismissed, as it was an important objective of the struggles of opposition and dissident movements. Yet this book emphasizes a more sociological standpoint which places justice in transition in the context of nation-building and a hegemonic project of state formation. A focus upon how the rule of law is established and maintained must be complemented by an analysis of the concrete ideological and administrative difficulties which new regimes found themselves in. This requires a greater awareness of how new regimes used human rights to re-imagine the nation by constructing new official histories, and how they sought to manufacture legitimacy for key state institutions such as the criminal justice system.

Human rights discourses and institutions in South Africa such as the Truth and Reconciliation Commission, Human Rights Commission and the Commission for Gender Equality are central to creating a new moral and cultural leadership, that is to say, a new hegemony. This new hegemony is initially asserted in relation to accountability of past state crimes and whether to punish and/or pardon previous human rights violations. The study of transitional truth and justice has been too dominated by philosophical discussions abstracted from specific contexts, and we should instead examine how the politics of punishment and the writing of a new official memory are central to state strategies to create a new hegemony in the area of justice and construct the present moment as post-authoritarian when it includes many elements of the past.

In South Africa, human rights talk became ever more compromised as it was dragooned by an emergent bureaucratic elite into the service of nation-building. Ostensibly, the language of rights represented a departure from old ethno-nationalist models of nationalism with their romantic images of blood and land. Post-authoritarian nation-building, in contrast, appealed to civic nationalism as the new basis for moral integration and a redefined conception of nation. Yet this process of nation-building also had its normative injunctions and included elements of moral coercion. The constitution and subsequent legislation deprived victims of their right to justice and retributive justice was defined as 'un-African' by some, such as former Archbishop Desmond Tutu. Human rights became the language of restorative justice and forgiveness of human rights offenders in South Africa, whereas at the same time in international contexts, human rights were developing in just the opposite (punitive) direction with the creation of an International Criminal Court and the prosecutions brought by the UN war crimes tribunal for the former Yugoslavia and Rwanda.

There were some unintended consequences of the reliance upon human rights talk for nation-building and state centralization. Due to amnesty laws and a lack of prosecutions of human rights offenders, the high expectations expressed in human rights talk by both politicians and citizens were left unfulfilled, as transitional institutions seemed to protect perpetrators more than they fulfilled victims' hopes for justice and reparation. Human rights came not to represent ideal and inviolable principles (such as justice for victims and punishment for offenders), but instead expressed the problematical nature of the elite-pacted political settlement. The new promises of the constitutional order outstretched the capacity of the legal system, as human rights were enshrined in the Constitution that were unrealizable by the majority of impoverished black citizens. Given the yawning gap between human rights ideals and the grim realities of criminal justice delivery, the conditions were ripe for a crisis of legitimacy. Rather than resolving the crisis of legal institutions, human rights talk came to symbolically epitomize the legitimation crisis of post-authoritarian justice. Finally, the place of human rights talk in a project of legal unification and centralization brought them into conflict with local justice institutions and popular legal consciousness in a legally plural setting.

These reflections on human rights institutions in democratization processes urge us to look beyond the formal, legalistic and normative dimensions of human rights, where they will always be a 'good thing'. A sociology or ethnography of rights will look instead at how rights are transformed, deformed, appropriated and resisted by state and societal actors when inserted into a particular historical and political context. This shifts our attention away from the transcendent moral philosophy of rights to a rigorous examination of the history and social life of rights.

This book results from a twelve-month ethnographic study (over a four-year period) inside and outside of one of the main human rights institutions in transitional South Africa – the Truth and Reconciliation Commission (TRC). During this time I was a lecturer and visiting associate in the anthropology department at the University of the Witwatersrand in Johannesburg. My research started in 1995, before the TRC began functioning, and continued into 1996–7, while it was in full swing; it ended in late 1998 after the main regional offices had been closed. I attended three weeks of Human Rights Violations hearings in

Klerksdorp, Tembisa and Kagiso and three weeks of amnesty hearings for Northern Province security policemen in Johannesburg. I interviewed nearly half of all the TRC Commissioners, the TRC executive secretary, and many staff workers, such as lawyers, researchers and investigators. I would also include as 'research' the conference evaluating the TRC which I co-organized with Merle Lipton at the University of Sussex in September 1998, which included a TRC Commissioner, members of the Research Unit and Investigative Unit and a former judge of the Constitutional Court of South Africa.

Much of my research, however, took place outside the TRC process and concentrated on the impact of the TRC on the African townships of the Vaal region to the south of Johannesburg. In the Vaal, I carried out in-depth interviews with over 50 victims of political violence, many of them members of the Khulumani Support Group, as well as local religious personnel, local court officials, political leaders, legal activists and policemen. In the beginning, my contacts were mainly aligned to the African National Congress, but as time went on I actively sought out leaders and ordinary members of minority parties such as the Pan Africanist Congress and the Inkatha Freedom Party. I also tried to glean views from those who were not aligned with any political tradition at all. As for 'perpetrators', it is worth pointing out that some of my 'victim' informants were also implicated in acts of public violence during the apartheid era. Only a few were willing to speak openly about their involvement in such acts, but I did interview three Inkatha Freedom Party members who had been convicted in the courts for their participation in the 1992 Boipatong massacre, as well as a policeman representing amnesty applications from within the Vaal police force, and an Amnesty Committee investigator of the TRC for the Vaal region. Finally, my interviews in the Vaal were complemented by several weeks' archival work in the William Cullen Library, which holds many useful historical records of human rights monitors such as Peace Action and the Independent Board of Inquiry which worked in the Vaal in the late 1980s and early 1990s.

Truth commissions are now standard post-conflict structures set up in over seventeen countries in the last 20 years to investigate unresolved cases arising from past human rights violations.[3] As one strand of the globalization of human rights, they have taken on a transnational validity as one of the main mechanisms for announcing a new democratic order. Truth commissions have fascinated international audiences and led to a voluminous literature acclaiming their promises of truth and restoration, mostly from law, political science and moral philosophy. The South African truth commission, as the largest and most ambitious in scope, is perhaps the zenith of this trajectory, and has attracted the most attention and discussion so far. The literature evaluating the achievements of truth commissions has mostly been positive and laudatory, claiming these commissions heal the nation by providing therapy for a traumatized national psyche. They break a regime of official denial of atrocities by ending the public silence on violence and violations. They expose the excesses of the previous political order and so discredit it, aiding in democratic consolidation. In Latin America, where disappearances were more widespread, they revealed the fate of the disappeared and led to exhumations of clandestine mass graves.

This book concentrates on the two main functions of the South African Truth and Reconciliation Commission: truth-telling about the apartheid past and the reconciliation of 'the nation'. The TRC Report published in 1998 on the gross human rights violations of a 34-year period provided a valuable starting point for discussions about moral responsibility during that era. However, the TRC's account of the past was constrained by its excessive legalism[4] and positivist methodology, which obstructed the writing of a coherent socio-political history of apartheid.

The TRC worked with many different understandings of reconciliation, but one came to dominate in the dozens of televised Human Rights Violations hearings held around the country. The religious-redemptive vision of reconciliation stressed public confession by victims, and it created meaning for suffering through a narrative of sacrifice for liberation. Finally, it encouraged the forsaking of revenge. Chapters 5 to 8 examine the consequences of the TRC's version of reconciliation for individual victims who appeared at hearings and others outside the TRC process in the African townships of Johannesburg. In many of these urban townships, political strife was ongoing during the period of fieldwork (1995–8), and it was possible to see the effect of the TRC on these conflicts.

At this point the book begins to shift its focus away from the TRC towards the surrounding social context, in order to evaluate the impact of human rights using ethnographic methods. This approach follows in the tradition of legal anthropology, documenting the moralities, discourses and everyday practices of ordinary citizens when they engage in rights processes and institutions. The TRC's language of 'reconciliation' elicited a variety of local responses and most could be placed in three categories: adductive affinities, where local values and human rights overlap and reinforce one another; pragmatic proceduralism, where survivors participate in human rights procedures to pursue their own agendas and without necessarily taking on human rights values; and relational discontinuities, where local actors are resistant to a restorative vision of human rights and assert a more retributive model of justice.

The variety of responses among the main ANC-supporting township constituency of the TRC demonstrates how human rights institutions are caught in a web of centralizing and pluralizing strategies simultaneously. Human rights talk is a contested discourse which draws popular legal consciousness closer to that of the state, while at the same time encountering resistance from localized organizations and moralities which assert the autonomous right to define and enforce justice. One of the main results of my ethnographic inquiries was the centrality of emotions of vengeance in popular legal consciousness and practices of revenge in local justice institutions. Despite the existence of many rarified national institutions dedicated to protecting human rights (not only the TRC, but also the Gender Commission, the Constitutional Court and the Human Rights Commission), enclaves of revenge controlled by militarized youth and punitive elders continued to shape the character of justice in the townships of South Africa. Because it was guided by a religious-redemptive notion of reconciliation, the TRC was never able to engage with, much less transform, these emotions and structures.

Understanding why the TRC struggled to accomplish its stated mission of 'reconciling the nation' requires a historical explanation which locates the TRC in a history of legal pluralism in South Africa in the twentieth century. The work of the TRC was shaped by the history of state attempts to consolidate the administration of justice and attempts by Africans to preserve control over local institutions of justice and social order. The racialized and dual legal system consolidated in the twentieth century led to a fracturing of justice and moralities which endured after the first multi-racial elections in 1994. The persistence of legal pluralism is closely linked to the historical failure to create a South African nation, reminding us of the concrete links between nation-building and state-building.

Instead of succumbing to state attempts at centralization, urban African residents continued to use local justice institutions to create social order in conditions of urbanization, industrialization and mass migration from rural areas. In the new South Africa, human rights talk was inserted into a context of a massive crime wave, profound social and economic inequality and disillusionment with ineffective criminal justice institutions. Human rights thus emerge as part of a pragmatic policy of state-building and centralization of justice in a milieu where state legality is still often perceived by township residents to be external and alien to the 'community'.

An ethnography of human rights evaluates new institutions of the nation-state 'from below' and compels us to understand them from a position of institutional fragmentation and legal pluralism. In concrete terms, it draws our attention to how human rights institutions and discourses in the 'new South Africa' have often failed to connect with local moralities and justice institutions and thereby transform them. As we come to realize that the new 'culture of human rights' is very thin indeed, we may need to temper celebrations of another seeming triumph for the model of liberal human rights. In a comparative perspective, the new human rights institutions of post-apartheid South Africa are impressive for their ability to shape the public debate on truth and reconciliation. It remains to be seen whether they have altered, over the long term, concrete social practices and discourses of violent conflict, justice and punishment.

ACKNOWLEDGEMENTS

This research was funded by two grants from the Economic and Social Research Council (UK) and an academic exchange funded by the British Council. It would not have been possible without the advice and assistance of many people in South Africa, including André du Toit, Patrick Kelly, Piers Pigou, Fiona Ross and Gerald O'Sullivan. Thanks are due to those at the University of the Witwatersrand between 1995 and 1999; Belinda Bozzoli, Carolyn Hamilton, Deborah James, Justine Lucas, Sakkie Niehaus, Joanne Pannell, Patrick Pearson, Robert Thornton, and Linda Waldman. In particular, Elsa van Huyssteen was a tolerant listener and constructive critic. At the Center for the Study of Violence and Reconciliation, I thank Brandon Hamber and Hugo van der Merwe. From the Khulumani Victims Support Group, I am grateful for the valuable help of Maggie Friedman and the late Sylvia Dhlomo-Jele. In the Vaal, my warm appreciation goes to Magouwsi Motau, 'Oupa' Tsoabisi and especially to Duma Khumalo, my main Vaal contact, drinking partner and merciless adversary on the chess board. During writing, I benefited from conversations with Jocelyn Alexander, Patrick Ball, Andy Carl, Jane Cowan, Marie-Bénédicte Dembour, David Dyzenhaus, Thomas Hylland Eriksen, Ralph Grillo, Stewart Lansley, Merle Lipton, Shula Marks and Neil Stammers. Saul Dubow provided experienced advice on the literature and incisive commentary on parts of the text. None of these people are responsible for any errors of fact or interpretation in the book, and some will undoubtedly disagree with aspects of the argument. At Cambridge University Press, my thanks are to Martin Chanock, Sharon Mullins and Paul Watt, also to Jean Cooney. Finally, Helene Kvale read many chapters and condoned my long absences, but most importantly encouraged me to pursue this whole new venture.

CHAPTER 1

HUMAN RIGHTS AND NATION-BUILDING

THE CIVIC STATE VERSUS ETHNO-NATIONALISM

The quest to build a 'culture of human rights' in South Africa after the multi-racial elections of 1994 needs to be understood in the context of a sea-change in global politics, and the rise of human rights as the archetypal language of democratic transition. A revived language of liberal democracy became increasingly prevalent in the mid-1980s, and was accentuated by the demise of the former Soviet Bloc and the rise of ethno-nationalist conflict in the Balkans. Since 1990, nearly all transitions from authoritarian rule have adopted the language of human rights and the political model of constitutionalism,[1] especially in Latin America and the new states of Eastern Europe.[2]

The end of the Cold War and the threat of irredentist nationalism led many intellectuals in Europe from a variety of political traditions to promote human rights and a return to the Enlightenment project. Among them, those as recondite as Jürgen Habermas (1992), as erudite as Julia Kristeva (1993) and as media-friendly as Michael Ignatieff (1993) advocated the establishment of constitutionalist states based upon the rule of law. All converge on the view that nations must not be constituted on the basis of race, ethnicity, language or religion, but should be founded instead on a 'community of equal, rights-bearing citizens, united in patriotic attachment to a shared set of political practices and values' (Ignatieff 1993:3–4). In this formulation, human rights are portrayed as the antithesis of nationalist modes of nation-building.

Habermas made one of the most influential constitutionalist statements of the 1990s in his paper 'Citizenship and National Identity' (1992). Here, he sees political change in Eastern Europe as having restored an older Enlightenment political tradition and recaptured the language of rights. Rights must do a great deal in Habermas' formulations: they underwrite an Aristotelian conception of participatory citizenship; they create a barrier to the totalitarian pretensions of states; and they resolve the awkward relationship between citizenship and nationalism:

> The meaning of the term 'nation' thus changed from designating a pre-political entity to something that was supposed to play a constitutive role in defining the political identity of the citizen within a democratic polity. The nation of citizens does not derive its identity from some common ethnic and cultural properties, but rather from the praxis of citizens who actively exercise their civil rights. At this juncture, the republican strand of 'citizenship' *completely parts company* with the idea of belonging to a pre-political community integrated on the basis of descent, a shared tradition and a common language [my emphasis]. (1992:3)[3]

Habermas' aim is to recover a republican tradition of rights from the grasp of the nationalist traditions which once seemed to own it. In his formulation, the rule of law and the 'praxis of citizenship' transcend nationalism in its cultural and tradition-bound form. The allure of rights in the post-Cold War era is that they prescribe basic human rights as an antidote to ethnic nationalism. As Ignatieff states: 'According to the civic nationalist creed, what holds society together is not common roots but law' (1993:4). The concrete practice of claiming citizenship rights creates a political culture which displaces ethnic nationalism and deflects the romantic politics of ethnicity, culture, community or tradition.

Constitutionalist discourse among political commentators within South Africa bears a close resemblance to its European counterpart. South African constitutionalists also see democracy as the antithesis of any sort of nationalist project, which is associated solely with the previous apartheid state.[4] Supporters of constitutionalism argue that an overarching moral unity cannot be achieved through cultural symbols since there is no 'ethnic core' in South Africa around which an overarching ethno-nationalism could be built, even if this were desirable. Instead of creating unity and identity out of cultural nationalism, the state should create a culture of rights based upon an inclusive and democratic notion of citizenship.

Some South African writers have gone a step further than their European colleagues by arguing that human rights should not be a form of nation-building at all. They argue that nation-building is not a guarantee of democracy, and they point to the failure of nation-building in other parts of Africa and the checkered history of nationalism in Europe. Instead of nation-building, they encourage the state to build legitimate and representative state institutions which respect fundamental human rights. Rather than attempting to build a nation, the new regime should build a working constitutional democracy so as to replace destructive nationalist sentiments with constitutional patriotism to a civic state. Fundamental rights and their protection by state institutions are an alternative to nationalism, but they perform similar functions – by creating national reconciliation and a sense of belonging and unity.[5]

National identity unfolds not through ancient symbols but through the practice of claiming basic rights. As Johan Degenaar wrote: 'In one sense we can still speak of the nation as the congruence of culture and power, but now culture has shifted from a communal culture to a democratic culture' (1990:12). South African constitutionalists were generally quite confident that the constitutionalist state would enjoy legitimacy and this would lead to a civic national identity. Over time, as the Bill of Rights, backed up by the legal system and Constitutional Court, protects citizens in a neutral manner, then a national consciousness and sense of belonging will emerge 'naturally' over time.[6]

Finally, human rights have the capacity to resist the limitation of rights to any one group of people; that is, they are seen as pan-ethnic, and irreducible to forms of ethnic particularism. The individualism of human rights chimes with the Charterist non-racialism professed by the ruling African National Congress[7] which won the 1994 and 1999 elections. Both political philosophies assume South Africa to be a society of individual citizens, not a society of racial communities with group representation and minority rights.

LEGAL IDEOLOGY AND NATION-STATES

My reservations about constitutionalism concern its sociological blindness to the pressures forcing transitional regimes to pursue a program of bureaucratic legitimization. Constitutionalists usually assume that national manifestations of human rights will remain true to their international orthodoxy, but instead human rights are dramatically redefined to suit national political constraints.

In the years following the first multi-racial elections there was a remarkable degree of consensus in elite circles that popular conceptions of democracy could be channeled into building a constitutional state based upon a bill of rights and the power of judicial review. Within this line of thought, there was a worrying unanimity of opinion that a constitutionalist project could be wholly distinct from expressions of 'pre-political' nationalism. Against this view, it will be argued that constitutionalism, state-building and the creation of what is a termed a 'culture of human rights' cannot be separated so easily from classic, communitarian forms of nation-building. Instead, human rights were subjected to the imperatives of nation-building and state formation in the 'New South Africa'.

Thesis

Political scientists writing on constitutionalism often operate with a set of over-rigid dichotomies; between nationalism and constitutionalism, between political society and civil society, and between the social processes involved in constructing a 'state of rights' and ethno-nationalist versions of culture. This means that they are often blind to how human rights talk is integrated into the nation-building project. Human rights talk does not, in the earlier phrase of Habermas, 'completely part company' with nationalist understandings of community. To the contrary, human rights talk has become a dominant form of ideological legitimization for new nation-building projects in the context of constitutionalism and procedural liberalism. Nation-building is not an end in itself, but a way to engender the necessary pre-conditions for governance. By contributing to the construction of a new notion of the 'rainbow nation', human rights advance certain pressing imperatives of the post-authoritarian state, namely the legitimization of state institutions and institutional centralization in the context of legal pluralism (which is explored in Part II).

Some constitutionalist conceptions of rights can involve a certain legal fetishism in that they often rely upon a conception of law as pristine and unsullied by surrounding discourses on culture, ethnicity and nationalism. This is apparent in recent debates on the character of judicial decision-making of Constitutional Court judges, between literal approaches aligned with Joseph Raz and interpretive frameworks influenced by Ronald Dworkin. A literal reading of legal texts such as the Constitution, has, for commentators such as Dennis Davis (1998:128), resurrected legal positivism in the South African context.[8] The main advocate of an ordinary-language approach to judicial decision-making, Anton Fagan (1995), draws upon Joseph Raz to say that legal texts are the source of all rules and that judges must do no more than give the text its ordinary meaning. Fagan advocates an apolitical vision of law as made up of universal and timeless principles where law is insulated from societal moralities, since moral reasoning must be guided solely by the moral position inherent in positive rules. Dennis Davis (1998) draws upon Ronald Dworkin to reject eloquently these positivist claims and states a political view of law close to the one being endorsed here:

> My argument is that there is no single meaning within the text and that the limits to meaning are not only imposed by the language chosen to be contained in the text but also in terms of legal and linguistic conventions, themselves informed by politics. Constitutional law is politics by a different means but it remains a form of politics. (p. 142)

Contrary to the myth of legal neutrality, the law is always a form of politics by other means, as it is normative as well as merely formal, rational and self-referential. Legal meaning is enmeshed in wider value systems, and is caught between other competing normative discourses which are political, cultural, and more often than not, nationalist.[9]

Against a view of law as a value-free process, legal ideology is a form of domination in the Weberian sense which is embedded in historically constituted relations of social inequality. In a legally plural context, as in South Africa where there are many competing justice institutions (such as township courts, armed vigilantes and customary courts), state law is one semi-open system of prescriptive norms backed by a coercive apparatus. If we conceive of law as an ideological system through which power has historically been mediated and exercised, then in a society where power is organized around racial/ethnic and national identities, we can expect rights talk also to be ensnared by culturalist and nationalist discourses. Constitutionalists hoped that a culturally-neutral Bill of Rights would transcend particularistic nationalist ideology, but in practice the reverse is often the case: rights are subordinated to nation-building.

HUMAN RIGHTS IN THE NEGOTIATIONS

In order to understand fully how human rights became enmeshed within a wider South African nation-building project, we have to look at the rise of human rights talk in the peace process between the years 1985 and 1994.[10] During this period, human rights emerged as the unifying language to cement the two main protagonists in the conflict: the ruling National Party (NP)[11] and the African National Congress (ANC). Human rights talk became the language not of principle but of pragmatic compromise, seemingly able to incorporate any moral or ideological position. The ideological promiscuity of human rights talk meant that it was ill-suited to fulfil the role of an immovable bulwark against ethnicity and identity politics. Because of its role in the peace negotiations, human rights talk came to be seen less as the language of incorruptible principles and more as a rhetorical expression of an all-inclusive rainbow nationalism.

By the end of the 1980s, the armed conflict between the anti-apartheid movement and the apartheid regime had reached a stalemate where neither side could annihilate the other. Key ANC leaders realized that a revolutionary victory could only be a pyrrhic one, where there would be little remaining of the country's infrastructure for building a new multiracial society. On the opposite side of the political spectrum, the rigid anti-Communist stance of the NP government began to soften after negotiations with the Soviet Union led to the withdrawal of Cuban troops in Angola and to an agreement on Namibian independence. The fall of the Berlin Wall further challenged the National Party elite to revise its ideological commitment to fighting the 'international Communist threat' which had for so long been the mantra to justify state repression. After the Cold War, authoritarian regimes across the South were coming under greater international pressure to liberalize.[12] Tentative talks between the government and opposition began in 1986 and gathered pace until they were formalized in 1991 in the Convention for a Democratic South Africa (CODESA) talks at Kempton Park, outside Johannesburg.

In the negotiations, constitutionalism emerged as the only viable political ethic that could bridge the chasm between seemingly incommensurable political traditions. The writing of the new Constitution at the Multi-Party Negotiating Process in 1993 functioned as a cement between the main actors. Despite the apparent discontinuities between National Party and anti-apartheid political thought, rights talk was indeterminate enough to suit the programs of both the NP and ANC, who came together to form a power-sharing arrangement. The ascendancy of human rights talk thus resulted from its inherent ambiguity, which allowed it to weld together diverse political constituencies. Constitutionalism became the compromise arrangement upon which the ANC and NP could agree a 'sufficient consensus'.[13]

During the negotiations, the NP was forced into significant concessions, notably to shift its position away from group rights to individual rights. Until late 1993, the NP had clung to an ideology of consociationalism which would entrench 'minority rights' through a compulsory coalition government. After the Record of Understanding[14] on 26 September 1992, liberal ideas of constitutionalism began to gain the upper hand over other strategies for power-sharing and 'group rights' for whites. The NP realized that a permanent white minority representation in government was not a realistic goal and the ANC would accept nothing less than a unitary state, full civil rights and majority rule.

The NP turned to a strategy of individual rights with liberal 'checks and balances' to secure the interests of a white minority and protect its economic and social privileges. The prospect of a political order based upon human rights reassured the business elite since they practically demanded a liberal political economy.[15] In the Bill of Rights of the 1993 interim Constitution,[16] classic individual rights (for example, of movement, free expression, and residence) are well entrenched, whereas those concerning socio-economic and welfare rights are weak and muted. The Constitution enshrined the right to private property and placed severe limitations on expropriation and nationalization.

The Left also went through its own Pauline conversion, with the social democratic current gaining preeminence over revolutionaries who had viewed rights with a Stalinist antinomianism.[17] In the late 1980s, many elements within the anti-apartheid movement espoused a 'people's war' in order to create a Soviet-style command economy. Rank and file activists as well as important leaders expressed cynicism towards a Bill of Rights, and Communist Party intellectual Joe Slovo wrote in 1985: 'In the South African context, we cannot restrict the struggle objectives to the bourgeois democratic concept of civil rights or democratic rights'.[18] (*Sechaba*, February)

Activists swung behind the constitutionalist position as the 1992 mass mobilization campaign fizzled out after several months. An awareness of the limitations of mass strategies led many activists in the ANC and South African Communist Party away from the insurrectionary seizure of power, thus marginalizing radicals and reinforcing the impetus for compromise and negotiation. The result, however, would be a very different kind of political order than the objective of popular democracy which many anti-apartheid activists had struggled for in the 1980s. Constitutionalism defines the law-government relationship in a specific way that is distinct from other models, such as straightforward Westminster parliamentary sovereignty. Constitutionalism places significant limitations on the exercise of governmental power, forcing legislation to comply with rules laid down in the Constitution as interpreted and enforced by the Constitutional Court.[19] Section 2 boldly states the supremacy of the Constitution: 'This Constitution is the supreme law of the Republic; law or conduct inconsistent with it is invalid, and the duties imposed by it must be performed.' However, according to section 74, the National Assembly can amend the Constitution if a bill has a two-thirds majority, and it has done so on numerous occasions since 1996.

The negotiations in 1991–3 leading to the new South African political order were among the most participatory and accountable seen in any recent transition from authoritarian rule. In the CODESA I and II talks, political parties and civil groups were able to intervene in significant ways in order to advance their agenda. The shape of the political system of the new South Africa (that is, the relationship between parliament and the Constitutional Court) and its economic structure (for example, whether private property should be protected in a Bill of Rights) were all hotly debated.

Yet the dilemma of how to deal with politically motivated human rights violations of the apartheid period was not subjected to the same process of democratic dialogue. In particular, the decision to grant amnesty to human rights offenders was eventually decided by an exclusive political deal between the NP and the ANC. The CODESA II talks did not address the issue[20] and outside the talks there was very little popular or open political party debate on amnesty. At the end of the Kempton Park negotiations on 17 November 1993, when all other issues were resolved and the interim Constitution was agreed, the question of amnesty was still outstanding. The National Party desperately wanted an amnesty, more so than the liberation movement which was in an advantageous position legally because of the two earlier Indemnity Acts.[21] At that point, Chief NP negotiator Roelf Meyer and ANC representative Cyril Ramaphosa mandated 'Mac' Maharaj (ANC) and Fanie van der Merwe (NP) of the negotiators' technical committee to draft a postscript to the Constitution[22] which would contain an amnesty clause. This occurred outside the official consultative process, in the hiatus between the end of the formal constitutional talks and the Constitution going to parliament in December 1993. NP negotiator Roelf Meyer reflected, 'At that point, there was just agreement that there should be an amnesty. There was a principle of agreement, but no details, apart from the point that both sides be given equal status. Apart from that, we left it up to the technical committee' (Personal interview, 16 February 1999).

The interim Constitution, with its last-minute postscript requiring an amnesty mechanism, went to parliament after 6 December 1993. There was never any open deliberation of the postscript at the plenary session of parliament, since it arose from a closed and secretive deal between the NP and ANC leaderships. Recognizing the exclusive character of the political deal done on amnesty is important as there is a strong moral argument that such an amnesty arrangement can only be entered into by victims themselves or their legitimate representatives and not by others on their behalf and with very little consultation.[23]

The statement on amnesty and reconciliation was criticized by smaller parties such as the Democratic Party, who denounced it as a cover-up pact. Roelf Meyer defends the exclusiveness of this process, saying, 'The Constitution wouldn't have gone through if the amnesty question had gone to other parties and through the consultation process at Kempton Park' (Personal interview, 16 February 1999).

The 1993 Constitution's postscript was titled, appropriately enough, 'National Unity and Reconciliation', as was the act passed in 1995 to establish the Truth and Reconciliation Commission (TRC). The Constitution's postscript explicitly rejected retribution and called for past injustices to be addressed 'on the basis that there is a need for understanding but not for vengeance, a need for reparation but not for retaliation'. The central meaning of 'reconciliation' was an amnesty law, rather than the later formulations advanced by the Truth and Reconciliation Commission. The TRC's motto would be 'Reconciliation Through Truth', not, as it happens, 'Reconciliation Through

Indemnity', which was more true to the 1993 Constitution's postscript. Early on, the Bill of Rights announced many new rights which could only be abrogated in extenuating circumstances, but the postscript unraveled the Constitution's commitment to human rights. In the postscript, the invocation of human rights did not express the determination to protect individual citizens as much as it did the willingness to sacrifice individuals' right to justice in the name of 'national unity and reconciliation'. The entreaty to human rights talk came to represent the final compromise of the negotiations; that is, amnesty for perpetrators of human rights violations.

After a turbulent negotiations stage, characterized by extremely high levels of political violence, a new Constitution was finally ratified in December 1993, leading to the first non-racial elections in South African history. In April 1994, the elections led to a 'Government of National Unity' (GNU), dominated by the ANC, but including high-ranking NP ministers such as Vice-President F W de Klerk. This limited power-sharing arrangement was to prove unstable and it collapsed in 1996, leaving the ANC to rule alone.

HUMAN RIGHTS, *UBUNTU* AND THE AFRICAN COMMUNITY

> God has given us a great gift, *ubuntu* ... *Ubuntu* says I am human only because you are human. If I undermine your humanity, I dehumanize myself. You must do what you can to maintain this great harmony, which is perpetually undermined by resentment, anger, desire for vengeance. That's why African jurisprudence is restorative rather than retributive.
>
> Desmond Tutu (Profile: *Mail and Guardian*, 17 March 1996)[24]

After the 1994 elections, the connections between human rights and nation-building became clear in the discourse of the Constitutional Court on reconciliation, restorative justice[25] and 'African jurisprudence'. One African word, *ubuntu*, integrates all these dimensions. *Ubuntu*, a term championed mainly by former Archbishop Tutu, is an expression of community, representing a romanticized vision of 'the rural African community' based upon reciprocity, respect for human dignity, community cohesion and solidarity. After the TRC was established in late 1995, the language of reconciliation and rights talk more generally became synonymous with the term *ubuntu*. *Ubuntu* became a key political and legal notion in the immediate post-apartheid order. It first appeared in the epilogue of the 1993 interim Constitution in the following famous passage: '... there is a need for understanding but not for vengeance, a need for reparation but not for retaliation, a need for *ubuntu* but not for victimization.' This same passage also appeared in the preamble of the 1995 National Unity and Reconciliation Act which established the Truth and Reconciliation Commission.

The term *ubuntu* also appeared extensively in the first Constitutional Court judgement on the death penalty (the State versus T. Makwanyane and M. Mchunu, 1995 (6) BCLR 605 (CC), hereafter *S v Makwanyane*), particularly in the judgements of Sachs, Mahomed, Mokgoro and Langa.[26] In all of these cases, as in the Tutu quote above, *ubuntu* was used to define 'justice' proper versus revenge; but the subtext instead reinforced the view that 'justice' in the new culture of human rights would not be driven by any desire for vengeance, or even by legally sanctioned retribution.[27] In *S v Makwanyane*, Judge Langa claims that *ubuntu* 'recognizes a person's status as a human being, entitled to unconditional dignity, value and respect …' (224) and sees the concept as 'a commendable attribute which the nation should strive for'. Judge Mokgoro seeks to create a nationally specific South African jurisprudence by referring to *ubuntu* as an indigenous South African value which militates against the death penalty and as a multicultural unifier; as 'a golden thread [which runs] across cultural lines' (307).

Judge Sachs' *S v Makwanyane* judgment relies upon an image of the static, ahistorical and remarkably compassionate African community. According to Sachs, African customary law did not invoke the death penalty except in the case of witchcraft, which Sachs saw as to do with spontaneous religious emotion rather than indigenous law (375–381). The existence of capital punishment in 'African communities', from witch-killing to necklacing in the 1980s, to mob lynchings in the 1990s, is more the product of irrational crowd hysteria than routine customary court justice, according to Sachs.

This interpretation of capital punishment in African communities results from a time-honored tradition in jurisprudence where the jurisdictional boundaries of law are defined by reference to law's opposite. Law excludes certain categories of persons (children, the mentally ill, and, in colonial contexts, slaves) and actions (violence without due process) from its purview. Law is cool, rational, and impartial, therefore the 'wild justice' of political cadres necklacing suspected police informers, of mob burnings of car hijackers, or customary courts killing 'convicted' witches simply are not allowed to be 'law'. *Ubuntu* expresses this rejection of revenge, and is explicitly linked in the TRC final *Report* to restorative justice (Vol.1, pp. 125–128), defined not as punishment but as resulting from reparations for victims and the rehabilitation of perpetrators.

However, there is a further slippage in the use of *ubuntu* that goes beyond simply supporting restorative justice in order to justify amnesty for perpetrators of apartheid-era human rights abuses. *Ubuntu's* categorical rejection of revenge also includes a rejection of the more moderate form of justice as 'retribution', even if it is based upon due process. *Ubuntu* is used to define just redress so as, in Tutu's words, to go 'beyond justice' to forgiveness and reconciliation (*Mail and Guardian* 17 March 1996). In this view, human rights justice is restorative justice is African justice. According to Tutu, 'Retributive justice is largely Western. The African understanding is far more restorative – not so much to punish as to redress or restore a balance that has been knocked askew' (quoted in Minow 1998:81).

Creating a polarity between 'African' *ubuntu*/reconciliation on the one hand and 'Western' vengeance/retributive justice on the other closes down the space to discuss fully the middle position – the pursuit of legal retribution as a possible route to reconciliation in itself. The constitutional right of citizens to due justice, to pursue civil claims against perpetrators, is taken away by amnesty laws, which preclude both criminal and civil prosecutions. This was justified in terms of a uniquely African form of compassion, or *ubuntu*. By combining human rights and *ubuntu*, human rights come to express compromised justice and the state's abrogation of the right to due process.

To see African law (or common understandings of justice in 38 states of the US, since *Gregg v. Georgia* 428 US 153 (1976), for that matter) as completely excluding violent revenge is an act of wilful romantic naïveté on the part of Sachs. Courts administered by Africans have often applied the death penalty for certain categories of persons (informers, witches and, in the 1990s, car hijackers) in numerous and successive historical contexts. The South African papers constantly report such cases of 'rough justice'.

Why, then, did the Constitutional Court judges express such romantic notions, given the actual historical record? After 1994, the Constitutional Court was seeking to legitimate its position as the sovereign institution in the land, and the judges were faced with the difficult task of making an extraordinarily unpopular first judgement. Judges invoked *ubuntu* to try to demonstrate that the Court was sensitive to popular values and to claim that these values were opposed to vengeance (even though every opinion poll showed overwhelming support for the death penalty).[28]

The judges adopted the strategy used by the authors of the interim Constitution's postscript; they sought to express the new 'culture of rights' in a popular idiom. In so doing they reinforced a wider propensity of state officials to connect rights and reconciliation to nation-building, through an appeal to Africanist ideas of unity and community. As Elsa van Huyssteen has argued, human rights are the 'main site for the reconciliation of constitutionalism with the aims of popular democracy' (1996:294). The concept of human rights, redefined as pan-Africanist reconciliation, is a bridge between an arid constitutionalism with little political purchase in South African society and the idea of popular sovereignty and representation.

Although the ANC consciously avoided constitutionalizing race in its first term, it still appealed to a pan-African identity to garner support for its policies, particularly among those who had highest expectations from the collapse of apartheid. Heribert Adam acknowledges the dominance of social democratic Charterists over African nationalists within the ANC (1994:45), but admitted that, 'A counter-racism would have great emotional appeal among a frustrated black township youth'. There is pressure from the ANC's politicized social base to adopt an increasingly African definition of the nation. Given the enormous expectations among impoverished black citizens coupled with the lack of a massive program for the redistribution of wealth and, therefore, the likelihood of a continued material disparity between whites and blacks, the pressure to adopt an Africanist language has been growing. Since 1994, Robert Price notes the growing salience of race politics as an important basis for political mobilization, the rise of racially exclusive forms of political association (black management groups, black chambers of commerce, Black Editor's Forum etc.) and 'the increased reliance on group rather than individually based notions of rights and rewards' (1997:171–2). By 2000, one commentator went so far as to state that 'African nationalism [has] triumphed as the philosophy of South Africa's new petit-bourgeois political elite' (Bond 2000:6).

According to Alfred Cockrell, *ubuntu* is indicative of 'the saccharine assertions of rainbow jurisprudence' in the new South Africa, 'Which state blandly that *all* competing values can, mysteriously, be accommodated within the embrace of a warm fuzzy consensus [his emphasis]' (1996:12). Instead, argues Cockrell, human rights and constitutionalism require hard choices to be made between the positions of citizens who will inevitably disagree about the common good. This truth seems to have been forgotten by judges in their effort to ideologically legitimate the Constitutional Court. 'African values', he continues (p.25), do not justify themselves by virtue of their being 'African', but have to be subjected to the same kind of second-order moral and legal scrutiny that any societal values receive. Critically, they must 'surmount a threshold of constitutional consistency' and be commensurate with international human rights law. Cockrell is right to object, and could go a step further to argue that human rights must become a language not of compromise and a phony reconciliation, but instead the means to pursue a well-defined political will guided by a program of social justice.

It is tempting to ask, Where did *ubuntu* originate – which is its true and authentic meaning from the diversity of uses? To attempt a definitive conceptualization of *ubuntu*, particularly one based upon real or imagined African communities, would be to reproduce the language of nationalism. One can only trace the trajectory of its concrete and ideological usage between the circles of human rights organizations, religious leaders, Constitutional Court judges and in popular usage. In a sense, it does not really matter where and how *ubuntu* originated, since one of the main characteristics of nationalist ideology is to historicize and naturalize 'cultural' signs as they are incorporated into the rhetorical repertoire of state discourse. To draw on a formulation of Althusser, *ubuntu* is just another 'always-already there' element of pan-Africanist ideology. *Ubuntu* should be recognized for what it is: an ideological concept with multiple meanings which conjoins human rights, restorative justice, reconciliation and nation-building within the populist language of pan-Africanism. In post-apartheid South Africa, it became the Africanist wrapping used to sell a reconciliatory version of human rights talk to black South Africans. *Ubuntu* belies the claim that human rights would have no culturalist or ethnic dimensions.

TRUTH, RECONCILIATION AND NATION-BUILDING

> The Commission of Truth and Reconciliation. It is the creation of a nation.
>
> Constitutional Court Judge Albie Sachs.
> (Quoted in Boraine 1995:146)

The Truth and Reconciliation Commission (1995–2001) was *the* archetypal transitional statutory body created to promote a 'culture of human rights' in South Africa. It was a key mechanism to promote the new constitutionalist political order and the reformulation of justice in human rights talk as restorative justice.[29]

The TRC was geared not only towards building a state of right, but also towards using human rights talk to construct a new national identity. This is illustrated in the discursive associations drawn between truth, reconciliation and nationalism. It is striking how, in documents such as the 1993 Constitution and the 1995 National Unity and Reconciliation Act, as well as in the proceedings of conferences on the South African TRC, discussions of truth seem to lead naturally into questions of reconciliation, national unity, and nation-building. This is a general feature of truth commissions worldwide. The final document of the Chilean Rettig Commission states that, 'only upon a foundation of truth [is] it possible to meet the basic demands of justice and to create the necessary conditions for achieving *national* reconciliation' (Ensalaco 1994:658).

Despite their assertions to the contrary, rights-based narratives bear many formal attributes of other nationalist narratives on the past and tradition. Truth commissions, like all nation-building processes, construct a revised national history and, in the words of José Zalaquett of the Chilean Commission, write into being a new 'collective memory'. Truth commissions are more than simply the correct functioning of a legal process – they are a national history lesson and, as Benedict Anderson (1991) has argued, the formulation of a shared national past is simultaneously the basis of the assertion of a shared national future.

There is a close affinity between nationalist history-writing and the construction of a new notion of the South African self, as illustrated in former ANC provincial minister Jessie Duarte's assertion: 'The main view within the ANC is "Let's have the truth and use the truth to build a nation" ... People need to know what happened to their loved ones and why – that's a South African *cultural dynamic*' (Personal interview, September 1995). Looking at experiences in other countries, it is evident that a 'need to know' is not culturally unique to South Africans, but in the 'new South Africa' national personhood became tied up in how to respond to past human rights abuses. Being authentically South African comes to mean sharing the traumas of apartheid and uniting in the subsequent process of 'healing the nation'.

Whereas other countries may have a Day of Remembrance to memorialize valiant national martyrs who fell defending the mother/fatherland from foreign invaders, South Africa now has a 'Day of Reconciliation' on 16 December which commemorates a new group of national martyrs who died at the hands of fellow South Africans. The TRC had its first meeting on this day in 1995, and Archbishop Desmond Tutu in his opening address stated: 'We are meant to be a part of the process of the healing of our nation, of our people, all of us, since every South African has to some extent or other been traumatized. We are a wounded people ... We all stand in need of healing' (1999:87). The notion of the South African citizen as victim of trauma was then welded to other more culturalist visions of national identity when Tutu went on to refer to 'we, this rainbow people of God', which portrays the nation as the multicultural amalgam of distinct racial colors (which are united but still distinctive).

Here we can see an intriguing discourse unfolding linking suffering, the body and the nation. Firstly, the nation is conceived of as a physical body, as a generically South African (that is, not generically human) individual projected onto the national scale. What type of body is it? A sick one – one that is in need of healing. Healing the nation is the popular idiom for building the nation. What is the healing treatment prescribed? Truth-telling and, flowing from this, forgiveness and reconciliation. How do these treatments heal the national body? They open the wounds, cleanse them and stop them from festering.[30]

Seeing the nation as a body is important for nation-builders, as it creates the basis of a new 'we', and it incorporates the individual in a collective cleansing. The TRC constructed a collectivist view of the nation as a sick body, which could then be ritually cured in TRC hearings. This is something which no South African could escape – as Tutu stated, 'we *all* stand in need of healing'. Individual psychological processes cannot be reduced to national processes dedicated to 'healing', since the 'nation' is not like an individual at all. The nation, according to Ernest Gellner (1983), is a political fiction invented by nationalists, who conjure up tenuous concepts such as a 'collective memory' or a 'collective psyche'. Nations do not have collective psyches which can be healed and to assert otherwise is to psychologize an abstract entity which exists primarily in the minds of nation building politicians. Nevertheless, it is remarkable how widely accepted this nationalist language is in the literature on truth commissions and post-Communist truth-telling.[31] Michael Ignatieff rightly challenges the notion of national psyches when he writes:

> We tend to invest our nations with conscience, identities and memories as if they were individuals. It is problematic enough to vest an individual with a single identity: our inner lives are like battlegrounds over which uneasy truces reign; the identity of a nation is additionally fissured by region, ethnicity, class and education. (1998:169)

All of these elements – truth-telling, healing, nation-building, history writing – were integrated by the South African TRC into a potent mixture. This process is not wholly unique, as national politicians have redefined human rights in expedient ways in many other countries. Philip Roth (1993) writes insightfully about how the trial in Israel of John Demjanjuk, a Ukrainian allegedly involved in mass murder of Jews during the Holocaust, became a theatrical public spectacle to 'educate the public'. Its message was not only part of the founding nationalist narrative of the state of Israel but also constituted an expression of the power of the Israeli state over its past oppressors. It theatricalized that shift in national identity from victim to adjudicator and broadcast the message live nationally. Demjanjuk was there to maintain the nationalist mythology of the state of Israel, and was part of the relentless institutionalization of the Holocaust, according to Roth.[32] Similarly, the trial of the high-ranking Nazi official Adolf Eichmann in Israel in 1961 was harnessed to the construction of Israeli national identity in various ways; for example when it was interrupted by two minutes' silence to those fallen in the creation of the Israeli nation (Douglas 2000), or when the prosecutor, Gideon Hausner, focussed upon harrowing personal experiences of victims in order to 'design a national saga that would echo through the generations' (Tom Seger cited in Osiel 1997:16). Despite the appeals to values of truth, justice or reconciliation, embattled politicians simply cannot resist the imperative to institutionalize past abuses in order to manufacture legitimacy for national bureaucracies.

The power of truth commissions is ultimately symbolic: they cannot prosecute and the evidence found or disclosed to them cannot be used in later prosecutions, so they can make only a weak claim to carry out 'justice'. They have little institutional power to carry out reforms of judiciary; they can make recommendations, but these are often ignored (as in El Salvador) and truth commissions cannot usually follow through on their recommendations. The symbolic impact of these commissions lies in how they codify the history of a period, the theme of the next chapter. Popular memories of an authoritarian past are multiple, fluid, indeterminate and fragmentary, so truth commissions play a vital role in fixing memory and institutionalizing a view of the past conflict.

Truth commissions publish reports which share a similar form with nationalist narratives in the way they render a discontinuity with the past.[33] The creation of historical discontinuity and periodization is part of the relational dimension of national identity-forming processes. It has been widely noted that nationalism constructs the nation in opposition to other nations through a variety of signs: flags, a place on the map, fallen heroes, landscapes, animal totems, rugby teams, deploying a proliferation of symbolic forms to distinguish itself. Every ethnic or national identity needs an 'other' against which to oppose and, therefore, define itself: it is what the other is not and will find difference no matter where it looks. The most significant site of otherness for the new South Africa has not been other nations, it has been itself. The relationality of constitutional nationalism is often constructed in an opposition between the present self and the past other. The old nationalism was based upon a particular view of history/culture/race/truth/rights, etc., which is ritually rejected in favor of revised formulations of those concepts.

Unlike some nationalist visions of the past in, say, Britain or France, the new South African nation is not naturalized by reference to its ancientness, but in its affirming of the uniqueness of the present. The new South African identity is constructed upon a discontinuous historicity, where the past is not a past of pride, but of abuse. The past history of the nation *qua* nation of rights is a history of a catalog of violations, and pride is only to be found in resistance, by those struggling to recover an 'authentic' democratic tradition. The TRC codified the official history of the martyrs of that struggle in order to institutionalize those shared, bitter experiences of apartheid, which were silenced before, as a unifying theme in the new official version of the nation's history.

MANUFACTURING LEGITIMACY

> There is a deep crisis of legitimacy of our political institutions. The moral fabric of society has been torn. Expediency and principle have been blurred. Society is now held together by obstinacy, goodwill and good luck, instead of an inclusive moral base.
>
> Johnny de Lange, ANC MP, Chair of the Select Committee on Justice of the National Assembly. (Cedar Park Conference, 21 September 1995)

Having established, contra procedural liberalism, that human rights talk is enmeshed in culturalist discourses on community and becomes an integral part of nation-building, we must then ask what is this nation-building for? It is not an end in itself, but a means to another end, which is to consolidate a new form of bureaucratic governance. The ANC, when it inherited the battered shell of an authoritarian and illegitimate state, became motivated less by a vision of popular sovereignty than by bureaucratic imperatives. Nation-building allows other processes to be carried out, such as the legitimization of the apparatus of justice which still remains tainted by the authoritarian past.[34] Legitimating the state's justice system in turn promotes a process of state-building, as the post-apartheid state has embarked upon a project of unifying the diversity of justice institutions in state and society.

The legitimacy of constitutionalism depends in turn upon the legitimacy and the capacity of the criminal justice system to deliver swift justice. Constitutionalism, in short, necessarily assumes a strong and developed state apparatus. As Ignatieff asserts: 'The only reliable antidote to ethnic nationalism turns out to be civic nationalism, because the only guarantee that ethnic groups will live side by side in peace is shared loyalty to a state, *strong enough*, fair enough, equitable enough to command their obedience' (1993:185) (my emphasis).

If civic nationalism requires strong states, then a general problem besetting transitional regimes is that they often inherit a significantly debilitated state in crisis, with unstable, illegitimate and impaired institutions (see Huyse 1995). Therefore the most immediate problems for constitutionalists concern both the lack of citizens' respect for rights talk, legal institutions and the judiciary, and an inadequate infrastructure of courts which cannot hope to respond fully to the demands of a new rights-based political dispensation.

Many fundamental rights in the 1996 Bill of Rights are simply beyond the capacities of the legal system, including 'just administrative action' (section 33), universal rights to access to courts (section 34) and state-provided legal representation (section 35.b-c). The constitutionalists' reliance on the praxis of citizenship as the basis of civic patriotism does not make a realistic assessment of the lack of material preconditions and institutional capacity in South Africa for that 'praxis' to take place. For example, after the 1994 elections, the Legal Aid Board budget expanded from 56 million Rand to 307 million in 1998.[35] Yet this figure is generally recognized, even within the Justice Ministry, as not even approaching the levels required to actualize the new range of constitutional rights.

The strain on the legal order emanating from its inability to even partially respond to the demands made upon it is exacerbated by the bureaucratic character and power base of the democratizing state. The rise of constitutionalism has been coupled with the emergence of a new bureaucratic class whose power is primarily exercised through the law and the institutional power of state. Thus the continued control of the economy by a traditional white elite and transnational corporations means that the state bureaucracy has become the most important site for the exercise of political power in the transformation of South African society. And so the importance of legitimate legal institutions takes on an even greater significance in South Africa than in Chile or Argentina, since South Africa has invested so much political capital in a constitutional arrangement, whereas Latin American regimes sought to establish strong executives.

The importance of legal–technical mechanisms in pursuing societal transformation renders necessary an equally strong program of bureaucratic legitimization. In a context where state power relies so heavily upon legality, one would expect the state to concentrate resources in seeking to legitimate the law. Yet a program of legitimization which relied upon formal rationality and a dry technocratic ethos would only appeal to intellectuals and bureaucrats. In South Africa, adherence to the rule of law alone would hardly mobilize the masses to identify with the state. Therefore it should not be surprising that state officials seek to identify the Constitution with popular conceptions of culture, community and nation, in a bid to construct overarching metaphors of national unity. Thus, we have to recognize how the weakness of the state, coupled with the rise of a new bureaucratic class, necessitates that state-building and nation-building remain conjoined in the 'New South Africa'.

TRUTH COMMISSIONS AS LIMINAL INSTITUTIONS

Truth commissions are one of the main ways in which a bureaucratic elite seeks to manufacture legitimacy for state institutions, and especially the legal system. How specifically do truth commissions generate legitimacy for democratizing regimes? They occupy a 'liminal' space, betwixt and between existing state institutions. I take the term used by sociologist Arnold van Gennep (1908) to describe rituals of transition (such as life-cycle rituals), during which individuals move from one status with its incumbent rights and obligations to another. This idea was developed further by Victor Turner (1967:93–5), writing about the Ndembu of Zambia, who saw liminality as an ambiguous process of 'becoming' which was 'interstructural' and transitional between two states (in our case, between apartheid and post-apartheid). During the period of liminality, the core moral values of society would be restated and internalized (it was hoped) by those participating in the process. Importantly, the ritualized and moral features of rituals of transition were the result of the failure of secular mechanisms (such as the law) to deal with conflict in society. These ideas have not only been applied to life-cycle rituals in African societies, but also to pilgrimage, hippies, and institutions such as asylums, the military and prisons (Morris 1987:260).

The South African TRC also exhibited a number of ambiguous and liminal characteristics which made it neither a legal, political, nor a religious institution. For a start, it was a transitory and fleeting statutory body functioning in its entirety for only three years.[36] It was poised in time between the apartheid era and the post-apartheid epoch. It was not the sole product of any one government branch and it was nominally independent, but it was located in an interstructural position, in between all three major branches of government.

The Commission had an ambivalent relationship to the legal order: it was not exclusively a legal institution in that Human Rights Violations hearings were not constituted as a court of law. It could not carry out prosecutions nor could it sentence. In fact the TRC bypassed the legal process by naming perpetrators before they had been convicted in a court of law and by granting amnesty before a perpetrator had been indicted or convicted. The amnesty hearings were an unusual kind of inversion of the law, as amnesty Judge Bernard Ngoepe described to me in an interview:

> The [Promotion of National Unity and Reconciliation] Act does not encapsulate the principles of common law, therefore we don't find guidance for legal precedent … I can tell you that I find it strange that I as a judge should listen to the gory details of how someone killed, cut the throat of another person and then

> ask that I let him go. Normally, I should punish him instead of grant *political* immunity (my emphasis). (Personal interview, 17 December 1996)[37]

Amnesty hearings, in contrast to the Human Rights Violations hearings, were constituted as court hearings with legal consequences; either a granting or refusal of immunity from prosecution. Procedurally, the amnesty process mimicked a court but did not use standard legal rules of evidence:[38] the Amnesty Committee sought to establish truth by hearing testimony primarily from perpetrators and information proposed by the TRC evidence leader who attempted to ensure that 'full disclosure' had in fact occurred.

The liminal character of the truth commission granted it a certain freedom from both the strictures of legal discourse and the institutional legacy of apartheid. This allowed it to generate a new form of authority for the post-apartheid regime. The amnesty hearings were a theatricalization of the power of the new state, which compelled representatives of the former order to confess when they would rather have maintained their silence. Perpetrators were compelled to speak within the confines of a new language of human rights, and in so doing to recognize the new government's power to admonish and to punish.

This theatricalization of power gives us one clue as to why democratizing governments set up truth commissions rather than relying upon an existing legal system: truth commissions are transient politico-religious-legal institutions which have much more legitimizing potential than dry, rule-bound and technically-obsessed courts of law. The TRC's position as a quasi-judicial institution allowed it to mix genres – of law, politics and religious – in particularly rich ways. This makes it a fascinating case to study in order to understand how human rights talk interacts with wider moral and ethical discourses. However, I shall argue that the mixing of different genres undermined the TRC's ability to carry out certain functions (such as writing an official history of apartheid) effectively. In particular, the TRC's liminal status facilitated a contradictory mixing of a narrow legalism and an emotive religious moralizing.

Legitimation is not only an end in itself, but a prerequisite for pursuing other state objectives in the post-apartheid order. The quest for legitimation needs to be understood within a wider context of centralization and consolidation in the area of justice. With regard to the areas where centralization affects the work of truth commissions, we must consider how state law is involved in a constant process of creating its own boundaries, its own area of jurisdiction, defining that which is 'justiciable' from those areas of social regulation which fall outside its purview (Strathern 1985). Law draws upon and maintains a distinction from other domains of social control and consent. To this extent, human rights bodies such as the TRC are part of an extension of those boundaries of the justiciable to incorporate, and expunge, that which stands in the way of a state strategy of centralization, unification and standardization.

The establishment of the rule of law is fundamental to the consolidation of state power as defined by a monopoly over the means of violence. Although they are not legal institutions, truth commissions have implications for the process of judicial reform. An explicit motivation for setting up truth commissions is, according to Aryeh Neier 'establishing and upholding the rule of law' (1994:2). Since 1994, successive ANC governments have engaged in a program of eradicating and assimilating other coercive structures. They defended criminals and former human rights violators from lynch mobs and local courts, not solely out of compassion, but in order to defend the principle of the complete and unchallenged sovereignty of the state. The truth commission was part of a general and long-term orientation within state institutions which asserted the state's ability to rein in and control the informal adjudicative and policing structures in civil society. This is explored in detail in Part II.

THE STRUCTURE OF THE TRC

The work of the TRC, which commenced in December 1995, was divided into three committees: the Human Rights Violations Committee, the Reparations and Rehabilitation Committee and the Amnesty Committee.

Throughout 1996 and early 1997, the Human Rights Violations Committee (HRVC) held 50 hearings in town halls, hospitals and churches all around the country, where thousands of citizens came and testified about past abuses. This process received wide national media coverage and brought ordinary, mostly black, experiences of the apartheid era into the national public space in a remarkable way. The TRC took more statements than any previous truth commission in history (over 21,000). The HRVC faced the daunting task of corroborating the veracity of each testimony, choosing which would be retold at public hearings and passing along verified cases to the Reparations and Rehabilitation Committee (RRC). The TRC also took an investigative role and, by issuing subpoenas and taking evidence in camera, it built up an expansive view on the past. In its final report published in October 1998, the TRC produced findings on the majority of the 21,298 cases brought before it, and it named the perpetrators in hundreds of cases (unlike the Argentine and Chilean commissions)

The efforts of the Reparation and Rehabilitation Committee to facilitate 'reconciliation' presented the weakest of the three committees' activities. Part of the problem was structural and lay in the fact that the TRC had no money of its own to disburse to survivors; instead it could only make unbinding recommendations to the President's Fund with regard to monetary compensation, symbolic memorials (e.g. monuments) and medical expenses. The TRC made it clear that victims should expect little from the process and only a fraction of what they might have expected had they prosecuted for damages through the courts. Such pronouncements were internalized by victims, many of whom have severe material needs. At the Human Rights Violation (HRV) hearings one often heard, for instance, a woman recount the murder of her husband or son by the security forces and then meekly request a tombstone as compensation. It remains to be seen whether the reparations process, a key element in reconciliation, will even begin to address the needs and expectations (however lowered) of survivors.

In the 1998 final *Report*, the TRC recommended that an estimated 22,000 victims should receive an individual financial grant of between 17,029–23,023 Rand (approximately US$2,800–3,500) per year over a six-year period. In late 1998, 'urgent interim relief' payments of about US$330, the first tranche of reparations, were made to about 20,000 victims. At the time of writing, no further reparations payments had been made. A year after the publication of the TRC's findings and recommendations, survivors' groups were demonstrating outside the Department of Justice offices in Johannesburg as reparations policy had still not been discussed in parliament. The reparations issue was very far down on the list of priorities of all major political parties. Many victims were still waiting for their urgent interim reparations. In the press release by the survivors' organization, the Khulumani Support Group, their frustration was apparent:

> The TRC has compromised our right to justice and to making civil claims. In good faith we came forward and suffered the re-traumatisation of exposing our wounds in public in the understanding that this was necessary in order to be considered for reparations. We now feel that we have been used in a cynical process of political expediency. (Khulumani press release 27 October 1999)

In January 2000, the Mbeki government stated its intention to offer only token compensation of several hundred US dollars (Rand 2,000), instead of the US$21,000 which the TRC recommended should be given to apartheid-era victims. Duma Khumalo spoke for many victims when he protested bitterly: 'We have been betrayed. The previous government gave the killers golden handshakes and the present government gave them amnesty. [But] the victims have been left empty handed' (*Guardian* 3 January 2000)

Finally, the South African TRC was unique in bringing an amnesty process within the truth commission, whereas in other countries it has been a separate legal mechanism. The TRC had received over 7,000 applications and at the time of writing, about 568 people had been granted amnesty and 5,287 denied.[39] To receive amnesty, the applicant had to fulfil a number of legal criteria. The act had to have been committed between the dates 1 May 1960 and 10 May 1994. The applicant had to convince the panel that the crime was political: i.e., not committed for personal gain, malice or spite. Crucially, the applicant had to fully disclose all that was known about the crime, including the chain of command ordering the act. Perpetrators were not required to express any remorse for their actions. If a perpetrator was facing legal proceedings at the time, these would be suspended until the appeal for amnesty was heard. If amnesty was refused (for example, because it was found that the applicant did not fully disclose all information relevant to the case), then the applicant could face criminal or civil prosecutions in future.

Although it faced public disapproval and violated victims' desire for punishment, the South African amnesty process had the most stringent legal requirements of any recent amnesty and will probably be seen as model for other countries. Rather than a blanket amnesty (as in Chile and El Salvador), it was individualized and applicants had to prove that the violation had a political objective and had occurred within a specific time period, and they had to fully disclose the nature and context of their actions. In the context of an unreliable judicial system, which in 1996 convicted security policeman Eugene de Kock (and sentenced him to over 200 years in prison) but acquitted former Defense Minister General Magnus Malan,[40] the amnesty process was probably the best opportunity for the majority of ordinary survivors and their families to learn more about their cases.

Yet the amnesty arrangements also had their drawbacks. The amnesty mechanism created a clash between the criminal justice system and the TRC over specific perpetrators, as in the case of five security policeman (Cronje, Hechter, Mentz, van Vuuren, and Venter) from the Northern Transvaal security branch. The Attorney-General, Jan d'Olivera, had carried out extensive investigations into the men's crimes and had issued warrants for their arrest in connection with 27 cases of murder, attempted murder and damage to property, when the men fled to the TRC Amnesty Committee (AC). The criminal investigation had to be suspended and in the end the security policemen received amnesty for their crimes (which included torturing an ANC activist with electrical shocks before electrocuting him to death), thus undermining the laborious efforts of the criminal prosecution service.

Behind amnesty for individuals was the less obvious program of indemnifying the state itself. The granting of amnesty extinguished citizens' constitutional right to sue for civil damages in compensation from the perpetrator and state: if a former agent of the government was granted amnesty by the Amnesty Committee, then the state is also automatically indemnified for damages. In the amnesty process, the state became a silent partner, shadowing perpetrators who came forward and benefiting when their amnesty request was successful. The state then would consider what reparations it wished to make to survivors. In this way, the slate would be wiped clean and state ministries would no longer bear responsibility for past actions of their agents.

The degree to which perpetrators came forward was generally disappointing since many believed that they would never be successfully prosecuted. Applications from the former South African Defense Force (especially Military Intelligence and Special Forces) and the Inkatha Freedom Party were particularly sparse. In many cases, such as the hearings of seventeen IFP applicants in 1998–9 on the Boipatong massacre, the lawyers for the victims seemed justified in arguing that applicants were not revealing the full story and were protecting their leaders.[41] Thirteen applicants were granted amnesty by the AC, however, in November 2000.

Yet there were also some breakthroughs and revelations. In the case mentioned above of Brigadier Cronje and four other former members of the security police, information never made public before was divulged about a covert body known by its Afrikaans acronym, 'TREWITS'. TREWITS was an intelligence co-ordinating body which reported to the State Security Council (SSC) over which the State President and civilian ministers presided. The structure of TREWITS showed the direct links and integration of military and police intelligence and the involvement of high-ranking National Party leaders in everyday counter-insurgency matters. At the same hearings, former Police Commissioner General van der Merwe admitted that in 1989 President P W Botha ordered the bombing of Khotso House, the head office of the South African Council of Churches, and the unofficial ANC headquarters in the country. This revelation led to ten amnesty applications in January 1997 and further insights into the apartheid security police apparatus.

There were benefits of placing the amnesty process within the TRC; for instance, information could be pooled between the various committees. Yet combining amnesty with truth-finding functions created a number of strategic and ethical problems, which might have been avoided if amnesty had been a separate legal mechanism, unrelated to the TRC. There was a large gap between survivors' expectations of justice and the reality, as they saw perpetrators getting amnesty straight away while their meagre reparations were many years away. Perpetrators could obtain amnesty without even expressing regret – since the Act did not legally require an apology. Many repeated worn apartheid-era ideological justifications for their actions with little self-reflection and analysis. The much vaunted truth of amnesty hearings was often the truth of unrepentant serial murderers who still felt that their war was a just one.

Public opinion surveys have shown a great deal of opposition to granting amnesty. The research of political scientists Gibson and Gouws based upon a national survey in 1997[42] concluded that: 'Only a minority is able to accept the view that those clearly engaged in the violent struggle over apartheid should be awarded amnesty' (1998:28). Indeed, where blame is established, the overwhelming majority of those interviewed preferred not forgiveness or amnesty, but punishment and the right to sue through the courts.

This dissonance between popular understandings of retribution/punishment and the version of restorative justice proposed by national political figures was one of the main obstacles to manufacturing legitimacy for constitutionalism using human rights talk. The redefinition (and some would say deformation) of human rights during democratic transitions to mean amnesty and reconciliation not only conflicted with widespread notions of justice in society, but also, it could be argued, with a state's duty to punish human rights offenders as established in international criminal law. International criminal law is highly ambivalent on the question of amnesty and the tension between national amnesties and international human rights treaties has a long history.[43]

In Latin America, the most important recent exchange was between the Argentine human rights leader Emilio Mignone (Mignone, Estlund and Issacharoff 1984), arguing for prosecutions of human rights violators to the full extent under international law, and Carlos Santiago Nino (1985), legal adviser to President Alfonsín on trials of military officers in Argentina's 'dirty war'. This debate was repeated in the pages of the *Yale Law Journal* between Nino who argued for a pragmatic acceptance of national political constraints on justice (1991) and legal scholar Diane Orentlicher who reiterated the international legal imperative to punish that transcends national political contexts:

> … the central importance of the rule of law in civilized societies requires, within defined but principled limits, prosecution of especially atrocious crimes … international law itself helps assure the survival of fragile democracies when its clear pronouncement

> removes certain atrocious crimes from the provincial realm of a country's internal politics and thereby places those crimes squarely within the scope of universal concern ... A state's complete failure to punish repeated or notorious instances of these offenses violates its obligations under customary international law. (1991:2540)

I am persuaded that Orentlicher has articulated correctly the ideal relationship between international human rights and national processes of democratization and the establishment of the rule of law. The international character of human rights laws and institutions exists to reinforce national processes of delivering retributive justice for victims of human rights violations.[44] The rule of law cannot meaningfully be said to exist if it is predicated upon impunity for gross human rights violations committed in the authoritarian past, since as Orentlicher states:

> If law is unavailable to punish widespread brutality of the recent past, what lesson can be offered for the future? ... Societies recently scourged by lawlessness need look no further than their own past to discover the costs of impunity. Their history provides sobering cause to believe, with William Pitt, that tyranny begins where law ends. (2542)

The appropriation of human rights by nation-building discourse and their identification with forgiveness, reconciliation and restorative justice deems social stability to be a higher social good than the individual right to retributive justice and to pursue perpetrators through the courts.[45] This image of human rights undermines accountability and the rule of law and with it the breadth and depth of the democratization process. The empirical evidence from other democratizing countries shows that retributive justice can itself lead to reconciliation (in the sense of peaceful co-existence and the legal, non-violent adjudication of conflict) in the long run.

John Borneman's comparative study of the post-socialist countries of Eastern Europe (1997) concluded that where there was little or no prosecution of the former authorities for past crimes, societies (in Russia, Romania and the former Yugoslavia, in particular) were characterized by high levels of violence, much of it sustained by the previous communist elite. Borneman argues that where there is no retributive justice there is no legitimacy to the rule of law, leading to 'serious internal criminalization' (1997:104). High levels of criminality have also been conspicuously in evidence in post-apartheid South Africa, as well as enclaves of ungovernability; for example, in KwaZulu-Natal and some townships of Johannesburg. Borneman advises that 'to avoid a cycle of retributive violence, it may be wise to go through a longer phase of painful historical reckoning with the past, that is, of retributive justice in the present' (1997:110). Tellingly, where there were successful prosecutions against high-ranking communists, the initial passion for retributive justice seems to have subsided and even disappeared, which suggests that trials lead to a 'thick line' being drawn under the past through the ritual purification of the political center.

The strategy of drawing upon international human rights to reinforce criminal trials of perpetrators within South Africa would not only have the advantage of fortifying the rule of law and indirectly addressing wider criminalization in society, but would also have linked human rights to popular understandings of justice and accorded human rights-oriented institutions much greater legitimacy in the process. This could in turn have helped resolve the wider legitimation crisis of post-apartheid state institutions in a more effective manner. A policy of allowing more prosecutions of offenders would have made the transformation of the judiciary clearer and more evident. My own ethnographic research in the townships of Johannesburg had led me to the conclusion that, contra the established view within the Truth and Reconciliation Commission, retributive understandings of justice are much more salient in South African society than versions emphasizing reconciliation as forgiveness. As Michael Walzer has noted, 'victims ... make elemental claims for retributive justice' (1997:13). This argument is developed more fully in the rest of the book, and especially in chapters 6–7 on the prevalence of ideas of vengeance and local institutions of retribution among urban Africans.

The above argument does not imply that any form of amnesty was unjustifiable during the negotiation process – it may well have been politically indispensable at the time. Again, it must be recognized that the amnesty arrangement brokered in the South African negotiations placed much greater legal limitations and obligations on perpetrators than amnesties in democratizing countries of Latin America. However, had there been a more widespread and open public debate of the issue, other alternatives may have been explored, such as a mechanism where the state could grant amnesty from criminal prosecution but not from civil prosecutions, which could have been brought by families of victims such as the Ribeiros, the Mxenges and the Bikos. Leaving open the possibility of legal action would have made the category of citizenship more meaningful in practice.

TRUTH COMMISSIONS AND IMPUNITY

The reality that post-authoritarian law is subjected to the systemic imperatives of nation-building and the centralization of the state does not mean that we should reject constitutionalism in its entirety. The constitutionalist agenda of democratizing regimes is decidedly preferable to that of states founded upon ethno-nationalist 'blood and land' myths of nation. Constitutionalism has important strengths, including its division of powers between different branches of government and the ways in which it provides the institutional structure to defend individual rights, an aspect so lacking under authoritarian legality.

Yet in addition to recognizing the desirability of constitutionalism's goals, we are required to develop an analysis of the systematic pressures upon human rights and what the consequences of this might be for writing official versions of the past and advocating certain notions and institutions of justice and reconciliation. Liberal readings of human rights often ignore some important truths, such as the fact that state officials continue to speak the rhetoric of cultural difference and nationalism even though the democratizing state is significantly more procedurally rational, accountable and representative than its autocratic predecessors. The ideological needs of new regimes do not go away, but are even exacerbated by political transitions. Constitutionalist visions can underestimate the very real crises of legitimacy which new regimes find themselves in; crises which push the emergent bureaucratic elite into subordinating individual rights to the goals of the new bureaucracy: stability, legitimacy and a new image of the nation.

This observation is more widely applicable if we compare the South African experience to the position of human rights in Latin America.[47] After decades of military dictatorship, many Latin American governments now vaunt their respect for human rights and have generated a plethora of new agencies to monitor and uphold them, including truth commissions, procurators and congressional ombudsmen. Yet the development of human rights bureaucracies is not to be universally applauded, argues Francisco Panizza (1995:181), since these agencies can serve as a substitute for a government's lack of commitment to the rule of law and independence of the judiciary.

At worst, new human rights agencies deflect responsibility and criticism away from governments. Panizza uses the notion of 'legal fetishism' to describe this phenomenon, which

> refers not only to the excessive legalism in which public debate is conducted in most countries of the region, but to the combination of legal provisions that regulate every aspect of social life, including constitutional and legal provisions for the protection of human rights, with the practical disregard for the rule of law ... as a rule, the return to democracy in most Latin American countries has not brought about judicial reform or resulted in a more assertive and independent judiciary. (1995:183)

In South Africa, the concept of legal fetishism has utility in referring to the increasing legalization of political issues and the chasm between constitutional rights and the ability of the legal system to deliver. There are very important rights contained in the Constitution, especially the right to legal representation, administrative rights, and a number of provisions against discrimination on the basis of sex, race and sexuality which, if realized, would alter the nature of really existing horizontal and vertical human rights in the country.

Despite the promises of rights talk, I would urge us not to engage in the mistaken separation of law, human rights, truth commissions and reconciliation from questions of nation-building, legitimization and the centralization of state power. Ignoring the ideological dimensions of transitional justice is the quickest route to entrenching legal fetishism. Ernest Gellner (1988) referring to the historical precedent of the French revolution, points out how 'Liberty, Equality and Fraternity' very quickly became 'Bureaucracy, Mobility and Nationality'. Without a critical understanding of the reformulation of human rights in the hegemonic project of states emerging from authoritarian rule, we run the risk of ignoring the conjunction between state-building and nation-building, and thus becoming inured to the real pitfalls on a constitutionalist and rights-based route to a new democratic order.

Although truth commissions have legitimization as an objective, it is not clear at all that these commissions actually can or do legitimate state institutions. The TRC's actual ability to generate legitimacy was questionable, and its implications for impunity were mixed. On the one hand amnesty allowed perpetrators indemnity from previous convictions or allowed them to escape the closing net of the attorneys-general, thus undermining accountability. And yet amnesty forced a minority of perpetrators to confirm important truths about the past and reveal new ones.

In many Latin American countries, the political constraints created by a negotiated settlement curtailed the search for truth and justice and ultimately led to the erosion of legitimacy. For instance, the *Report of the Truth Commission* (1993) in El Salvador recommended an extensive program of judicial reform, which was patently ignored; and the amnesty law passed shortly afterwards undermined its potential as an instrument for reform of the security apparatus. Because of this and similar experiences, Panizza writes,

> It would be tempting to sum up the legacy for human rights of the processes of transition to democracy in Latin America in a single word: impunity … Politically impunity eroded the legitimacy of the new governments by blatantly violating the principle of

> equality before the law which every democratic government is bound to uphold. (1995:175)

Whether a truth commission challenges impunity and generates legitimacy for the legal system depends on the contribution it makes to a process of legal reform and, more specifically, whether it enhances the capacity of the criminal justice system to pursue prosecutions of human rights abuses. Yet often truth commissions are established as a substitute for prosecutions and represent the compromises made on human rights during the peace negotiations. Nation-building and a version of justice as reconciliation then come to inhabit the vacuum of impunity left by amnesty laws. This means that human rights function in the opposite way to which they were intended in international conventions, and can actually undermine the rule of law, the legitimacy of constitutionalism and the rights of citizens.

PART I

HUMAN RIGHTS AND TRUTH

CHAPTER 2

TECHNOLOGIES OF TRUTH: THE TRC'S TRUTH-MAKING MACHINE

Whereas the last chapter framed the overall place of the TRC in the South African transition, this chapter examines how the Commission operated on a day-to-day level, and in particular how the Commission sought to fulfill its mandate to provide a truthful account of human rights violations over a 34-year period.[1]

In the press and in public debate, there was a great deal of opposition to the truth-finding mandate of the TRC, particularly from former apartheid political parties such as the National Party and Conservative Party, as well as from some central-right liberal quarters. Anthea Jeffery (1999), for one, asserted that the TRC was neither objective nor neutral but was biased in favor of the ANC and liberation movements, and that it did not adequately uphold legal standards of investigation. These debates are dealt with in chapter 3, where I contend that political party bias was not the most pronounced or significant feature of the TRC. Moreover, concentrating solely on the overt, high politics can divert attention from a close examination of the TRC's methods. Before looking at observable political conflict over past truths, we need to look at logically prior questions of the conceptualization and formulation of official truths – classifications upon which other distinctions and assertions were made.

The hidden policy decisions on truth-making and the invisible technologies of bureaucratic truth production have so far received little elucidation or analysis either in the South African case or in truth commissions elsewhere. As truth commissions proliferate, it becomes increasingly necessary to interrogate the ways in which human rights violations are formulated and investigated as part of a wider assessment of the genre of human rights reporting for documenting violent histories. I argue that human rights methods of investigation, if not accompanied by other more historical methods of documentation and analysis, can be a poor avenue for accessing the experiential dimensions of violence.

After considering the TRC's methods of fact-finding, the chapter ends with a critical assessment of the final five-volume *Report*. Its limitations result from an over-legalistic perspective and a statistical methodology which were not accompanied by a conceptual framework which could integrate and synthesize the massive amount of information provided by the tens of thousands of testimonies. A critique of the TRC being developed in different ways by André du Toit (1999a, 1999b), Deborah Posel (1999) and Lars Buur (1999), looks at how the bureaucratic production of truth was dominated by a factual-forensic model. A positivist approach to truth decontextualized acts, dissected people's narratives of the past and stripped them of their integrity and meaning. In the end it led to an incomplete report which lacked any overarching and unified historical narrative, only a moralizing narrative predicated upon a notion of 'evil'. Why was this version of truth adopted by the TRC? As the last chapter sought to presage, truth-finding, like all functions of the TRC, was subordinated to the overriding nation-building objectives of post-apartheid regimes.

THE LIMITATIONS OF THE MANDATE

The South African TRC had the widest remit of any truth commission to date. The Uruguayan commission (1985) solely reported on 164 disappearances during military rule but ignored the more common offences of torture and illegal detention. The Chilean National Commission for Truth and Reconciliation (1991) only included in its remit violations which resulted in death. In the South African case, section 1(ix) of the Promotion of National Unity and Reconciliation Act mandated the Commission to investigate 'gross violations of human rights' between 1 March 1960 and 10 May 1994. Gross human rights violations were defined as:

a) the killing, abduction, torture, or severe ill-treatment of any person: or
b) any attempt, conspiracy, incitement, instigation, command or procurement to commit an act referred to in paragraph (a).

Notably, the South African TRC included all cases of torture as well as the category of 'severe ill-treatment', allowing Commissioners wide discretion. Nevertheless, the TRC attracted opprobrium for only including cases that exceeded the wide latitude of abuse permitted by apartheid laws. Detention without trial, pass laws, racial segregation of public amenities, forced removals and 'Bantu' education policy were all legal under apartheid but were excluded under the terms of the Act.[2]

The Commission focused primarily upon the extreme events and not upon the everyday, mundane bureaucratic enforcement of apartheid. Judging the past in terms of itself hinders the development of a new democratic conception of 'justice' and prevents an understanding of how violence became a routine part of state and social practices. The exclusion of acts which were legal under apartheid created a false distinction between the normative aspects of a racialized and authoritarian order (deemed to be outside the mandate) and illegal forms of violent physical coercion, when the latter implied the former.

This point has been developed by Mahmood Mamdani (1996), who bitterly criticized the TRC for avoiding the issue of the beneficiaries of apartheid, and the Commission's inability to see apartheid as a system, not dedicated towards individual gross human rights violations *per se*, but towards dispossession of Africans and their forced removal from their land. Because of its narrow, individualistic and legalistic view, in his opinion the Commission actually obstructed the wider project of ensuring social justice for the majority of Africans:

> [w]hereby injustice is no longer the injustice of apartheid: forced removals, pass laws, broken families. Instead the definition of injustice has come to be limited to abuses within the legal framework of apartheid: detention, torture, murder. Victims of apartheid are now narrowly defined as those militants victimized as they struggled against apartheid, not those whose lives were mutilated in the day-to-day web of regulations that was apartheid. We arrive at a world in which reparations are for militants, those who suffered jail or exile, but not for those who suffered only forced labor and broken homes. (1996:6)

To their credit, however, Commissioners addressed aspects of the institutional context in which apartheid operated through nine institutional and special hearings on different sectors of state and society. At these, evidence was heard on the maintenance of an environment in which human rights violations could thrive. Institutional hearings were held for business and labor, the religious community, the legal community,[3] the health sector, the media, and prisons and special hearings dealt with compulsory military service, children and youth, and women. The results, published in Volume 4 of the *Report*, were often damning. Business was centrally involved in 'state security initiatives … specifically designed to sustain apartheid rule … Business in turn benefited directly from their involvement in the complex web that constituted the military industry'.[4] The judiciary is blamed in the *Report* for upholding apartheid legislation and for unquestioningly granting police search warrants and turning a blind eye to the causes of death in police custody.[5] Some Christian churches are condemned for giving their blessing to the apartheid system, doctors and surgeons are accused of regularly misrepresenting forensic evidence and the media is savaged for being a docile tool of the National Party government. Through these institutional hearings, the TRC transcended some of the limitations of its narrow human rights mandate and did address, albeit in a fragmented fashion, certain important elements of the social context and institutional structure of apartheid.

RAINBOW TRUTHS

At the launch of the TRC, Commissioners made some quite extraordinary claims for truth, abetted by an advertising company which came up with the slogan 'Reconciliation Through Truth'. They claimed that the truth would heal suffering, deter future violations and serve as a form of reparation and compensation for victims. Commissioners later scaled down their claims as they grew more aware of the magnitude of the task facing them. Truth shrank from a single emancipatory Truth to smaller, multiple truths and in the final *Report*, there were only four fragmented types of truth remaining.

The TRC's truth-finding work was not organized through a set of unified procedures consistently applied throughout the life of the Commission. The fact that no overall, coherent conception of truth dominated from beginning to end in part resulted from the fissured internal organization of the Commission. The distinct constituencies – the Investigative Unit, the Research Unit, and the Human Rights Committee – all defined truth differently. Each made different types of input into the Informational Management System of the TRC (Infocomm) and each consumed different parcels of truth coming back from Infocomm.

The pressures from distinct truth constituencies were reflected in the TRC's final formulation of its guiding truths. The TRC's final *Report* (1:100; hereafter referred to as the '*Report*') defined four notions of truth which had guided the Commission:

1 *Factual or forensic truth:* is 'the familiar legal or scientific notion of bringing to light factual, corroborated evidence'. This category includes individual incidents, as well as the context, causes and patterns of violations.

2 *Personal or narrative truth:* refers to the individual truths of victims and perpetrators, attaching value to oral tradition and story-telling. Healing often takes place as narrative truth is recounted.

3 *Social truth:* is established, in the words of Judge Albie Sachs, through interaction, discussion and debate. Social truth acknowledges the importance of transparency and participation and affirms the dignity of human beings.

4 categories of Truth

4 *Healing and restorative truth:* repairs the damage done in the past and prevents further recurrences in the future. The dignity of victims is restored by officially acknowledging their pain.

Sociologist Deborah Posel has criticized the TRC's definition of truth as a 'wobbly and poorly constructed conceptual grid' not adequate to the task which it was set (1999:12). Like Desmond Tutu's vision of a rainbow nation, the plural model of truth is made up of discrete elements, and it is unclear how the elements are meant to relate to one another. The *Report* gives no guidance about how the four categories of truth might be connected, integrated and synthesized.

There were, broadly speaking, only two main paradigms of truth under which all others congregated: forensic truth and narrative truth. Forensic truth focussed upon creating the knowledge for the final product (findings and the *Report*) and the next three categories emphasized instead narrative, subjectivity and the experiential dimensions of truth-telling. These two truths were regularly counterposed to one another and each was dominant at different times. Narrative truth was hegemonic at the beginning of the Commission's life as public televised hearings had an unexpectedly dramatic effect, but it was displaced by a more legalistic forensic paradigm after the first year.

Only one of four types – forensic truth – is granted any epistemological value in the process of creating knowledge about the past. Forensic truth is a means to produce knowledge and an end in itself, whereas the other three truths are means-directed towards other ends, and specifically towards healing or affirming dignity. The three types of narrative truth are not given any epistemological standing – they are there for emotional 'catharsis' and nation-building. They do not contribute to the history of South Africa, nor to an improved understanding of the context, patterns and causes of past violations.

Since Max Weber's discussion of *Verstehen* (or interpretation) (1949), narrative truths are indispensable to a full understanding of the reasons why social agents act in certain ways. One cannot only look at empirically observable actions but also at the subjective meaning of social actors.[6] One can hardly understand the causes of past conflict in South Africa if the political narratives of race, ethnicity and nationalism (whether Afrikaner or white, African or Zulu) are not taken seriously in an attempt to grasp how ideology was internalized by actors and motivated certain types of behavior. Without encompassing the meanings associated with ethno-nationalist discourse in the picture, one gets no sense of how racism was an essential element of the background 'lifeworld' (or ongoing flow of experience) in which human rights violations occurred. Yet there seemed to be no conceptual place for subjectivity and political identity formation in understanding macro-historical events. Instead, narrative and social truths were included in public HRV hearings and in the *Report* solely for their healing potential. They were so much emotional window dressing, while the serious business of investigative work was carried out under the rubric of factual/forensic truth.

THE RISE AND RISE OF INFOCOMM

> ... the law selects among these voices, silencing some and transforming others to conform to legal categories and conventions ... Most voices are silenced; those that do survive do so in a barely recognizable form.
>
> J. Conley and W. O'Barr (1990:168–9)

At the end of the first year of the TRC in late 1996, public hearings, catharsis and healing began to give way to statement-taking and legal findings. There was a sea-change in the TRC's activities which were refocussed from victims' narratives to perpetrator findings. The information management system, or 'Infocomm', became entirely dedicated to investigating amnesty applications and making perpetrator findings, taking the emphasis away from victims' narratives. The rise of the forensic model transformed everything from the statement form to the controlled vocabulary of data coding, all of which profoundly affected the final *Report*.

Infocomm was a large-scale human rights database project created by Patrick Ball of the American Association of the Advancement of Science, and adapted from use in other places, such as El Salvador and Haiti. Just as human rights talk is becoming more globalized, then so is the technology of human rights information management. Infocomm was based upon logical positivism and quantitative statistical methods. A positivist approach was defended by sociologist Janice Grobbelaar, Information Manager in Johannesburg:

> Positivism is the best way to present the truth to the majority of South Africans, for reasons that most South Africans would not understand. Truth will be delivered by methodological rigor and scientific findings. The legitimacy of the TRC depends on its ability to create a truth that is acceptable, and that means a scientifically valid process that people can buy into. (Personal interview, TRC office, Johannesburg, 16 October 1996)

This comment shows a confident recognition of the mythical power of positivist rhetoric, and the assumption that ordinary South Africans will believe in facts produced through a positivist methodology mostly because they recognize its authoritative style. Janice Grobbelaar seemed to revel in the mystique of her powerful technology, which used the testimonies of the masses as its grist to magically produce graphs and bar charts which enjoyed an unassailable (since not fully understood) validity. In this in-house governmental positivism, a scientific elite controls society according to principles which the majority may not share or understand.

Grobbelaar's comment also expresses a pragmatic evaluation of the political conditions in which the TRC was working. Commissioners were caught in a hailstorm of political disputes and initial evaluations of its methods were withering (Jeffery 1999). The TRC was widely seen by opposition parties (such as the NP, DP, IFP and PAC) as an ideological advertising campaign for the ANC's version of the past. Although the hearings had a pro-ANC resonance to them, the *Report* was not an unreconstructed liberation narrative. However, the constant political pressure pushed Commissioners further down the positivist route. If they succeeded in having impartial methods, then they could fulfil Desmond Tutu's vision to be a one-nation institution embracing all political parties and favoring none. Facticity and impartiality were the foundations for the TRC's hegemonic project and nation-building mission.[7]

To silence its critics, the TRC's technologists of truth adopted a muscular, hard-hitting language. Whereas STRATCOM was the quasi-military agency entrusted by apartheid politicians with a mass disinformation campaign,[8] Infocomm was the post-apartheid strategy that would wage a quasi-military campaign of truth-finding. The statement form used to take the victim's stories down was called the 'protocol', a term sometimes used to describe a code of ceremonial agreement between heads of state. The information from the protocol was passive data to be 'captured' by the front-line data processors and then 'structured' in a uniform manner by the analysts.

The three main objectives of Infocomm were to identify a systematic pattern of abuse through statistical analysis, to describe the nature and extent of gross human rights violations and to evaluate its own activities.[9] Although it had seven stages from statement-taking to making findings, Infocomm was motored along by individual acts of violation. As Patrick Ball stated, 'the human rights event drives the whole process' (1996:4), and by event, he meant *act*, and by act, he meant:

> any act of violence that can be classified according to the data processors' controlled vocabulary … An act is the smallest unit of analysis in data processing and consequently in the database,

The Information Management System (Infocomm)

1. Statement-taking
300 designated statement-takers in offices and communities

↓

2. Registration
Register statement on database
Copy each statement and archive originals

↓

3. Data processing
Each narrative broken into number of discrete human rights violations and categorized in terms of 48 violation types. Names of perpetrators, witnesses and victims recorded. Brief narrative summary

↓

4. Data Capture
Data from processing entered on database shared between 4 offices

↓

5. Corroboration
60 investigators corroborating basic facts of each case

↓

6. Regional pre-findings
Findings made by commissioners and committee members. Either rejection because outside of date or mandate of Act or seen as untrue, or acceptance on the basis of the evidence and the balance of probability

↓

7. National findings
Findings ratified on basis of recommendations from regional offices
National Findings Task Group reviewing sample of each region's findings to ensure consistency

> and it is the basic working tool of the data processors and data analysts. This is what we count, for example, when we do statistics of different kinds. (1996:9)

The whole system was designed to break down the narratives contained in statements into quantifiable acts. Complex events and people were divided up into constituent components – either 48 distinct acts in the case of events, or three categories in the case of persons – victims, perpetrators or witnesses. It is interesting to note what was left out of the 'information flow', notably the victims' testimonies at public Human Rights Violations hearings. Hearings were not conceptualized as having any input into the production of knowledge – they had no epistemological status at all. I asked Janice Grobbelaar whether information from the hearings was recycled back into the database and she replied: 'No ... Hearings have to do with legitimation and recognizing people's experiences.'

TRUTH IN CRISIS

The logic of the information management system, combined with an internal sense of crisis, led to a wholesale restructuring towards making findings on individual acts. In late 1996, Commissioners were panicking. There was a policy vacuum for the first half of the Commission's life, when there was still no definition of basic categories such as 'victim' or 'gross human rights violation'.

Further, the TRC had originally expected thousands to flood into its four regional offices and give up to 150,000 statements. But deponents failed to materialize due to a poor public education campaign and by September 1996, the TRC had only taken 4,276 statements, when it should have had about 20,000. The Amnesty Committee was acting as if it were a separate institution and refused to hand over material from amnesty applications on the grounds of confidentiality. Crucially, there had as yet been no findings, and without findings, the Reparations and Rehabilitation Committee could not make reparations policy nor grant urgent interim reparations to those suffering acutely.

Infocomm designer Patrick Ball, in an internal document 'Evaluation of TRC Information Flow and Database' written on 8 September 1996, recognized the extent of the difficulties:

> We who designed the system failed to consider the profound effect the hearings have had on all aspects of the TRC's functioning. We failed because we did not foresee the importance hearings would grow to have. Thus the TRC has adopted as its principle function a task for which this organizational design is ill-suited. (p. 1)

The problem, however, did not just lie with the information management system design. Ever since the TRC's establishment, there had been a tension between two competing visions: whether the TRC was a legal process or an instrument of moral and emotional catharsis for the nation. This tension reached a breaking point and the 'legalists' eventually won out over the 'moralists', at least in the area of information management and the production of legal findings. The HRVC, which included a preponderance of forceful lawyers and intellectuals, steered the institution towards the production of legally defensible findings through positivistic methods.

Committee members perceived that all the public hearings were to the detriment of making findings and the number of public hearings was scaled down. They then turned their energies to reshaping Infocomm to produce individual findings. Following the Chilean model, it was felt that each deponent of a statement had a statutory right to have their case investigated. Human Rights Committee members began their massive restructuring with the first stage in the process – statement taking – so it would facilitate the Investigative Unit's 'low level' legal corroborations.[10] This enormous organizational transformation took another year to produce results and by early 1998 the TRC was making regional pre-findings.

It is important here to distinguish between legal positivism and sociological positivism. As stated in chapter one, legal positivism sees law as made up of rules which can be recognized and analyzed according to certain observational tests. As Dworkin writes, these tests are not concerned with content but with pedigree, that is, the manner in which the rules were developed (1977:17). For legal positivists, the set of valid legal rules is exhaustive of the 'law' and there are no legal obligations without a valid legal rule. Sociological positivism, on the other hand, asserts that knowledge cannot be based upon anything apart from systematic empirical observation and experimentation. Both forms of positivism share certain characteristics which create affinities between them: both use the same view of the natural sciences and its iron laws as their model; both eschew metaphysical reflection; both engage in a radical separation of fact and value or, in the case of legal positivism, law and morality (see Hart 1958, 1961). The South African TRC, once it adopted a more legalistic direction, did not have to adopt a more positivistic information system, but the affinities between law and sociological positivism made this more likely.[11]

TAKING ON THE STATEMENT-TAKERS

The new legalism of the Commission led to an expansion, redeployment, and retraining of statement-takers and a change in their relationship with the Investigative Unit. Further, its increasing reliance on sociological positivism altered the experience of giving and taking statements irrevocably.

In the beginning there were 40 statement-takers in the four offices and more volunteers (mainly from the churches) in the communities. The first group of statement-takers in Johannesburg had been trained for two days by psychologists Brandon Hamber and Thulani Grenville-Grey. In their training, there was an emphasis on preserving the victims' narrative whilst being aware of their psychological needs. Statement-takers were collaborators, in the intricate weaving of narrative, as well as counsellors to those traumatized by political violence.

Most deponents were Africans, but all statements were written in English, requiring statement-takers to carry out an ongoing translation. The statement-takers were not just invisible ciphers or neutral translators: instead, they were continually prompting and reminding deponents of events and wider histories. With the original statement form, statement-takers listened, sometimes for an hour or more, as deponents retold their experiences. Chief Johannesburg statement-taker Ollie Mahopo told me, 'To dig straight into the form from the outset was cold-blooded. We were dealing with people from an era of repression who had nowhere else to go and we had to be humane.' Only when the deponent told the narrative for a second time would statement-takers begin writing. At the end, the statement would be read back to the deponent, with the entire process taking up to three hours.

Within the TRC hierarchy, statement-takers received much of the blame for the information crisis. They were seen as slow and inept in obtaining, in the mantra of the legalists, 'the facts of the case'. Members of the IU often had a derisory view of statement-taking and data-processing. A Johannesburg investigator commented:

> Statements were coming in with no date of the violations, no names of victims or witnesses, and meanderings in the story. We should have had trained lawyers taking statements ... they were of very poor quality. I would read the statements and just want to cry. And the information management system was too complicated for the information being entered. You put shit in and you get shit out. (Personal interview, Johannesburg, 10 November 1998)

The 'designated statement takers program', made possible by a donation from the Netherlands government, was launched in Johannesburg in 1997. It added an extra 100 statement-takers to the office's jurisdiction and another 300 for the whole country and within a year dramatically increased the number of statements. The new wave of statement-takers were trained in a way very different from that of the initial cohort; that is, by investigators who wanted to turn out efficient para-legal clerks.

Control was taken away from statement-takers as the form became a checklist, not one requiring listening and an inter-subjective construction of a narrative. Statement-takers began to feel the strain of a new regime of urgency and legal precision. As Ollie Mahopo put it, 'there is a lot of pressure on us to get the facts, the cold facts'.

These changes sparked a struggle between victims and statement-takers over the relevance of testimonial evidence, whereas before the process was more collaborative.[12] Vaal statement-taker Thabiso Mohasoa said: 'we were told to keep it as brief as possible and only focus on the major points ... we had to get the facts, but people wanted to tell their story in broad terms.' Under the new positivist regime, statement-takers I interviewed reported more incidents of resistance as some deponents refused to sign their statements, contending that vital information had been omitted.

THE NEW PROTOCOL

Over the life of the Commission, there were five successive versions of the statement form, or 'protocol', until by the end the protocol had become a highly structured questionnaire. The protocol also was altered to give designated statement-takers less room to make 'mistakes' and to force them into the 'cold facts' approach desired by the Investigation Unit.

The first version of the statement form used in early 1996 began with an open section for narrative which often ran to 15–20 pages. Ernest Sotsu, an ANC leader in the Vaal, showed me his statement form completed in early 1996 with a 20-page narrative containing a blow-by-blow account of the circumstances leading up to a massacre in Sebokeng in 1990, when the army and police fired upon an ANC crowd which had surrounded a group of IFP supporters. Sotsu gave the background to the event and described his own role on the day, insisting that he attempted to avert the impending disaster in negotiations with the security forces and ANC leaders.

In August 1996, a new statement form designed by Dr Ruben Richards, executive secretary of the HRVC, was piloted. It adopted a mass survey style of format which completely abandoned the original opening narrative section. The form could be completed in 30–45 minutes, and even by deponents themselves.[13] Complexity was lost, and one member of the Research Unit I interviewed likened it to a vehicle registration license, and then an information manager present less charitably revised that to 'maybe more like a dog registration license'.

With each revision, the protocol forms became more and more like the data base that statements were 'captured' on to. The closer resemblance between paper form and software program meant less slippage between the protocol and inputting on the database. It also meant a severe curtailing of deponents' narratives. In the final *Report*, the TRC openly recognized the pitfalls in this move to a more legal and administrative focus: 'Such institutional reorientation is not easily achieved ... and there was also considerable concern that it would become driven by technical rather than moral considerations' (1:156).

For some deeply involved in the functioning of the information system, the consequences of these changes to the protocol were deleterious. Themba Kubheka, chief data processor in the Johannesburg office, acknowledged this:

> When we started it was a narrative. We let people tell their story. By the end of 1997, it was a short questionnaire to direct the interview instead of letting people talk about themselves ... The questionnaire distorted the whole story altogether ... it destroyed the meaning. (Personal interview, 9 November 1998)

For Weber, the replacing of moral considerations by technical ones and the loss of meaning was characteristic of bureaucratic rationalization (for example, Gerth and Mills 1991:196–244). Purposive rationality impoverishes the life-world of social agents as it increasingly renders the communicative practices of everyday life in instrumental and bureaucratic terms. With the South African TRC, we have another example of this rationalization of society by the state, but in this case it is a human rights commission (rather than law and bureaucracy generally, *pace* Weber) which is the transformer of the lifeworld of social agents.

In the Weberian tradition, Jürgen Habermas has also formulated an important critique of the technocratic consciousness of states and the hegemonic place of 'scientism' in modernity. For Habermas (1986), 'scientism' results from the unshakeable belief in science held by certain scientific constituencies.[14] Scientism reduces all knowledge to that provided by empiricist natural sciences and is blind to how its so-called facts are components in a changing historical framework of understanding.

Habermas' work is very useful in seeing how human rights are part of a wider and progressive rationalization of the lifeworld of social agents. In opposition to positivist science and a forensic legalism, Habermas seeks to maintain the place of subjectivity and interpretation in the creation of knowledge. Habermas' subject is social and conditioned by both historical experience and reasoning. Knowledge depends as much upon its inter-subjective construction as it does upon rationality and reason. Law is a transformative catalyst situated between system and lifeworld which can facilitate the colonization of the lifeworld by systemic imperatives (such as nation-building, in the South African case). This approach has useful things to say about how a public, official version of the past might be constructed, as it insists upon knowledge being intersubjectively created within a political community.

THE DATABASE DRIVING THE MODEL

> A gross violation is a gross violation, whoever commits it and for whatever reason.
>
> TRC Chair, Desmond Tutu (*Report* 1:52)

Patrick Ball's information system Infocomm was a significant improvement on many previous large human rights databases. For a start, it had a more sophisticated means of coding multiple acts, and did not just deal with the worst act, as other databases do. Further, it allowed for a person to be a victim and a perpetrator at the same time which is important in the South African context, where many activists who suffered at the hands of the police or army also committed violent acts of resistance.

Data processors proceeded along the following lines. They would read the statement through once, highlighting key persons and events and then break the narrative up into discrete acts which could be put into the database. Each violation to be counted was time-and-place-specific, and was separate from the other violations. If a person had been detained for three months, then tortured and then killed, there were three separate violations rather than a composite narrative (the harassment and killing of Ms X).

The first database screen displayed the date, the TRC office, and the names of deponent, witnesses, victims and perpetrators. Under 'person details', the data processor had to summarize the statement in 30 words or less. This called for an extreme condensing of the statement, which made many data processors uneasy, as Themba Kubekha commented,

> The emotional part of the story wouldn't go on the computer, remember it was just a machine. You'd lose a lot – we couldn't put style or emotion into the summary. We were inputting for counting purposes. We lost the whole of the narrative … we lost the meaning of the story. It was tragic, pathetic. It became dry facts. (Personal interview, 9 November 1998)

The second database screen contained the details of the acts of violation. There was tabulation for the victim, place, date, time, and category of violation. The data processors chose from a coding list, informally called the 'Bible'. They could not deviate from this classificatory scheme which Ball portentously referred to as the 'controlled vocabulary'. The initial 200 categories were seen as too complex and the Bible was whittled down to 48 violations. All information had to be classified according to this grid, which rigidly fixed how complex statements could be interpreted. As one data processor put it: 'in the beginning there was lots of interpretation of the statement but by the end we were just like robots. You read it and put it in the computer as it is.'

For the purposes of the information management system, information did not exist unless it conformed to the controlled vocabulary and coding frame. This is a clear example of how a statistical grid can selectively classify social reality and in turn shape how that reality is analyzed.[15] Violations are irreducible acts which conform to all the other acts within their category in the controlled vocabulary. This allows comparison of 'like with like', but one must remain aware of the degree to which comparability itself is a result of the process of coding. It is only possible to compare and statistically analyze these acts if the acts are decontextualized and treated as just the same. Statisticians and human rights organizations both require that events be categorized in a way that is universal and generalizable: quantitative sociology needs to count and human rights needs justiciable violations.

In the contingency and flow of social life, however, each act is not the same as every other in its category. Instead, each is unique, and irreducible, part of specific personal and community histories. Some acts happened to men, some to women, some to activists fighting apartheid and others to security police. The controlled vocabulary levelled contextual differences – all cases in a category are presented as the same act. To take one of the classifications used, all killings by shooting are the same as all others, regardless of the aims of the person pulling the trigger. In his pragmatist critique of legal positivism, Tamanaha states that positivism's urge to categorize is problematic since 'social reality is gloriously complex and chaotic, filled with phenomena and variations of phenomena in shades and degrees that do not come in categorical boxes' (1997:62).

These criticisms do not imply that statistical analysis cannot be done, only that it must be accompanied by a recognition of the limits of the process. There is little or none of this critical epistemological reflection in the *Report*. As Habermas has noted, this lack of reflection on the conditions of knowledge is characteristic of the positivist reduction of knowledge to scientific methodology. In fact it is a defining attribute, as Habermas writes, 'That we disavow reflection is positivism' (1986:vii).

What was lost in the data processing and the urge to generate acts that could be counted were the existential truths contained within complex narratives. The processors destroyed the integrity of the narrative by chopping it into segments and 'capturing' discrete acts and types of person. What was lost was the arc of a personal history, the sense of the trajectory of the story, where, to return to the instance used above, killing by shooting might have been the culmination of a long process of detention, harassment and torture.

As I have argued elsewhere (1997a), human rights reporting is characterized by a stripping out of subjectivity in order to construct a minimalist realist account in general, not only in truth commission reports. In fact, truth commission reporting has been one of the areas which has occasionally proved the exception to this rule, as some truth commission reports made a serious attempt to integrate the consciousness of social actors into wider historical contextualization and political analysis. Yet as a rule, human rights institutions tend to favor the bare minimalist style (dealing only with forensic truths) which is endemic in the law. In 1998, this point was apparent during the longest trial in French history, the trial of Vichy bureaucrat and Nazi collaborator, Maurice Papon. The verdict which convicted Papon of complicity in crimes against humanity and gave him a suspended sentence of ten years did not go far enough for many French citizens in dealing with the historical questions of collaboration. The historian Denis Peschanski commented: 'Society expected a whole regime to be put on trial. The problem is that this verdict is about the responsibility of an individual involved in the criminal acts of a regime' (*Guardian*, 3 April 1998).

EXPERIENCES OF TRUTH-TELLING

> For most black people it is apartheid that is on trial, but that is not how the TRC was conceived. It was mandated to document the gross human rights violations committed during the maintaining and fighting against apartheid.
>
> Russell Ally, Human Rights Committee Member. (Personal interview, Johannesburg, 28 October 1996)

By looking at Infocomm from the perspective of victims, it becomes apparent that there were fundamental differences between popular expectations of the TRC's work and the narrow human rights mandate of the TRC. After giving their statements, many deponents expressed dissatisfaction at the way in which their individual narrative seemed not to fit into the model of information management. Their story was frozen in time, stripped to its 'essential characteristics' and that which was outside the 'controlled vocabulary' was discarded.

I first got a sense that all was not well in victims' experiences of Infocomm when I heard deponents say that they had left something vital out of their statement. Many wanted to return to make a new or additional statement. Julia Mulutsi of Pimville, Soweto, forgot to mention that the judge at the inquest into her daughter's shooting had named a police constable who had not even been mentioned in the case (Personal interview, October 1996). She wanted the TRC to clarify the judicial error which had haunted her for over a decade. The late leader of the Khulumani Support Group, Sylvia Dhlomo Jele, echoed many victims in saying, 'Most of the things I wanted to say I couldn't say' (Personal interview, 8 October 1996). She reported being told by the statement-taker that all the pages were full, and she should tell the rest to the investigators, who never came.

Further, many were dissatisfied that they did not formulate their request for reparations. For instance, what was most important to Hilda Mokoena of Soweto was to see the police cell where son was alleged to have hung himself while being detained for his political activities. 'How did he do it? What could he have tied his blanket to?' she asked, with incredulity (Personal interview, 2 October 1996). The 'cold facts' approach to statement-taking exacerbated these kinds of silences by diverting deponents away from their own personal agendas.

In order to generate statistics and findings, the TRC required a clear chronology which furnished only relevant evidence within a constrained time period. Information was only needed on the period immediately before and after an act. The long historical run-up to the actual event was seen as superfluous. Moreover, victims' testimonies were often characterized by a lack of the rigorous chronology essential to the factual/forensic model. Instead, testimonials were jumbled, elliptical. They were partial and fragmented, not magisterial. They were full of interpretation and enmeshed in lived memory.

The narratives of victims and witnesses almost always began with the critical event itself – the phone call, the sound of an explosion. A survivor of the Sebokeng Night Vigil Massacre in 1991, Cecilia Ncube, told of the sound of explosions and the screaming of neighbors (Personal interview, 30 October 1996). Trudy Shongwe of Soweto began with the moment when she was called from work to go to the hospital where her son lay dead (Personal interview, 8 November 1996). After the critical moment, testimonies go in one direction or the other – either into the aftermath and consequences of the event, or they detail at length the events preceding the event. Many testifying at TRC hearings showed no regard for chronology at all, jumping from one episode to another.

Persons historically excluded from power in South Africa – women, the uneducated, the poor – often adopt a relational view of their own subjectivity and place themselves within social networks. Almost all the victims I heard spoke of the relationships between families of victims, and often between victims and perpetrators. There was very little room for this in the statement form or in the data processing, which decontextualized by excluding community networks and complex social dynamics. The statement form only referred to the party political or institutional allegiance of a victim or perpetrator. There was little room for including the immediate family and wider kinship networks which may not have been 'party political', but which were often central to the organization of disputes. The vocabulary of human rights violations often excises social context, and with it a perspective on local power relations. Human rights investigations are characteristic of the legal process in general; Conley and O'Barr have written about the same kind of extraction of individuals from their social contexts during court proceedings:

> Many litigants speak of their place in a network of social relations and emphasize the social context of their legal problems. They assign legal rights and responsibilities on the basis of social status ... By contrast, the official discourse of the law is oriented to rules. (1995:172)

One consequence of law's propensity to exalt rules over relationships was a de-politicization of local histories.[16] In her account of the HRV hearings in Alexandra township in Johannesburg, Belinda Bozzoli (1998) argued that the format and content of the hearings, and I would add also the format of information management, created a depoliticizing narrative which left out the excesses and local dynamics of the anti-apartheid struggle. The role of the youth in leading a revolt was marginalized, as were the organizational forms of street committees and strategies of boycotts, barricades, and marches. Less savory aspects, such as petrol bombing, punishment at people's courts and necklacing of alleged police informers, were often omitted entirely. Bozzoli writes, 'One unintended consequence ... was to exclude from the communally constructed narrative the main "public" story of the revolt of the 1985–6 period' (1998:185). The TRC hearings only presented a sequence of individualized victims, as opposed to a richly complex and layered history of a state of war.

Finally, positivistic approaches to the past organize a narrative in quite distinctive ways from individual memories, which are quite fragile and idiosyncratic. In a manner that is distinctive from a legal chronology, an individual or more social form of memory relies on information which may be considered irrelevant to the investigation of the act, but is highly relevant to the victim's ability to remember. These mnemonic devices are key events or symbolic images upon which whole segments of narrative hang. Sometimes they can seem quite bizarre and expressive of states of extreme psychological dissonance. They are the personalized symbols upon which the structure of the narrative hinges, and emotional associations tend to pivot.

This point may be quite generalizable to the way people tell narratives, as I first realized it when interviewing victims of state terror in Guatemala. In one case, a man returning to his village of Plan de Sanchez in 1982 came across a cooking gas bottle in the middle of the path. He elaborated greatly upon this gas bottle, as it was of some significance to him, being the first sign that something was out of place, and that things were generally amiss. He then proceeded to the village where he encountered the grisly scene of a massacre of over 200 people by the army. In an account (Poniatowska 1984) of the Tlatelolco massacre in Mexico in 1968 discussed by Grandin (n.d.) individuals sought cognitive refuge from the uncanny and incomprehensible by grasping at tiny and bizarre details. One survivor, Elvira B de Concheiro, remembers how in the midst of the slaughter by the military, who had closed off streets and set up gun encampments, a woman handed her an empty milk bottle before disappearing into the crowd.

THE BANALITY OF 'EVIL'

> We realized quite soon that we could not, as our mandate demanded, write the history of the years between 1960 and 1994.
>
> TRC Research Unit Director, Charles Villa-Vicencio
> (*Mail and Guardian*. 'TRC admits it missed the full story'. 14 August 1999)

The TRC's final *Report* has to be understood as being the direct result of the methodology used, and its limitations must be linked with that methodology. The main shortcoming, noted by many observers, is that there is no overarching and unified historical narrative linking together the various fragments of the *Report*.

As André du Toit has commented, the truth commission did not try to write a history (1999a:2), instead it was led by the need to make perpetrator findings. He, too, has noted a crucial shift in the TRC's work 'from a narratively framed victim-oriented conception of the TRC process to a perpetrator-focused quasi-legal approach'. Because of this shift, it ended up on the terrain of the courts, not on the terrain of the historians. This surprised observers who expected that the *Report* would put 'apartheid on trial', but the TRC opted for a more narrow, legalistic sequence of findings on single gross human rights violations. This, of course, was the product of the compromise made during peace talks which required the TRC to fill the legal vacuum (for example, in naming perpetrators) left by the amnesty provisions.

The primacy of the amnesty requirements resulted in a report with no internal unified narrative form and which did not deal with the structural nature of apartheid: instead it is like the compendious work of a nineteenth-century Victorian scientist obsessed with a comprehensive social or biological classification. A lack of history and contextual explanation can also be found in truth commission reports from Latin America. The Argentine commission report, *Nunca Más*, provided no historical context to the political violence of the 1976–83 period, and the Chilean Rettig report offers very little political history leading up to the coup in 1973 and the murderous regime of General Augusto Pinochet.

The South African *Report* is a multilayered document drawing upon many different types of material, from quantitative sociological analysis of findings to the testimonies of victims at hearings. There are many different messages and ways of delivering these messages, thus allowing contradictory interpretations. There is no authoritative perspective on the past arranging the diverse material into a progressively structured exposition of an argument. Instead, the various sections – statistical analysis of patterns of abuse, chunks of testimony from hearings, and short background research pieces – lie side by side, unconnected.

The disassociated nature of the information in the *Report* derives from the lack of coherence between the four types of truth. There is in particular a lack of integration between statistics and testimony from hearings. The lack of an integrating structure emerged from the pluralist methodology; statistics were based upon statements and were a central part of Infocomm, whereas testimony came from hearings transcripts which were excluded from the informational management system.[17]

In the *Report*, victims' voices were limited to extracts from public hearings and their statements were never quoted. Thus subjectivity was contained and controlled; it had a photogenic emotive impact, but it was not incorporated in a way that contributed to knowledge about the past. Subjectivity had no epistemological status, but came into the *Report* as a flavoring, as a spice to give an idea of the testimonial character of the hearings.

The *Report*'s vision of the apartheid era emerges through a series of chronologies and typologies. Chronology was the only attempt made at narrative, but it is the most unimaginative, impoverished and barren form of narrative. A sequence of events, unless it is explained how one event led to another, or how all were produced by a set of complex factors, is a version of history as 'just one damned fact after another'. Lacking an explanatory historical framework, simple chronologies were in the end too weak conceptually to integrate the various dimensions of the *Report*.

The document did not have an underpinning narrative template to bind together the distinctive chronologies of separate areas. The most important part of the *Report* for history-writing purposes is Volume 3, which contains five regional profiles (Eastern Cape, Natal and KwaZulu, Orange Free State, Western Cape and Transvaal). Violations are placed into a set of categories (torture, murder, etc.), and told in chronological order per region, so there is a historical progression of facts for each designated area but no overarching discussion of the relations between regions. Violations are analyzed according to statistical models, but not theoretically analyzed. There is no integrated explanation of the (personal, ideological and structural) reasons for the violence, nor how it was structured and organized. In particular, there was no theory relating to the violence which explained 'the inherently violent nature of apartheid itself: 'violence is not merely the result of apartheid, but necessary for it ... apartheid has actually made use of violence to sustain itself' (Mervyn Bennun 1995:38). Bennun rightly concludes that 'accounts which do not locate the violence firmly in both the social structures created by apartheid and in the political processes of aparheid itself are at best incomplete and inadequate' (37). Political scientists such as Bennun and Rupert Taylor (1991) came up with sophisticated theories of apartheid violence, but they were largely ignored by the TRC.

The lack of a central narrative exacerbated other tendencies in the *Report* to decontextualize cases. The grouping together of cases under themes (detention, deaths in custody, banishment, etc) meant that violations were taken out of their context, and the voices taken from hearings are left hovering in the ether. The fragmentation and decontextualization is noted also by du Toit, who writes:

> In terms of its structure ... the TRC *Report* somewhat unexpectedly opted for a determinedly non-narrative framing of its material: instead it relied on a positivist methodology for constructing a systematic database ... aimed at making perpetrator findings on a case by case basis ... in practice this led to an analytical decontextualizing and deconstruction of historical incidents. (1999a:3)

Du Toit then considers the 'zero hand grenades' case of the East Rand in the Report as his example of fragmentation and decontextualization. This story of the highest levels of the government ordering security police operatives (again, Joe Mamasela) to deliver booby-trapped hand grenades to youth activists was not told in its entirety in the *Report* – instead it was broken into different sections. This was a common treatment of single stories in the *Report*.

Du Toit sees the lack of a principal narrative in the *Report* as an advantage (1999a:3), since it avoids an exclusive reading of apartheid which could have caused more conflict. Yet in applauding the absence of an 'authoritarian version of the truth', du Toit presents us with a stark choice between either an 'authoritarian' truth or no overarching truth at all. Anthea Jeffery also adopts this liberal position and condemns a publicly sanctioned history as 'an Orwellian notion, paving the way for renewed political indoctrination' (1999:5).

There are, of course, other possibilities between these too extremes. Authoritative does not necessarily mean authoritarian or 'Orwellian'. Du Toit's argument acquits the TRC for its failure to enter into significant historical debates about apartheid and racism. The TRC treated the collected work of historians of apartheid as 'factual data' to be duly archived but it did not weigh up important theoretical debates (Was apartheid a recent expression of centuries-old white settler colonialism? Or was it a racialized structure of capital accumulation?). Applauding the lack of narrative on minimalist liberal grounds comes very close to celebrating the *Report*'s inability to make clear its theoretical assumptions about apartheid, violence and the complexities of race, gender and class.

Deborah Posel suggests another way of looking at the *Report* when she writes that there *is* a master narrative and an overarching structure, but it is not one a historian would recognize (1999:3). Instead, it is 'more a moral narrative about the fact of moral wrongdoing across the political spectrum, spawned by the overriding evil of the apartheid system'. This is an interesting insight and goes some way in explaining the relationship between fact and analysis in the *Report*, and the relationship between individual acts of moral wrongdoing and 'evil' as the structure of understanding.[18] The *Report*'s disconnected bodies of information and findings, unattached to any unifying narrative, allow the moral narrative to serve as the explanatory framework. The legal-forensic method therefore gelled nicely with an overarching nation-building project with strong religious and moralizing overtones.

An in-depth understanding of the social conditions (racism, class inequality, gender hierarchy, poverty) of wrongdoing is bypassed in favor of the moral category of 'evil' which resolves the problem of meaning: Why did people commit gross human rights violations? Because of the evil system of apartheid. End of story. The litany of moral transgressions in the *Report* all add up to the evil of apartheid. Yet strangely, as Posel notes, 'The TRC *Report* sheds remarkably little light on apartheid' (1999:23). This is only intelligible if we accept that the *Report*'s overall narrative is a moral one dedicated to national reconciliation, rather than the type of account one might expect from historical and sociological research and analysis.

The *Report* is primarily to be understood as a chronicle of acts embedded within a moral framework of denunciation. The nation-building project relies upon recognizing moral wrongness; in fact, it is a new criterion of moral citizenship. Further debate about apartheid is placed in abeyance, in favor of constructing this new moral unity. This is not to be lightly dismissed, but we should be aware that South Africans are not united by a shared political understanding of apartheid, but by their shared moral denunciation of wrong acts.

A MORAL RESPONSE TO APARTHEID VIOLENCE

Perhaps we should have expected from the beginning that an official version of the past would end up with just such an overarching moral narrative rather than an historical one. Richard Rorty writes of national histories:

> I think there is no point in asking whether Lincoln or Whitman or Dewey got America right. Stories about what a nation has been and should try to be are not attempts at accurate representation, but rather attempts to forge a moral identity. (1998:13)

The emphasis on a moral response to atrocities in South African history leaves open the question of which socio-political explanatory framework one might use to understand the causes of violations. Certainly, in pragmatic terms, it is more difficult to create a consensus (even though in some ways it is more consequential) on an historical understanding of apartheid violence and a political vision of the future than it is to create a consensus that apartheid was morally wrong. In short, it is more politically expedient to allow those who supported apartheid in various ways to adopt a moral demeanor of denunciation than it is to insist upon a complex political understanding of injustice developed by the anti-apartheid movement.

Apart from just politically expedient reasons, it could be argued that a moral response was necessary from the TRC due to the weak ideological appeal of constitutionalism. With constitutionalism, the loyalty of citizens is to the rule of law, but also to the ethical values motivating legal rules. It could be argued that the idea of human dignity is logically a precondition for the list of rights contained in the Constitution. To have any legitimacy, constitutionalism requires not only procedural fairness but a minimal framework of basic shared values. The content and level of shared values might be drawn in a strong, social-democratic or a weak liberal manner, depending on the political moment and actor. In any case, it can be argued that there must be a moral line which cannot be crossed by state officials under any conditions (for example, legal officials may not torture criminal suspects) or, in the words of one writer, 'a consensus concerning the intolerable'.[19] The TRC succeeded in drawing that line in its moral response to apartheid and this was a significant contribution to a 'culture of human rights' in the sense of promulgating some of the values necessary for constitutionalism to actually function.

The moral accounting of apartheid by the TRC contributed, though only time will tell to what degree and with what consequences, to a wider attempt of post-apartheid governance to integrate respect for human rights into the everyday beliefs and practices of ordinary South Africans and engender a respect for, and identification with, state legality. Perhaps more importantly it expressed a commitment to political accountability on the part of state officials, who reiterated their undertaking to not abuse human rights, even if they could not realize all the other constitutional commitments to justice in the Constitution.[20]

A number of writers, such as Allen (1999), Borneman (1997), Minow (1998) and Shklar (1990) have emphasized the importance of a 'moral reckoning' with atrocities in order to affirm the dignity of the victims, ritually purify central state institutions and construct the state as a legitimate moral agent. The first stage of this reconstruction is moral recognition. Allen (1999) argues that the South African TRC could be justified on the grounds that it articulated a general moral position – the denunciation of apartheid legality – which would have been out of place in a court of law. Here, the TRC is a form of recognition not captured by legal justice which acknowledges the historical fact of exclusion from legal recognition of the African majority, and demonstrates the consequences of a lack of commitment to the rule of law.

An appropriate moral response is necessary in order to generate the moral context for democratic constitutionalism. The legitimization of the state, and especially the law, cannot just be left to the rational and impartial functioning of the law in a society so ravaged by conflict. The state cannot maintain a position of neutrality on the past if it wants to be an efficacious arbiter of conflict in the present, and the TRC was the institution that forcefully articulated a moral position. An astringent liberalism which sees legitimacy as arising solely through procedural fairness does not seem wholly appropriate to the reality of the South African justice system.

In sum, it is important to recognize that a moral response to apartheid violence is a necessary component in creating respect for legality and enhancing the legitimacy of democratic constitutionalism. This recognition complements the critical evaluation of the TRC's truth-making project made in this chapter, since a moral response would be even more persuasive and enduring if linked to a political response to the past which is integrated into a vision of social justice in the future; that is, if the moral denunciation of apartheid were combined with salient elements of the politics of the anti-apartheid struggle.

A moral response to atrocities should also be linked to a legal response – an obligation to pursue offenders who do not participate in amnesty procedures sanctioned by the 1994 political settlement. A moral response on its own is not enough, as Borneman argues, 'if the state wants to establish itself as a moral agent with legitimacy in the entire community, it has an obligation to pursue retribution where wrongdoing has occurred' (1997:7). Therefore the moral response advanced by the TRC is a necessary but not sufficient condition of successful democratization. Crucially, it is important that the legal and political responses to apartheid-era violations do not get lost in the religious paradigm of moral denunciation.

THE HUMAN RIGHT TO A HUMAN STORY

My evaluation of the TRC's approach to truth is less a critique of the information management system than it is a critique of the changes to that system during the life of the TRC, the pre-eminence which 'scientism' enjoyed, the emphasis on perpetrator findings, and the inability of the TRC to integrate positivist sociology within a wider historical understanding.

My point is not that forensic and positivist forms of documentation do not have their place. In the legal setting of a criminal case, a forensic method is essential for producing the evidence necessary to evaluate guilt or innocence reasonably. Nor is law condemned in all circumstances to exclude context and banish the subjectivity of victims and perpetrators. Writers such as Mark Osiel (1997) and Lawrence Douglas (2000) have demonstrated how many liberal 'show' trials, in cases of mass atrocities such as the Holocaust and the 'dirty war' in Argentina, have included historical context as well as seeking to investigate the state of mind and intentions of alleged perpetrators.

The law must do what it is good at in a legal setting: criminal prosecutions. Because prosecutions were obstructed by amnesty laws, the TRC became for a time the only forum in which perpetrators could be 'investigated' and named, and this facilitated the intrusion of a narrow legalism combined with sociological positivism into the writing of an official national history. The legal method is important for anchoring core assertions, but it cannot provide the overarching structural narrative to explain *why* violence occurred. Had there been separate legal mechanism for indemnity from criminal prosecution only, and the door left open for civil claims, then this would have facilitated more prosecutions of offenders and the truth commission would have been freer to write an historically informed account of apartheid-era violence.

In considering the contribution of sociological positivism to the TRC *Report*, I would argue in a similar vein, since the *Report* includes some valuable demonstrations of the sociological database. Graphs show peaks in violence in 1976 after the Soweto uprising, during the state of emergency in 1986, and in 1992 during the crisis in peace talks. There is a sharp rise in torture between 1984 and 1988, which supports the view that it became a widespread policy of the security apparatus at that time, and particularly during the state of emergency. The opening to Volume 3 provides a very good macro-level picture of violations and tells us a variety of salient truths: that most victims were African males between 13 and 24, and that most killings were perpetrated by the Inkatha Freedom Party, followed by the South African Police; and most acts of torture were perpetrated by the South African Police. These are useful insights which can be used to support or refute general assertions, as long as we comprehend that they do not, in themselves, *explain the reasons for* the violence. In fact they cannot and we should not expect statistical methods to generate a complex theoretical understanding of the past.

So my objections are less directed towards quantitative sociology than the inability of the Research Unit to subject it to a wider vision of writing history and to their opting instead for a heady mixture of narrow legalism and an unreflective quantitative sociology. Meaningful knowledge about the past is only possible when scientific positivism assumes its proper, subordinate place within the more profound application of historical analysis. Infocomm was allowed to cannibalize all other approaches to truth, and this left a vacuum of analysis which was eventually filled by a moral-theological narrative on good and evil. Technology and law came to drive the truth-telling process and to shape the manner in which the official version of history would be constructed. History came to increasingly occupy an excluded middle, wedged between a moral narrative on the one hand, and a legal-positivist methodology on the other. Fact and value remained separate, and there was no historical narrative to harmonize and synthesize them.

There is a direct link between a forensic method and the moral language of nation-building. Individual and community narratives as expressed in ethnographic interviews often express a range of levels of intention behind acts, where personal and political motives are difficult to distinguish one from the other. Law unbundles these different levels of intentionality so as to separate out different motivations (for example, political versus a crime of passion) and identify those which are legally relevant. It filters subjectivity so as to individualize responsibility and attribute blame to offenders. The TRC only focussed on intentionality at one level – the victim–perpetrator dyad – which fits into a nation-building project. It selectively focussed on individuals and acts as part of the construction of a new type of South African citizenship.[21]

Despite the centrality of law to the TRC's mission, the legal standing of the TRC's findings (the main purported objective of the information management system) is highly uncertain. The *Report* states that: 'the Commission was a legal institution with the responsibility of making defensible findings according to established legal principles' (1:144). Yet, as we have noted, the TRC was not a 'legal institution' in the conventional sense. It was a liminal institution only verging on the legal, or perhaps it is better described as 'legally established', with certain limited legal powers. Du Toit (1999b) refers to the 'quasi-legal' nature of the TRC and he questions the legal status of the findings. He argues rightly that they have no legal standing as the TRC was not a court of law following due process. It emulated but did not strictly follow legal principles of evidence. The criteria for evidence that would constitute the basis of a finding were not those of a criminal case ('beyond a reasonable doubt') but instead a loose burden of proof closer to the 'balance of probabilities' required of a civil court (Jeffery 1999).

Du Toit writes, 'it may be questioned whether truth commissions, as non-judicial bodies and not following legal procedures, are properly qualified to make such (quasi-legal?) determinations. Strictly speaking, "perpetrator findings" is not their business but that of the courts or other qualified institutions' (1999b:16). It is still not clear how the evidence produced by the TRC might or might not lead to criminal or civil prosecutions for those who did not receive amnesty. In the *Report*, Commissioners did not recommend that findings should be taken up by the courts. The findings amount to little more than the stigmatizing of individuals, former state institutions, and political parties.

There was a shift here in the findings from legal 'guilt' to moral 'responsibility', as the *Report* backtracked from a watertight legal position, stating that 'a perpetrator finding' is 'not a finding of [legal] guilt, but of responsibility for the commission of a gross violation of human rights' (1:157d). All that effort put into mimicking the law, only to discover that the findings do not have any legal standing after all! Perhaps it would have been better to have abandoned the legal-positivist paradigm early on in order to pursue a more historical-sociological one, which would have involved the TRC accepting that it was a human rights commission of enquiry, *not* a legal body.

I am not arguing for a greater emphasis on the moral-therapeutic dimensions of its work as there was enough of this already. Instead, the

TRC could have combined more effectively its important moral response to the past with its task of writing a nuanced socio-political history of the past. Given that it was not a legal institution *per se*, it could have integrated both statistical analysis and oral history into a wider theoretical framework for understanding violence. In so doing, oral history could have been made more central to the TRC's information system. This might have led to an account that preserved, rather than stripped out, the subjectivities of victims and a history that retained narrative and context and meaning. This has been achieved by other truth commissions (for example, the two recent commissions in Guatemala) which perhaps underlines the uniquely legalistic character of the South African TRC *Report*. The Guatemalan Commission for Historical Clarification report, *Memoria del Silencio* (1999), dedicates the first volume to the 'causes and origins of the internal armed conflict' and offers a damning narrative of how violence emanated from hundreds of years of economic exploitation, racism and political exclusion. The third volume (*El Entorno Histórico*) of the report of the Catholic church project *Guatemala: Nunca Más* (1998) gives an excellent account of the socio-political conditions from the 1870s to the 1990s, portraying a complex scenario constituted by US foreign policy and periodic military interventions, guerrilla insurgencies and popular movements, Guatemalan elites and transnational capital (especially the United Fruit Company), military dictators and the Catholic and Protestant churches. Interviews and more systemic analysis were integrated into an overarching narrative of economic injustice and violent racial oppression and a popular struggle for liberation. A more cautious brand of 1990s' liberation theology provided the single narrative to bring together different types of information. Now one might disagree with this historical perspective, but at least it contributes to the debate about the future social order.

My emphasis on oral history methods does not emanate from the disciplinary chauvinism of an ethnographer touting his own particular methodology. If anything, this is an argument not for the centrality of anthropology but of oral history and social history. One main policy recommendation for others, in Sierra Leone, Bosnia and elsewhere, who are thinking of setting up truth commissions is to learn from the inability of the South African TRC to incorporate and integrate historians.

Southern Africa has many excellent oral and social historians – they are perhaps the most vibrant intellectual community in the country. Why were they excluded? Because they could not produce the kind of history amenable to the preferred model of nation-building. This was entrusted to the lawyers and the quantitative sociologists, which perhaps suggests that we should revise Eric Hobsbawm's (1992) comments that nationalists are like heroin addicts and historians produce the opium to fuel their political habits. In South Africa, civic nation-builders dismissed historians and relied instead on lawyers and statisticians to supply their opium.

CHAPTER 3

THE POLITICS OF TRUTH AND HUMAN RIGHTS

The last chapter demonstrated how a positivist methodology led to a particular version of truth in the TRC's final *Report*, one which lacked an overall explanatory framework apart from the moral language of denunciation. The substitution of a morality tale for a rigorous analysis of the organization of violence resulted from the requirements of the post-apartheid nation-building project and the need to legitimate new state institutions. This chapter extends our examination of the tensions between truth-telling and nation-building by looking at the content of the *Report* and specifically how it dealt with accusations that high-ranking apartheid-era state officials fomented violence during the 1990–1994 negotiations period.

First, this chapter contends that the TRC stopped short of finding that there was a centrally directed plan of violent destabilization since it eschewed theorizing the link between violence and the apartheid state; it opted for the wrong periodization of the past and failed to see continuities in counter-insurgency strategies of the 1980s and 1990s. Secondly, the TRC balked at issuing a subpoena for Inkatha Freedom Party leader Mangosuthu Buthelezi and fully investigating his responsibility in the public violence of his members, either through his actions or neglect. This it did largely out of deference to the ANC's consolidation of state power and its political overtures to its old enemy, the IFP.

The chapter then turns from the 'high politics' of the Commission to an examination of the hidden politics of human rights and the assumptions behind committee rulings that one crime was 'political', whereas another was 'criminal'. One case is examined in detail, that of four Afrikaner brothers, white right-wingers who claimed that 'racism' provided the political motivation for their killing of two African security guards. Understanding the contradictions between the Amnesty Committee's ruling which rejected racism as a political objective, and a later ruling, which accepted amnesty applications made on similar grounds by four black youths who murdered a white American student, Amy Biehl, requires us to look again at the way in which the imperative to nation-building through reconciliation dominated the TRC's activities.

WAS THERE A THIRD FORCE?

The most intense violence and terror of the whole apartheid era occurred when political conditions were meant to be improving; between the unbanning of the ANC, the SACP, the PAC and other liberation movement organizations by State President F W de Klerk in February 1990, and the first multiracial elections in April 1994. More were killed in those four years than in the whole of the 1980s, a period of mass insurrection and state repression. Over half of all the reports of killings which the TRC received concerned the 1990–4 period. Human rights monitors estimated that 14,000 people were killed in political-related incidents in the country (TRC *Report* 2:584).

In July 1990, political violence exploded in the Transvaal townships as a number of factors coincided: the Zulu nationalist organization Inkatha became a political party – the Inkatha Freedom Party (or IFP) – and started organizing in the migrant hostels, and liberation movement parties were unbanned and extended their military and political organization. The parties became locked in a struggle over membership and during the same month that peace talks commenced, four days of clashes between ANC and IFP members left 30 dead.

Within a year, the political violence became routine, and swept whole communities into a maelstrom of random terror. Violence levels surged upwards in the year talks began and reached their zenith in the year talks ended: there were 1,000 fatalities in 1990 on the 'Reef' around Johannesburg, and this figure doubled in 1991 to 2,000 (Shaw 1994:82).

Although it emerged from the structures of the 1980s, the violence of the 1990s was of a qualitatively different kind. It was less targeted at individuals and leaders of political organizations but was randomized, creating a climate of terror and intimidation. In urban townships, especially in Johannesburg and around (the 'Reef'), there were drive-by shootings, armed attacks on commuter trains and beer halls and indiscriminate massacres of residents regardless of ethnic identification or political affiliation. This violence had serious political consequences and threatened to destroy the peace process altogether, and the ANC walked out of talks after the Boipatong massacre on the night of 17 June 1992. Boipatong was the high point in accusations that there was a covert 'Third Force', centrally directed by the government as a strategy of violent destabilization. Much of the validity of the Third Force theory rests upon the involvement of the security forces in planning and participating in the random attack on Boipatong residents.

A number of bitterly contested theories were offered to explain the violence of the transition. One such theory, put forward by the ANC,[1] human rights monitors[2] and the *Weekly Mail and Guardian* newspaper, was that there was a 'Third Force' bent on destabilizing the negotiations. The government was accused of following a twin track strategy – participating in the negotiations at Kempton Park while continuing to wage war on the ANC in the townships. In the strong version of this theory, the Third Force was a covert strategy of state terrorism. The Third Force was an integrated network of security force and ex-security force operatives who, in conjunction with the IFP, sowed terror in order to undermine the position of the ANC in the talks and prepare the way for a victory of a National Party–IFP alliance in the first democratic elections.[3] In a climate of fear, the ANC would not be able to engage in normal political organization and mass voter mobilization and would appear weak, failing to defend its political bases. This strategy had been used successfully by the South African military in the decolonization of Namibia in 1989 and had reduced considerably the support and vote of the liberation movement there, SWAPO.[4]

Within the Third Force theory, there were different views on the role of senior National Party ministers and President de Klerk. In the 'strong' view, the Third Force was a continuation of counter-insurgency policies of the 1980s and was centrally directed by the State Security Council (SSC), of which de Klerk was a key member. Nelson Mandela was one of the first to use the term 'Third Force' a few months after his release in 1990 and in 1991 he directly accused de Klerk of letting 'loose his hounds against the people' (*Business Day* 8 October 1991). ANC officials and human rights monitors argued that violence was turned on and off to the maximum political advantage of the ruling National Party as levels of violence seemed to decrease when de Klerk left the country.

A diluted version of the Third Force theory asserted that de Klerk and other ministers were not personally directing state agents to carry out repression, but they assembled a decentralized command structure which covertly armed and deployed security agents and IFP members. The clandestine system was consciously designed so ministers could not be held accountable. Although ministers did not direct events on a day-to-day basis, they cultivated an environment where security operatives could act with maximum lawlessness. Thus, de Klerk was complicit, a willing accomplice in violence, as he never decisively acted to restrain his own security forces.

De Klerk himself responded to the upsurge in conflict by famously saying that it was the result of 'black-on-black' ethnic animosities. There was no 'hidden hand' of the police or army in the war between the IFP and ANC. The government was an innocent bystander in a history of hostilities between Zulus (IFP) and Xhosas (ANC) which went back centuries, even to before the arrival of whites.[5]

An 'ethnic animosity' explanation for the violence received media support from those such as Johannesburg *Star* reporter Rian Malan. Malan wrote in the immediate aftermath of the Boipatong massacre that the IFP had carried out a revenge attack after months of provocation and persecution by the ANC.[6] In his view, the ANC concocted the story of white police involvement in Boipatong to justify walking out of the peace talks, to gain international sympathy and to bolster an undemocratic mass action strategy.

There were others who placed the blame for mass violence on the ANC: the South African Institute of Race Relations director, John Kane-Berman (1993) wrote that the violence was the result of the ANC's instigation of a 'people's war' which targeted Africans accused of being 'apartheid collaborators' and produced a violent backlash which found expression in the IFP. Random violence was the inevitable consequence of a policy of making the country 'ungovernable'. For Kane-Berman:

> The people's war, directed in theory against the state, in fact helped to unleash massive violence within black communities. Black people, who were the victims of apartheid itself, became also the victims of the struggle against apartheid. (1993:12)[7]

In defending itself from Third Force accusations, the government repeatedly pointed out that the Harms[8] and Goldstone[9] Commissions, set up to investigate accusations of state participation in violence, did not initially uncover any evidence. Both commissions of enquiry were under-resourced, overly legalistic, misled by police evasions and political party cover-ups, and were disappointing in their conclusions. Each commission in turn rejected the idea of a covert Third Force. The commissions were too legally-minded in their search for *prima facie* evidence and, had they embraced a wider political analysis, could have revealed more about state involvement in informal repression.

However, in its report just before the April 1994 elections, the Goldstone Commission confirmed that senior police officers were involved in arming the IFP and in subverting the commission's investigations. Goldstone named police generals, such as General 'Krappies' Engelbrecht, who had been in charge of the Harms Commission's investigations, thus throwing profound doubt upon the findings of that earlier commission of inquiry.

The criminal courts proved more conclusive than governmental commissions of enquiry in establishing evidence on the National Party's role in state structures of terror. Despite the rogue elements and sometimes decentralized and delinked nature of informal repression, irrefutable evidence emerged that the government, right-wing, security forces and the IFP were allied in a strategy of covert violence during negotiations. Many of the unverified allegations of the human rights movement during the early 1990s were confirmed in the trial of Colonel Eugene de Kock, the former commander of the C1 security police unit at Vlakplaas, outside of Pretoria. In late 1996, in the most important criminal trial in post-apartheid history, de Kock was sentenced to 212 years, having been convicted of dozens of offences, including eight murders, numerous counts of attempted murder and supplying arms and bombs to the IFP to wage war against anti-apartheid activists.

During his trial, de Kock confirmed that the security forces trained IFP hit squads in Ulundi, Natal and Caprivi in Namibia, so as to destabilize the position of the ANC. De Kock claimed that high-ranking cabinet ministers, including Minister of Law and Order Adriaan Vlok, Minister Louis Le Grange, Foreign Minister Pik Botha and Defense Minister Magnus Malan all had knowledge (at least in outline) of dirty tricks operations (*Star* 16 September 1996 and 18 September 1996). The SADF and Security Branch police were involved in train violence, and in the arming and training of IFP hit squads.

Although conclusive evidence had emerged after 1994 that IFP regional leaders, such as Themba Khoza, orchestrated a campaign of violence in conjunction with Security Branch policemen, such as de Kock, neither the leadership of the National Party nor IFP Chief Mangosuthu Buthelezi confessed to wrong-doing. Nevertheless, the accusations continued to fly in 1995–6, and it was in this highly charged atmosphere, with a fragile Government of National Unity (containing the ANC, NP and IFP), that the TRC began its investigations.

WAS THERE A THIRD FORCE? 'WELL, NO, YES, SORT OF, MAYBE'

The TRC's final *Report* took what could be described as a 'middle position' on the Third Force. It lay somewhere equidistant from strong ANC accusations of high-ranking security force and ministerial involvement *and* National Party evasions which blamed a 'few bad apples' with their own private agendas. On the one hand, the Report produced evidence of state planning of violations, arming and directing of hit squads and complicity in cover-ups. At the same time it stopped short of referring to a centrally planned policy of state terrorism as the ANC and others had alleged. Perhaps surprisingly, its condemnation of the leadership of the anti-apartheid movement – the ANC and PAC – was more categorical than that of the main perpetrators of violence, the state and IFP.

The *Report*'s findings on state involvement in conflict during the transition are found primarily in chapter 7 of Volume 2, titled 'Political Violence in the Era of Negotiations and Transition (1990–94)'. The chapter begins with the acknowledgment that the Commission was relatively unsuccessful in uncovering violations in this period compared with the 1980s, primarily because of the low levels of amnesty applications it received. Applications from the South African Defense Force were significantly lower than from the South African Police Service. There were, for instance, no applications from members of the military's National Intelligence Service. In the vast majority of cases where there were no accompanying amnesty applications, the 60 or so investigators could do little other than 'corroborate' that violations had indeed occurred, by matching them to death certificates, inquest documents or police dockets.

Not only were there very few amnesty applications for the 1990–4 period, but the TRC did not try to use the few amnesty applications it had received to prise the lid of impunity and silence off other events and violations. Thus the TRC never fully pursued investigations into this era and never developed a general picture of events, according to one senior TRC investigator. This left the Commission's investigations in a highly unsatisfactory state with regard to certain incidents of the violence in the 1990s. For instance, it was not able to confirm or deny evidence claiming security force involvement in train violence in which 572 people died between 1990 and 1993. Only three perpetrators were convicted in more than 600 incidents of train attacks, in which hundreds of armed attackers usually participated. One of them, Felix Ndimene, an IFP member and former soldier, claimed that military Special Forces (5 Reconnaissance Regiment) and others (including former Selous Scouts, and RENAMO fighters from Mozambique) planned and executed the massacres he was involved in, but the TRC did not confirm or deny such allegations (TRC *Report* 3:707).

Nevertheless, on other incidents, the *Report* made bold findings on security force involvement. Perhaps the most important was on the Boipatong massacre, the climax of accusations of a Third Force, and the one act of violence with the most profound political impact. All previous investigations into Boipatong from the Waddington Inquiry (sanctioned by the Goldstone Commission) to the criminal trial of IFP members convicted for the massacre had found no evidence to support accusations of white or police involvement in the attack.[10] In striking contrast, Volume 3 (pp. 683–689) of the *Report* on the former Transvaal region largely accepted the ANC/human rights monitor[11] version of police involvement and complicity in the Boipatong massacre. The Commission found that the slaughter of 45 people had been carried out by IFP residents of KwaMadala hostel – this much was already known from the criminal trial.[12] But the Report went much further in linking the IFP attackers to the police:

> The Commission finds that KwaMadala hostel residents, together with the police, planned and carried out an attack on the community of Boipatong ... The Commission finds that white men with blackened faces participated in the attack. (3:689)

Note that the Report does not conclusively establish that the armed white killers were policemen. The Commission accepted the testimonies of witnesses from Boipatong and the neighboring factories (ISCOR, Cape Gate and Metal Box) that police transported attackers to the far side of the township (the squatter settlement of Slovo Park) where the attack began, and then escorted them back across the road to the hostel. The wording 'carried out' is therefore ambiguous – it could mean actually killing residents, or it could mean just ferrying around IFP killers. The *Report* goes on to make the weaker charge that the police had 'colluded' by failing to respond to the alarm raised by a petrol station attendant who saw hundreds of armed IFP members streaming across the main road into Boipatong. Afterwards, the police engaged in a cover-up by erasing crucial tapes from the radio control room of the Internal Stability Unit.

Having established the involvement of the IFP and police in the 1990–94 violence and confirmed the link between the two in a number of different scenarios, the next most important question became higher-level responsibility within the government: Who ordered the attacks? Who orchestrated the violence which seemed to be carried out with military precision in incidents such as the train massacres? There was no reference to higher level authorization in the case of the Boipatong massacre – the *Report* completely avoided raising this issue. In other cases, it traced a direct chain of command to the main security body, the State Security Council which included the State President, cabinet ministers and military and police generals. This was the case in the October 1993 raid on Umtata, Transkei, by 45 Parachute Brigade (military Special Forces) in which five youths were killed, including two only 12 years old. Orders for the raid came from a meeting of the State Security Council to 'neutralize the target' – authorizing the assassinations in a language of deniability. Present at the meeting were, *inter alia*, State President F W de Klerk, ministers Kriel, Coetsee and Pik Botha, and SADF chief Georg Meiring. All were held accountable for the violation (*Report* 2:600–2).

The complicity of State President de Klerk was much harder to establish in other cases. Even where the Commission was confident in its findings and ready to go to print, de Klerk managed to successfully outmaneuver the TRC in the courts. The *Report*'s most widely publicized omission at the time of its release resulted from a last-minute injunction obtained by de Klerk. The former head of the last apartheid regime had been accused of having 'contributed to a culture of impunity' and also of having been an accessory to the bombing of two office blocks in Johannesburg which housed the South African Council of Churches and the Congress of South African Trade Unions in the mid 1980s.[13] The *Report* stated that de Klerk was present at a meeting of the State Security Council where former State President P W Botha congratulated [then Law and Order Minister] Adriaan Vlok for the successful bombing. De Klerk's recourse to the courts meant that segments of pages 225–6 of Volume 5 of the *Report* were blacked out before release. One journalist wryly referred to the pages as 'an ironic memorial to apartheid censorship in the TRC *Report*' (Beresford, *Mail and Guardian* 2 October 1998).

In contrast the ANC and PAC leadership were held much more directly accountable for their part in the post-1990 violence, even though their role was disproportionately much smaller than that of the police, army and IFP. Ironically, this was because the ANC was much more forthcoming in their public admissions to the TRC and co-operative with the TRC investigation process. With its limited resources, the TRC could more easily trace a direct line of command for ANC violations, because the ANC had a widely-known policy (Operation Vula) of internal armed struggle. Operation Vula was publicly known and recognized and had a definable command structure of high level co-ordinators and middle- and low-ranking operatives, whose names are now public knowledge. Because of the literalism and legalism of the TRC and the weakness of its own investigations, the fact that the ANC had a stated policy of insurrection and chose to admit this was to its detriment in terms of its share of the blame in the *Report*. The ANC was disadvantaged by its relative openness while most National Party leaders[14] continued to deny any illegal activities at all, rejecting the idea that the Third Force was official government policy. The IFP leadership completely boycotted the Commission and urged its supporters to do likewise.

The exact charge that the ANC had made against the National Party government – that it was pursuing a twin track strategy of negotiating while still waging war – was leveled against the ANC in the *Report*:

> Under the banner of Operation Vula, the ANC continued with its clandestine activities while engaged in the process of negotiations. Vula was seen by some ANC leaders as an insurance policy: if the negotiation process failed, the ANC would still have some capacity to mount armed resistance. (p. 666)

In the *Report*, we are told how Operation Vula was created and structured, how it resulted from the South African Communist Party

(SACP) camp within the ANC which centered upon Chris Hani, and how it was seen as the Maoist third stage of the revolution. There was no such analytical discussion of the Third Force or the internal organization of violence within IFP or NP structures at the time. The ANC leadership was excoriated for setting up Special Defense Units (SDUs) after 1990 and accused of being irresponsible for arming and training such a force. At the end of the section on the ANC in chapter 7 of Volume 2, there is a set of damning findings which concluded that '... the leadership should have been aware of the consequences of training and arming members of SDUs in a volatile situation and in which they had little control over the actions of such members' (p. 684).

The ANC National Executive Committee[15] was incensed over these comments, and more still over the allegations made about torture and murder in ANC detention camps such as Quatro. It too, like de Klerk, sought a last-minute gagging order to block the *Report*'s publication, but the court ruled against the ANC. This was seen as an 'own goal' by many commentators – a case of the party in power attacking the truth body it had itself set up because it did not like the truth being told. Given the strong language of the TRC's condemnation of the ANC leadership and the reaction it evoked from the National Executive, I cannot agree with Jeffery's conclusion that the TRC was somehow lenient on the ANC while demonizing other parties, 'The effect of the TRC's approach ... is to heap the blame for violence on the former police, the former army, and/or the IFP. At the same time, any possible culpability of the ANC is downplayed or ignored' (1999:147).

In fact, the same treatment which ANC leaders received was patently not meted out to the IFP leadership in volume 2, and the section on the IFP does not end with a set of findings at all. There is no overall statement of the role of the IFP in the violence of the 1990–4 period, unlike all the other parties considered in chapter 7 (i.e., security forces, homelands, liberation movements and the white right wing). This is astonishing considering that according to the Human Rights Committee, Inkatha members were responsible for 34 of the 49 massacres between 1990–2 (Taylor and Shaw 1998:20). The *Report* never even raises the question of the link between local and regional actions and the leadership in IFP headquarters in Ulundi, as it does in all the other sections. Even if it did not resolve them, it at least raised these questions of intellectual authorship when considering the role of other party leaders in the conflict. Of the IFP, it never even asked the question.

This avoidance of high-level blame within the IFP is surprising given the evidence which the TRC held proving that middle- and high-ranking IFP officials, such as Themba Khoza, Celani Mthethwa (both members of the first Gauteng Provincial Legislature) and Phillip Powell, collaborated with the police in fomenting public violence. At the de Kock trial it emerged that all three were given arms by the Security Branch (SB) policeman, the arms having been procured from the counter-insurgency unit Koevoet ('Crowbar') in Namibia. De Kock's arming of IFP Youth Leader Khoza was sanctioned by three high-ranking SAP generals, Engelbrecht, Smit and van Rensburg.

The Report also published evidence of the involvement of IFP leader Chief Mangosuthu Buthelezi in the post-1990 violence, but revealed little more than was already known in the press. On page 630, it referred to a memorandum of a meeting between two military intelligence colonels and Buthelezi which emphasized the deployment of offensive actions against the ANC and the use of 'hit squads'. In 1991, a more operational meeting was convened by Captain Langeni of the KwaZulu Police and attended by Buthelezi's personal secretary, M Z Khumalo, which created the Esikhawini hit squad comprised of IFP members trained in 1986 by the SADF in Caprivi, Namibia. The hit squad's targets were all ANC leaders. In 1993 and 1994, in the run-up to the first democratic elections, IFP leaders threatened to wreck the electoral process and on 14 February 1994, Buthelezi made an inflammatory call on all Inkatha members to 'defend and fight back and resist the ANC and its communist surrogates' (cited in TRC *Report* 2:638)

Despite the mounting evidence against him, Chief Buthelezi was not found responsible by the Commission for authorizing one single violation of the 9,000 gross human rights violations committed by members of his political party between 1990 and May 1994. Over the whole 34-year period covered by the Commission, IFP members were responsible for nearly 4,000 killings in KwaZulu-Natal alone (compared with 1,000 perpetrated by the ANC) (TRC *Report* 3:326). Yet despite the massive involvement of the IFP in the violence and the evidence that Buthelezi and his personal secretary attended meetings where hit squads were proposed, the *Report* does not hold Buthelezi accountable for ordering or sanctioning even one violation. In Volume 3, the regional profile of Natal and KwaZulu, Buthelezi is only mentioned in findings twice – as one of a number of others who are collectively responsible for the training of IFP members in Caprivi and for the setting up of the Special Protection Unit project to confront the ANC's Special Defense Units.

In the Volume 2 chapter on 1990–94 violence, Buthelezi was not even accused of the lesser charge of being responsible for violations through his neglect as Chief Minister of the KwaZulu government and head of the IFP. Unlike his NP, ANC and PAC counterparts, he was not held accountable for failing to rein in and control his own armed units – the KwaZulu police, Special Protection Units and covert hit squads operating in KwaZulu and on the Reef. Yet the IFP is notoriously controlled in virtually all its aspects by one man with an iron will – Chief Mangosuthu Buthelezi. It is not known as a decentralized organization with a loose structure but more as a 'personal fiefdom'.[16] At a prayer breakfast in Durban in 1990 at the outset of the transitional violence, Buthelezi recognized his own position of accountability when stating, 'Although I have not orchestrated one single act of violence ... as the leader of the IFP, I know that the buck stops right in front of me' (quoted in Kane-Berman 1993:83).

Even if the TRC felt that there was not enough evidence to claim that Buthelezi had authorized gross human rights violations, as the leader of a party which had carried out the majority of such acts brought before the Commission, it might have been expected that the Commission subpoena Buthelezi under section 29 of the Act. All other prominent party leaders had given evidence, and 1980s President P W Botha was subpoenaed to give evidence. P W Botha famously flouted the Commission's request, was convicted of defying a court summons and was sentenced to a suspended court sentence, but then acquitted on a legal technicality.[17] Having tangled with the old 'Crocodile', why then was the TRC so feeble in its evaluation of Buthelezi's accountability, especially in its section on the 1990–94 period? In addition, why did it ignore evidence given in 1997 during in-camera testimony by former IFP central committee member Walter Felgate that Buthelezi had collaborated with state security service structures, such as the notorious Bureau for State Security (BOSS) for decades and had participated in a conspiracy with right-wing whites to prevent the 1994 elections by triggering a civil war? (*Mail and Guardian*, 27 November–3 December 1998)

The TRC adopted a policy of non-provocation of the IFP, and of Buthelezi in particular. It feared that if it called him to testify, then at the least its work in KwaZulu-Natal would be made more difficult than ever, and if Buthelezi felt threatened, then he still had the ability to unleash further public violence. In short, the Commission was intimidated by the leader of the political party most responsible for recent violence in the country. As the Commission itself replied when asked to explain why it had failed to subpoena Buthelezi:

> The only defence that can be offered is that the ... commission ultimately succumbed to the fears of those who argued that Buthelezi's appearance would give him a platform from which to oppose the commission and would stoke the flames of violence in KwaZulu-Natal. (*Guardian* 30 October 1998)

Secondly, the Commission, although no simple instrument of ANC policy, was committed to the consolidation of state institutional power in the post-apartheid order and, in the case of Buthelezi, deemed this to be a priority over truth-finding and investigation. Since winning the 1994 elections, the ANC had adopted a canny strategy towards Buthelezi and the IFP; it was one directed at neutralizing and containing its implacable foes. The ANC was aware of the immensely debilitating effects of the conflict between ZANU and ZAPU in post-independence Zimbabwe and sought to avert this dismal scenario. It saw shrewdly that the greatest threat to political stability was the IFP and its calls for federalism, not the white right, which had been trounced at Boputhatswana in 1993. It therefore sought to build bridges with Buthelezi, and kept him on as Minister of Home Affairs even after the Government of National Unity had collapsed in 1996. The ANC regularly gifted him the ornamental role of acting President when Mandela and Mbeki were abroad and played to Buthelezi's famous vanity.

The dominant disposition in the ANC leadership is towards a long-term absorption of the IFP into an ANC-dominated political bloc. In a television interview in 1997, Nelson Mandela supported the idea of making Buthelezi deputy president of the ANC and urged him to return to the party.[18] In early 1998, ANC deputy President Jacob Zuma and Mangosuthu Buthelezi had a number of meetings and Zuma was said to be in favor of an alliance. Newspapers also reported a number of secret meetings between Buthelezi and President-to-be Thabo Mbeki, at which Mbeki called for a merger between the two parties.[19] The ANC in KwaZulu-Natal proposed a blanket amnesty as part of the peace talks in the province and to reinforce the thaw in relations with Buthelezi. The TRC avoided jeopardizing this political reconfiguration by delving too far into Buthelezi's role and by calling him to give evidence, even at the cost of being economical with the truth in the final *Report*. In the TRC's dealings with the IFP the *realpolitik* of the post-apartheid order impinged most heavily on the quest for truth, deforming it beyond all recognition.

THEORIZING THE THIRD FORCE

Since the TRC made little progress in uncovering the forces behind the violence of the early 1990s, it stopped short of the accusation that the 'Third Force' was government policy: 'Beyond the specific violations ... a major issue the Commission was unable to determine was the degree to which the involvement of the security force operations was part of a government strategy at the time' (TRC *Report* 2:705).

In its findings at the end of Volume 2, it made weak findings on central authorization and high level complicity:

> The Commission finds that, while there is little evidence of a centrally directed, coherent or formally constituted 'Third Force', a network of security and ex-security force operatives, acting

> frequently in conjunction with right wing elements and/or sectors of the IFP, were involved in actions that could be construed as fomenting violence and which resulted in gross violations of human rights, including random and targeted killings. (p. 709)

The vital link to higher levels of government, it argued, was unproven. There was a 'network' of perpetrators, but no 'centrally directed' chain of command emanating from the higher levels of the National Party regime. Having abandoned a strong Third Force theory, the Report ends up blaming 'high levels of political intolerance' (ibid.: 710). This recourse to morality was a strategy which the Commission repeated elsewhere – where the forensic evidence does not extend and the TRC's limited powers of analysis would not reach, the *Report* invoked 'political intolerance' to fill the gaps. This was, in my view, a rather fainthearted term used to avoid allocating responsibility. Violence was not centrally directed, but was amorphous, ineffable and nameless, welling up from a culture of violence. There are certain parallels here with postmodern theory, which also portrays all-encompassing and unutterable cultures of violence, but the implications of both are politically conservative, since they ignore how certain agents directed violence and others (including former Archbishop Desmond Tutu) did their best to prevent it. Worse still, there are echoes of apartheid government denials in this ambiguous terminology, as the ANC submission to the TRC noted: 'This terror campaign against black civilians was ascribed to "political intolerance" in much the same way that covertly directed violence was deliberately portrayed as "black-on-black" violence in the 1980s' (1996:42).

In the moralizing formulation of violence as the outcome of 'intolerance', everyone is ultimately to blame. The problem is seen to be values and attitudes, not identifiable institutions, individuals and organizations. 'Political intolerance' was well suited to the value-oriented perspective of the TRC's theological component, and also to the objective of nation-building. If the violence of the past could be ascribed to wrong beliefs, not individuals or organizations, then anyone could change their beliefs, reinvent themselves as 'politically tolerant' and become part of the new South Africa.

In contrast, a more sociological approach would try to provide a theory as to how the violence was systematically organized inside and outside of the state, and how violence was central to the apartheid order. This theorizing would raise its head above the dull litany of facts to see the patterns and make deductions which went beyond the visible forensic facts, exactly what the TRC *Report* avoided. It was determinedly anti-theoretical, opting instead for a positivist legalism with occasional flights of theological fancy when its forensic method broke down. The *Report*'s blunt realist language made it difficult to evaluate the thinking behind some of its claims – for this it needed to make its theoretical understanding of apartheid violence more explicit.

Had it operated with a more complex theory of violence, a defensible historical periodization and a less legalistic notion of causality, the TRC may have come to different conclusions regarding the Third Force. While many observers of the South African transition have relegated violence to a footnote in a miraculous story, writers such as Taylor and Shaw (1998) and Bennun (1995) have argued that violence during the negotiations was the product of the political will of the state and that the apartheid apparatus used violence to sustain itself.

If in the TRC's findings there had been more analysis of the state as a perpetrator, through looking at the integration of actions between various sectors of the security services and IFP, then the TRC would have been able to find that that the behavior of state operatives was 'coherent'. The demonstrable cohesiveness and coherence of actions of different parts of the security apparatus lends support to the strong Third Force theory. How could different sections of the police and military have acted in such concerted unison if there was not some form of centralized co-ordination? If there had just been many maverick splinter groups with separate agendas, then how was it that their efforts managed to interlock during specific operations with such precision?

If we start our analysis a little earlier and look at the 1985–1992 period, it is remarkable to see how consistently and coherently different sections of the security forces and IFP worked together. This alliance was forged in the war in the Natal Midlands (Kentridge 1990) from 1985 onwards. If we examine just one locale, the Vaal region to the south of Johannesburg, a remarkable picture of coherence between distinct branches of the state apparatus and the IFP exists. In the Vaal, C10 Security Branch policeman Eugene de Kock supplied to the IFP Youth League leader Themba Khoza the guns and hand grenades which were used during the Sebokeng hostel massacre in September 1990 in which 19 people were killed. The SADF defended the 137 IFP members from angry ANC supporters who had them cornered, and soldiers shot four dead.

Judge Stafford leading the enquiry recommended that soldiers be prosecuted but the Attorney-General brought no legal action. Even though an assortment of weapons were found in the trunk of Khoza's Nissan Sentra, he was acquitted because of the collusion of three Vaal policemen from different branches of the police; J F Conradie, head of the Security Branch, A J van der Gryp of the Unrest and Violent Crime Unit and J Jacobs head of the Murder and Robbery Unit. These three acted as 'sweepers', clearing up after incidents in the 'dirty war'.[20] Each has applied for amnesty from the TRC, admitting that they deliberately conspired to secure Khoza's acquittal by altering statements and tampering with forensic and ballistic evidence so weapons could not be linked to those IFP members arrested.

So in one incident alone we have a variety of state security agencies and departments – the Security Branch police from Vlakplaas, the SADF and the local Vaal police – all acting in concert to favor the IFP in its war against the ANC. The police and criminal justice system failed to bring appropriate legal action against the perpetrators. To my mind, this is more than enough evidence to justify the use of the word 'coherent' which the TRC mistakenly refrained from using in its findings.

And this is just one event in a pattern repeated again and again at different times all over the country. For example, Vaal policeman van der Gryp was also a 'sweeper' in the Boipatong investigation and is allegedly responsible for destroying crucial ballistic evidence that would have implicated the IFP and possibly the police, who some witnesses claimed participated in the massacre. In the Boipatong massacre, again in the Vaal, there is evidence of intimate involvement in the planning and execution on the part of the Vaal Internal Stability Unit (ISU), other units of the Vaal police service, Security Branch agents from Vlakplaas again supplying weapons to Themba Khoza, and the SADF which escorted IFP units back across the road. Finally, there is evidence of high-level police complicity in the cover-up and failure to properly investigate the massacre. Such unity of purpose would have required a significant degree of co-ordination and supervision to ensure that different elements of the security forces were not getting in each other's way.

Part of the reason that the TRC rejected the notion of a Third Force was because it chose to distinguish the violence of the 1990s from earlier 1980s State Security Council plans to establish a Third Force. The TRC asserts that it treated these periods as separate and distinct, but does not explain why (2:703). Yet seeing the 1990s in isolation from the 1985–86 period deprives the Third Force theory of the historical aspects of its explanation. The Third Force of the 1990s can only be understood as an extension of the policies of the 1985–86 period. This continuity between the 1980s and 90s was argued by one of the TRC's own researchers, Stephen Ellis, in an article in the *Journal of Southern African Studies* (1998), but his important conclusions were seemingly ignored by Commissioners.

Ellis locates the origins of the Third Force in the establishment of the State Security Council (SSC) in 1985 and its ideology of reversal of the ANC's doctrine of 'total onslaught', which it learned from

Argentinian generals and other international counter-insurgency experts. The SSC worked on the principle of an insurgency war in reverse, adopting its illegal means. From the overall SSC policy emerged a number of other notoriously violent state security institutions which would wreak havoc into the 1990s. In 1985, Strategic Communications (STRATCOM) was established to blackmail, manipulate the media and engage in a war of propaganda. In 1985–86 TREWITS[21] was created as an intelligence co-ordinating unit based in the counter-revolutionary Section C of the police Security Branch, with representation from the National Intelligence Service and Military Intelligence which reported to the Coordinating Intelligence Committee.[22] In 1986 the Civil Co-operation Bureau was created to carry out various illegal actions, including political assassinations. In 1986 the SSC ordered the SADF to train IFP paramilitary units in Caprivi, Namibia, and these would become the core of the IFP hit squads of the 1990s.[23] Finally, security personnel and operational networks of Security Branch police in the former Rhodesia (Selous Scouts) and Namibia (Koevoet) and SADF Special Forces, such as 32 Battalion, were integrated into South Africa's internal war in the late 1980s.

With the personnel came the strategies used in the war and decolonization of Namibia (in 1989) and the policy of weakening the ANC so as to negotiate from a position of power. Namibia was the model of a controlled transition which de Klerk had in mind when he unbanned the ANC and SACP. As Ellis writes: 'Here lay the origins of the Third Force, among professional counter-insurgency specialists with long experience of border wars, which as the years went by, they increasingly applied in South Africa itself' (1998:270).

This burgeoning security apparatus in the late 1980s was highly systematized and centrally planned. Operations were co-ordinated through the National Security Management System (NSMS)[24] which could oversee a range of state functions; from arranging assassinations to improving local social services. The violence of the 1985–1992 period was a result of this centrally planned and directed state strategy of counter-insurgency. In particular, the massive eruption of violence in 1990 was directly linked to the structures put in place in the mid-late 1980s.

Of course, this co-ordinated counter-insurgency structure was not public government policy, nor was there an overt command structure. Just because there were not formal lines of accountability does not mean that there was no centrally directed Third Force, as the TRC concluded. The whole strategy of covert violence relied upon hidden lines of accountability. This does not mean that violence was not centrally authorized at the ministerial level. Up to 1992, there is plenty of evidence that it was. In minutes of SSC meetings civilian leaders, including Law and Order Minister Vlok and Presidents Botha and de Klerk, used a variety of ambiguous terms, such as 'neutralize', 'eliminate' and 'wipe out', when giving their subordinates in the security service orders to kill. The terms of the orders were intended to avoid direct responsibility in a court of law while their intended meaning was crystal clear to the security agents. Secret tapes of security police lectures in 1990 report Minister Adriaan Vlok telling senior police that he sanctioned assassination techniques: 'I support you in these things but you must know I will be committing political suicide if they come to light' (*Sunday Times* 5 March 1995)

When middle-ranking police or military operatives followed through on the assassinations, they were not upbraided or punished by their generals, but given medals and financial rewards.

In this context, the TRC's wording seems to miss the point. The Third Force was indeed not 'formally constituted' because this implies an officially-recognized and publicly stated policy. There was nothing formal about it. Instead, the Third Force was a covert strategy, the hidden hand of the state in seemingly random violence between rival black organizations. The whole point of the Third Force was that it was *informally* constituted (but no less officially organized because of this) so as to escape detection, and denunciation and indictment in a court of law. The TRC tied itself in knots because of its weak analysis of the relationship between covert and overt strategies, and because it took a literal line which obstructed the wider picture beyond the facts of individual violations. The Third Force only begins to be plausible as a theory if violence is seen in the wider historical and contextual trajectory of apartheid state terrorism.

A centralized edifice of violence did not remain intact until the 1994 elections, but fragmented and disintegrated from late 1992 onwards, and this seemed to have caused the greatest analytical problems for the Commission in its quest for visible lines of causality. It did not come up with a theoretical model which could elucidate the qualitatively different periods of the violence under the same explanatory framework. In late 1992, after the signing of the Record of Understanding on 26 September 1992, the NP dropped the IFP and shifted its allegiance to the ANC. In December, President de Klerk partially dismantled the 'securocrat' structures put in place in the mid-1980s, retiring eighteen SAP generals in August and sixteen senior SADF officers. Taylor and Shaw note that from the end of 1992, hit squad activity and train attacks dropped off completely (1998:24).

The strategy of violence after late 1992 became increasingly fragmented. Covert security force units fractured into smaller autonomous groupings. There was decentralization and separation from the main command structures and lines of authorization. The link to the central organs of the state became more untraceable, as there were multiple command structures operating in decentralized ways. Operatives such as Eugene de Kock used more discretion and became more embedded in, and reliant upon, criminal networks.[25] At this point, we could describe the networks as 'official-informal' groupings.

The TRC rejected the notion of a Third Force because it opted for the wrong periodization of history, one which rendered a sharp discontinuity between the 1980s and 1990s, when this discontinuity did not exist. Instead, any plausible theory of the Third Force requires that we see the continuity between 1980s structures and 1990s violations. A more adequate theory of Third Force violence would run as follows: between 1985 and 1992 there was a NP–IFP political alliance which relied upon a coherent, centrally authorized but covert policy of violence (i.e., a Third Force mark I) which was designed by the State Security Council and co-ordinated by the National Management System. Its central aim was not to sabotage negotiations but to use violence to undermine the ANC in the negotiations and politically in the townships so as to ensure the hegemony of an apartheid conservative alliance. From late 1992 until the 1994 elections the NP–IFP alliance broke down and was replaced with a new dominant political axis, between the NP and the ANC. At this point, another political alliance[26] gelled between units of the security forces, and ex-security forces, the IFP and the white right (the Third Force mark II), which sowed random terror and sought to trigger a civil war and derail the first democratic elections. This alliance itself disintegrated shortly before the elections when the IFP decided to participate, and remnants of it carried on into the first two years of the Government of National Unity.

The 'Third Force mark I' was exactly as the ANC and human rights monitors described it, but the TRC rejected this version. The post-1992 Third Force mark II was exactly as described in the TRC report, a loose network with high-level complicity, but no central authorization. Volume 2, therefore, is only an accurate description of the post-1992 era. For 1985–92, the TRC findings were often mistaken and confused: during this period there was a Third Force in the sense of a centrally directed government strategy of concerted violence against the liberation movement. This Third Force mark I was the concerted strategy of the criminal apartheid state which relied upon terror and violence to sustain itself.

HUMAN RIGHTS VIOLATIONS AND COMMON CRIMES

The first part of this chapter considered the overtly 'political' dimensions of the TRC. It is hardly contentious to say that human rights talk is 'political' in that there are public disputes between human rights agencies and political parties, or between political parties over responsibility for human rights violations (as in the case of the Third Force). The South African press regularly reported on the fraught relationship that the TRC had with political parties. One of the first confrontations was over the statements of senior ANC leaders that ANC members responsible for criminal acts in fighting a just war need not apply for amnesty, prompting a threat by Desmond Tutu to resign as chair of the TRC (*Star* 11 November 1996). Next came a furore over the political party submissions made to the TRC on the offences committed during the apartheid era, when many political parties admitted very little in the way of organizing and directing violence.[27]

Throughout the Commission's existence, Chair Desmond Tutu exhorted political leaders – Mandela from the ANC, de Klerk of the National Party, Buthelezi of the Inkatha Freedom Party and Stanley Mogoba of the Pan Africanist Congress – to apologize for bombings and other abuses carried out by their followers. All the politicians were reluctant and remained silent. Further, both the ANC National Executive and former State President F W de Klerk sought High Court injunctions

De Klerk (NP) and Mbeki (ANC) make their fulsome apologies (11 November 1996). This cartoon is republished by permission of the *Star*, a Johannesburg-based newspaper of the Independent News & Media Group. Also with permission of the cartoonist, Dov Fedler.

to block publication of sections of the Report in October 1998, and de Klerk was successful in his court action.

The rest of this chapter, however, focusses less on high politics than it does on the hidden politics of human rights, which lay in the assumptions and everyday categorizations of the TRC, which shaped how human rights were defined and debated. Human rights always rely upon a distinction between politically motivated abuse (and therefore a human rights violation) and a simply criminal act (which is therefore not a human rights violation). Separating human rights and common crime is the first distinguishing act of all human rights institutions. In so doing, they establish what a human rights violation is, decide on what issues and incidents they can intervene, and what is outside their mandate as established in national or international law. Here politics operates at the level of assumptions about what is 'political' and what is not.

In many human rights institutions, these decisions are unstated and implicit – say, when a prosecutor at a United Nations war crimes tribunal reads about a crime in the former Yugoslavia, decides that it appears to be a common crime and excludes it from her or his consideration. At the South African TRC, in contrast, this level of decision-making was more transparent since it was essential to the whole public functioning of the Commission. At HRV hearings, cross-examination ascertained whether the person testifying was a victim of a politically motivated crime and therefore could be designated a 'victim' with the right to receive reparations. At amnesty hearings, practically the entire thrust of cross examination by Amnesty Committee judges was directed towards deciding whether there was a political objective to the violation. If not, then the applicant would be refused indemnity, as many thousands were.

The distinction between a politically motivated act and a common crime is not wholly arbitrary, but it is often indistinct and ambiguous. Different human rights agencies (from the International Criminal Court, to the South African TRC, to non-governmental organizations) will delineate the boundary in contrasting ways. Often perpetrators are involved in both criminal acts and politically motivated abuses at the same time. In South Africa, this occurred all along the political spectrum. Anti-apartheid organizations such as the ANC, UDF and PAC often included gangs who were fighting the police at the barricades and enforcing boycotts, as well as murdering each other in personalized rivalries, as well as committing conventional crimes such as burglary. In many areas – such as the West Rand, East Rand and Vaal townships around Johannesburg – the criminal activities of the gangs came to outstrip whatever political functions they might have fulfilled. The ANC itself recognized this when referring to its own armed Special Defense Units (SDUs): 'Some SDUs became little more than gangs of criminals at times led by police agents, and inflicted great damage on popular ANC aligned community structures' (TRC *Report* 2:676).

In its section in Volume 3 on 'Criminalization of Political Conflict', the TRC accurately described not only how the liberation movement came to rely upon criminals in the post-1990 period, but also how covert police *agents provocateurs* fomented conflict, further blurring the lines of politics and criminality:

> During 1990, criminal gangs became increasingly drawn into the political conflict in the PWV[28] [now Gauteng province], becoming extremely effective participants in the contest for political power and territorial control. For criminal gangs, association with political organizations also provided valuable protection for and legitimated their criminal activities. Many gangs had become alienated from communities and 'anti-crime' campaigns, often initiated by ANC-aligned youth, sometimes led to violent retribution against gang members. Criminalization of political conflict was further facilitated by the police who frequently failed to intervene in the violence ... and more directly ... in supplying weapons to the IFP. (3:712)

The apartheid security apparatus was responsible for an astonishingly high volume of crime, especially in the post-1992 period when its activities became more fragmented and decentralized. Significant information emerged in the trial of security policeman Colonel Eugene de Kock that during his one-man war on behalf of the apartheid state and the National Party, he was also involved in extensive criminal activities.[29] He was not just murderously enforcing apartheid, but was found guilty on 66 fraud charges, robbery, handling false dollar notes, selling banned rhino horns, gun-running to the Inkatha Freedom Party for financial gain, and illicit diamond buying. De Kock was not alone in his criminal underworld. In Jacques Pauw's 1996 South African Broadcasting Company documentary, 'Prime Evil', it emerged that the quiet, Christian and 'shy' de Kock did not deal cocaine like his Vlakplaas police colleagues, nor visit prostitutes at a brothel run by members of Military Intelligence.[30] Ellis (1998) insightfully charts the criminalization of the security agencies after 1990, and quotes de Kock as saying to his judges (review in *Mail and Guardian*, 18–24 October 1996) that a person with a curriculum vitae like his could only choose between becoming a drug smuggler or a mercenary.

It is difficult to disentangle the complex motivations to the extent that one could say with absolute certainty: this is political, that is criminal.

There are multiple determinations to behavior and it is problematical to prioritize one over the other. Yet this is what the TRC's committees were mandated to do. There were significant incentives for amnesty applicants to retrospectively re-cast their motivations (for example, if the potential reward is release from prison), and this was a continual challenge for the Amnesty Committee. Similarly, the Human Rights Violations Committee had to decide if suffering was connected to political crimes in order to determine which victims were 'real victims' and qualified for reparations. Suddenly all the political issues surrounding past acts come to the fore and other motivations disappear in a legally induced amnesia.

One case at the HRV hearings in Klerksdorp on 26 September 1996 illustrated very well the ambiguities surrounding the category of a human rights violation, and the way in which Commissioners sought to untie the knotted rope of causality which led to the murder of Jackson Molete. At first glance, the murder seemed to be a straightforward politically motivated human rights violation. At about 9 pm on the night of 13 August 1992, a group of IFP supporters entered the largely ANC 'Moscow' section of the tiny Tigane township on the West Rand. They attacked house number 1201, throwing rocks and shouting 'Come out you bastards!' Inside were Daniel Molete and his brother, Jackson. Daniel Molete escaped through the back door but Jackson was caught by the attackers and brutally murdered with steel *pangas* (machetes).

As the testimony wore on, however, the plot thickened and the political motivation of the killers became more difficult to discern. Daniel Molete denied any political involvement or membership in the ANC, and reported that he had studiously avoided politics all of his life. Indeed, he had been ejected from a shantytown for refusing to join a political party. He categorically rejected the idea that the murder was an act of revenge for previous political activity on the part of himself or his brother. Further, his evidence that the killers were IFP members was very thin, as he never actually saw them. The attackers never revealed any political affiliation, and Molete just assumed the attackers were IFP. In largely ANC-supporting townships, the term 'IFP' was synonymous with 'the enemy' generally. After he heard stones being thrown, Molete stated in his testimony, 'I shouted with a loud voice, I said, "Gentlemen of the IFP! I am the owner of this house!"'

Further, it was not at all clear that Jackson Molete was the intended target of the killers. Jackson lived in Pretoria and had returned for a rare weekend visit. Vital but confused information came out in Daniel Molete's cross-examination regarding Johanna Molete, Jackson's daughter. Before the murder, she had been quarreling with her violent and abusive husband. She requested support from a group of men, who she claimed were IFP supporters, to prevent her husband from beating her. It was Johanna's husband they were looking for, not Johanna's father, Jackson, who appears to have been the unfortunate victim in a violent domestic dispute. A crime of passion had been re-cast as a political murder for the purposes of bringing it before the TRC.

By the end of the hearing, an exasperated Commissioner Randera asked the befuddled Daniel Molete:

> CHAIRPERSON: Do you think that this incident has got anything to do with politics?
> MR MOLETE: I do not understand.
> CHAIRPERSON: The stoning of your house and the killing of your brother, do you think that had anything to do with politics?
> MR MOLETE: No, M'Lord.

What the case also shows are the multiple lines of causality and motivational opaqueness of an act. The murder of Jackson Molete was both 'criminal' since it stemmed from a domestic dispute, and 'political', since it involved (allegedly) IFP supporters killing a man in an ANC-supporting area.[31] It was also neither, since the wrong man was killed. Despite the outcome of the cross-examination, Jackson Molete was included on the TRC's list of victims in the final *Report*. The circumstances pointed to a different interpretation of the murder, but the Commissioners found that the act was politically motivated because of the context of the township at the time, even though this case does not appear to be straightforwardly linked to the ANC–IFP conflict.

RACE CRIMES AND POLITICAL MOTIVES

Much of the distinction between political objective and common crime hinges upon a bipolar distinction between public ideology and private belief. The NURA fixed and authorized this dualism[32] when it required that the Amnesty Committee take into account the following factors in deciding whether an act was associated with a political objective: motive of the perpetrator, the gravity of the act, the proportionality[33] of the act and whether the act was executed on the orders of a political organization (for example, the state or a liberation party). It expressly excluded acts committed for 'personal gain' or 'out of personal malice, ill-will or spite'. The terms of the act set up an either/or distinction rather than a both/and continuum.

The difficulty in distinguishing between political violations and those undertaken for personal gain was most evident when amnesty applicants invoked racism as their political motive. Given the history of apartheid and the degree to which racism is at the center of state policies of racial superiority, segregation and denationalization of blacks, it would seem fairly obvious that racism constituted a political motivation *per se*. This view was reinforced by the TRC *Report* which cast racism as a primary component of apartheid. Apartheid and racism were even used interchangeably by the Chair Desmond Tutu in his foreword:

> ... we cannot hope properly to understand the history of the period under review unless we give apartheid and racism their rightful place as the defining features of that period ... Racism came to South Africa in 1652; it has been part of the warp and woof of South African society since then. (1:15–16)

Early on, the Amnesty Committee heard an application from four brothers which would define how the committee would deal with race and racism. In September 1996, the Amnesty Committee had hearings in Potchefstroom to decide the case of the four van Straaten brothers who had been convicted of the murder of two black security guards and the theft of a Ford truck from Terblanche Transport in Vereeniging on 17 June 1989. At the time of the hearings, the brothers were all in the minimum security section of Zonderwater prison serving a 13-year sentence.[34]

The van Straaten brothers (Adriaan, Gideon, Willem, and Dawid) based their appeal for amnesty on the grounds that their actions were racially motivated and therefore politically motivated, and the entire hearings revolved around whether race constituted a political motive in and of itself. The brothers began by adopting the strategy used by nearly every self-designated 'Afrikaner' amnesty applicant – they put their actions in the context of a strict Christian upbringing and an authoritarian father who was a member of Ossewa Brandwag (a whites-only political organization). They were raised in a social climate of racism where they were taught to hate blacks and regard them as little more than slaves. They were poor, as their father died when they were young, leaving their mother to raise eight children. All spent periods in the South African armed forces, where they learned, in their words, that 'blacks were the enemy' and Adriaan saw combat duty.

All four brothers professed to being supporters of the white supremacist Afrikaner Weerstandsbeweging (AWB) movement led by Eugene Terre'blanche They had attended AWB meetings, although they had not formally joined the movement. Adriaan claimed that he had been approached by an AWB member, Robbie Coetzee (now deceased), to set up a cell which would engage in terrorist activities, destabilize the National Party regime and ultimately establish a *volkstaat* for 'the

Afrikaner people'. Coetzee encouraged Adriaan to carry out a preliminary act of violence which would prepare them for greater acts of terrorism, such as planting explosives at government installations. Adriaan claimed that this was the incentive for hatching a plan to tie up two night security watchmen and steal a truck, in order to demonstrate that blacks were not capable of the job and unemployed whites should be hired instead. As Amnesty Committee member Sisi Khampepe dryly commented, their actions were presented as a form of 'job creation for whites'. On the night of 17 June 1989, the brothers entered the transport depot premises and encountered unexpected resistance from the two security men. The brothers killed them both with a chisel and rocks they found on the premises, and stole a Ford truck, but left it 300 meters from the gates.

Under cross-examination from the amnesty judges and TRC evidence leader Mpshe, the van Straatens' account began to unravel and another story emerged. The brothers had only come up with their plan after an all-day drinking session at the National Station Bar. They had taken no rope to the transport depot, so could not have been planning to tie up the guards. All had previous criminal convictions and the eldest, Willem, had been imprisoned for repeatedly driving under the influence of alcohol and theft of a motor bike trailer. They admitted that they were not actually members of the AWB, and Willem was a member of the right-wing (but closer to the center than the AWB) Conservative Party. They had no official order or direct instruction from the AWB to commit the act. The AWB disassociated itself from the four men, did not arrange their legal defence, and in the end they had to rely upon legal aid. They were defended by Advocate Isaks who is, ironically (given their racist beliefs), an Asian woman. In their confessions, they pleaded guilty to robbery, therefore acknowledging that the act had criminal intent. In the eyes of the committee implementing the either/or terms of the Act, the murders could not have had a political intent also. In the end, the amnesty applications of all four applicants were rejected and the brothers were condemned to serve out the rest of their sentences.

In determining political motivation, membership of a political organization came to outweigh all other factors. 'Political' relied on politics in the narrow liberal sense of formal membership of a political party. The personal desire to create a white state or bring about the downfall of apartheid was not enough, unless it was accompanied by membership in a political party which had given explicit instructions for the act. The TRC *Report* spelled this out for race cases, and was written with the van Straaten case in mind:

> There were cases in which people were victims of racist attack by individuals who were not involved with a publicly known political organization and where the incident did not form part of a specific political conflict. Although racism was at the heart of the South African political order, and although such cases were clearly a violation of the victim's rights, such violations did not fall within the Commission's mandate. (1:84)

This narrow view of politics forced Amnesty Committee members to take party political policies at face value. This led them to ignore the more informal, less institutionalized connections between private racism and public ideology. When I put it to Amnesty Committee Judge Bernard Ngoepe that racism might be considered 'political', insofar as the apartheid state organized society on racial lines and people were killed in the war simply for being white or black, he replied:

> But political parties never recognized this. In fact they denied it and because of this racism cannot be included in the Act. Even the AWB never accepted this. They said, 'we're not against blacks, just communism'. When the [National Unity and Reconciliation] Act was drafted, political parties such as the National Party could not have included killing on the grounds of race. If I as a judge were to say that people were killed because of their color and this was politically motivated then I'd be doing their dirty work for them. (Personal interview, Cape Town, 17 December 1996)

The emphasis on politics being party political led to a reductive literalism where, if the National Party denied that it was racist, then the racism of its members could not be political. Yet the Amnesty Committee's logic was disingenuous since it contradicted positions adopted elsewhere within the TRC – for instance the *Report*'s finding that apartheid was a form of racism, and a crime against humanity. Since the National Party, despite its denials of racism, was the party which constructed and maintained apartheid for 46 years, then surely it could be seen as a racist party with racial superiority at the core of its ideology. Far right breakaway parties from the NP were even more explicit in building racist rhetoric into their public statements and policies. An initial list would have to include the Herstigte Nasionale Party which broke away from the National Party in 1969 in protest at the minor attrition of social apartheid, the Conservative Party which broke in 1982 over the attempt to co-opt 'Coloureds' and Indians into a subordinate position in a white-led tricameral parliament. Finally, the AWB, with its swastika insignias and neo-fascist politics, publicly incited racist violence in the early 1990s. In all of these parties, public and private racism were bound up together in a heady and violent mixture.

In the van Straaten hearings, the Amnesty Committee's distinction between political racism and private or 'pure' racism clashed with the brothers' understandings of their political motivations:[35]

> TRC ADVOCATE MPSHE: Do you agree that the fact that you refer in this letter to the fact that it arose from pure racial hatred, that that once again shows that it had nothing to do with politics?
> MR VAN STRAATEN: Well, as I understand politics, it was the way I was raised, and in my experience the various races were pitted against each other and these were the consequences.

At one point AC Chairman Judge Hassen Mall became utterly incensed with the brothers' use of racism as a defence:

> CHAIRMAN MALL: Are you saying to us that you don't distinguish between murder committed through political objectives or motivation, on the one hand, and murder committed as the result of pure racial hatred, you don't distinguish between the two, is that what you are saying to us?
> MR VAN STRAATEN: That is correct, Mr Chair.
> CHAIRMAN: Are you serious? You are saying that you are motivated, you didn't even say you were motivated by racial hatred, you said by pure racial hatred?
> MR VAN STRAATEN: Because we grew up in this way, I can say that at that time it was difficult to accept the situation.

In defending their judgment, Judge Bernard Ngoepe spelled out clearly the Amnesty Committee's logic, which confined and reduced racism to the domain of personal prejudice:

> The Act says that one should not be motivated by ill-will, malice or spite. My interpretation is that racism is ill-will and malice and therefore is not a political motive. The van Straaten case was outrageous. They were saying that if you kill on racial grounds, then it is political. They don't distinguish. (Personal interview, 17 December 1996)

What the brothers did not correctly distinguish between was 'political' racism according to the public stated policies of political organizations and the 'private' racism in their own world view as individuals. In the legalistic view of the Amnesty Committee, the two are not linked.

The Committee's reasoning on race was inspired by the combination of human rights talk and the ANC's non-racial constitutionalism discussed in chapter 1, where race, ethnicity and culture are not allowed (at least formally) any political connotations. Expressions of cultural or ethnic identification are reduced to the level of private belief and cannot enter the public political sphere and are therefore not 'political'.

Price describes well how the post-apartheid ANC has taken 'every opportunity to project its vision of an inclusive nonracial definition of South African national identity' (1997:167). Civic universalism can express, however, some extraordinary blind spots towards the socially embedded aspects of race beliefs. It places any discussion of race firmly in the past and asserts a radical break with old apartheid thinking, despite the fact that race still plays a significant role in the organization of South African politics and society.[36] The van Straaten brothers, always rather slow on the uptake in life, failed in their application because they were still caught in an apartheid *mentalité* and could not speak the new race-blind language of human rights.

There were clear contradictions between the stance on race/culture of different sections of the commission, with the Amnesty Committee adhering much more closely to classic liberal constitutionalism, while the Human Rights Committee pursued a nation-building agenda that combined culture and rights in the language of reconciliation. Using the language of rainbow nation-building, TRC officials at HRV hearings fused human rights talk to culturalist visions of *ubuntu* and the romantic 'African community'. The TRC would only accept these weakly pan-Africanist expressions of race and nation from those testifying, and it rejected discourses on race associated with the apartheid era. Amnesty applicants could not dredge up the old political language of racism to explain their past actions, as this clashed with the nation-building vision of multiracialism in the present.

In the legal terms of the Amnesty Committee then, racism belonged to the category of the 'personal' and Committee policy was to reject applications made on this basis. In political terms, this may have been defensible, insofar as it prevented a swathe of easily-secured amnesties for convicted racist murderers claiming their acts had some elevated political goal. In post-authoritarian contexts, truth commissions and amnesty processes inevitably have to distinguish between political crimes and criminal crimes. Yet psychologists of violence have argued that this distinction is meaningless at the level of the individual psyche (for instance Simpson and Rauch 1991).

Sociologically the distinction is nonsense, as 'politics' is about the operation of power in both public institutions and society and racism always operates at both levels simultaneously. It is fair to say that the whole thrust of social science studies of racism from the 1960s to the present day is towards understanding how public and private understandings of race are linked and how political and societal organization of racism rely upon one another.[34] Racism emanates not from isolated state policies but from the interaction between policies and societal and cultural assumptions, categories and ways of talking about racial distinctions as well as from racialized material inequalities.

In apartheid South Africa, in the words of liberal politician Helen Suzman, 'the political, economic and social status of every individual is conditioned, if not predetermined, by his race. Indeed the whole pattern of an individual's life – from the cradle to the grave – is circumscribed by his race' (quoted in Boonzaier 1988:58). There are a million examples of how government officials orchestrated the patterns of individuals' lives according to racial criteria, but I will briefly consider one: a meeting of apartheid government ministers at 9.30 am on 17 September 1975, almost nine months before Soweto erupted in the 1976 riots.

The high-ranking officials were drawn from a number of departments – Justice, Environment and Planning, Community Development, Indian Affairs, Sport and Recreation, and Bantu Affairs. They had serious matters to deal with, as the crumbling of segregation was challenging the very constitution of the political order. Johannesburg wanted to integrate racially its municipal bus service and Pietermaritzburg had done this already. Worse still for the mandarins of racial separation, whites, 'coloureds' and Indians were playing cricket together in Maritzburg, Natal. The Aurora Cricket Club, which had an Indian captain and a white vice-captain, had joined the second league. To comply with the law, the players brought their own refreshments and did not use the club house so that 'different races' would not use the same toilets.

Despite cricket's reputation as a benign gentleman's game, the multiracial playing of cricket was the thin edge of the wedge as far as the government was concerned. The State President issued a complicated proclamation extending the Group Areas Act to tearooms and club houses, hoping to discourage multi-racial sport, but the small-town cricket team ignored it and played on (*Sunday Independent* 5 January 1997). Records released after 20 years from state archives show the bumbling attempts of apartheid bureaucrats to enforce policies which were absurd, but which nevertheless had significant effects on people's everyday lives. As observers of South Africa have noted before, the administration of apartheid was not just about the formal policies of political parties, but also about the 'lived experience' of racism.[38] It must be understood as a detailed minute-by-minute bureaucratic enforcement of a totalizing racial paradigm which obliterated any easy distinction between political and personal racism. Likewise, resistance to apartheid entailed both formal political opposition and everyday acts of non-compliance, sabotage and non-co-operation.

Due to the interweaving of personal and public racism during apartheid, the Amnesty Committee could not always neatly separate the two domains and this led to inconsistencies in their approach to racist crimes. It was perplexing that in the van Straaten case the two murdered night watchmen[39] were included in the report as victims of gross human rights violations and their surviving relatives were therefore eligible for reparations. Although their murders were vicious and cruel, they were judged to be outside of the mandate of the commission. Since they were judged to be common crimes rather than human rights violations, the victims should therefore have been excluded from the designated list of victims of gross human rights violations on grounds of consistency. Including them implied that the act was political all along. Can there be a political victim without a politically-motivated perpetrator? It does not seem that the Act allows for this.

Perhaps a more serious breach of the Amnesty Committee's ruling on racism came in the Amy Biehl judgment. Amy Biehl was a bright and promising 26-year-old American student on a Fulbright scholarship pursuing a PhD in political science at the left-wing University of the Western Cape. On 25 August 1993, she drove three black colleagues from the Community Law Center to their homes in Guguletu township, where her car came under attack from an angry black mob. The windows and windscreen were smashed with stones. Amy Biehl, bleeding from the head, fled from her car and attempted to reach a garage across the road. Her pursuers showed no mercy, despite her desperate pleadings. She tripped and fell, and was quickly surrounded by 7–10 youths who stoned and stabbed her until the police arrived. Biehl died from a stab wound to her chest.

Four Guguletu youths (Ntamo, Peni, Nofemela and Manqina) applied for and received amnesty in relation to the murder for which they were serving a prison sentence. Their case bore more than a passing resemblance to the van Straaten case and raised the same issues concerning the politics of racism. The youths were not members of any political party and their act was therefore not authorized. They were sympathetic to the black nationalist PAC party, and had been impassioned by a rally earlier that day where APLA[40] (the armed wing of the PAC) speeches were punctuated by the slogan 'One Settler, One Bullet!' To the applicants, this slogan meant that all whites were the enemy of black people, a mirror image of the AWB's politics of racial hatred. The amnesty applicants were, in sum, motivated by a racial prejudice that did not distinguish between their personal ill-will towards all whites and a 'politically' selective strategy to attack whites who represented particular parties or political institutions (the government, the security forces, etc.). Personal malice and public politics blurred into one another, as they always do in violent nationalist ideology.

The murder of Biehl was not premeditated nor was it on the explicit instructions of a public political organization. According to Nancy Scheper-Hughes' account of the trial, the boys hardly came across as hardened cadres driven by political ideology (1995:149–151). Manquina sucked his thumb throughout the trial and Ntamo was so confused by basic biographical questions that he was sent for psychiatric evaluation. There was a criminal element to the act as the personal effects of Biehl and the passengers were stolen. The attack occurred in the context of a township uprising against white domination, but the van Straaten murders also occurred in a locale (Vereeniging) where many whites were organized into far-right white supremacist organizations and random acts of violence against blacks were commonplace.

However, the van Straaten brothers lost their case and Ntamo et al. won theirs. The contradictory nature of these two judgements can only be explained in terms of the Commission's efforts to project 'national reconciliation' in the media. The van Straaten brothers were parochial, unsophisticated Afrikaner males who could not speak the new language of reconciliation and nation-building. The Biehl case was one which commanded international attention and massive media coverage since it seemed to epitomize reconciliation. Racist murderers confessed, expressed regret at their actions, built 'racial harmony' with a white family and all achieved political and spiritual redemption.

The PAC, although not accepting responsibility for the gross violation, expressed its condolences to Amy Biehl's family in a letter to the US ambassador. Biehl's parents, Linda and Peter, came over from America to attend the hearings in Cape Town in 1997. They were remarkably forgiving in public and stated in press conferences that they did not oppose the amnesty decision. Their press statements appealed to *ubuntu* and principles of human dignity, called for all to 'link arms', to build reconciliation and to further the cause of 'social progress' in South Africa. In this context, granting amnesty for the killers of Amy Biehl was a public relations coup which the TRC could not afford to pass by. In this way, if amnesty applications appealed to the ideals of nation-building and national reconciliation, they stood a much better chance of success than those that failed to articulate the new language of human rights.

From its inception in December 1995, to the day it submitted its Report on 31 October 1998, the TRC was buffeted by tenacious opposition from entrenched political groupings, including those political parties which had given the TRC its mandate in the first place, the NP and ANC. To its credit, the TRC battled in the courts and in the media to tell unpalatable truths that political parties would rather it glossed over. This included the ANC, whose National Executive failed to secure a court injunction to prevent the TRC from publishing certain accounts of ANC violations. The TRC was not simply a rubber stamp on an ANC version of the past, as Jeffery (1999) and others have claimed.

Nevertheless, we need to be aware of how certain political imperatives, such as nation-building and state consolidation by the ANC, distorted the TRC's publicly stated commitment to objective truth-telling. This was apparent when the language of values and moral norms came up against the cold, dispassionate language of the TRC *Report*. Morality ventured where analysis feared to tread, as when violence was not deemed to be the inherent product of state structures and social inequality but 'political intolerance'. The *Report* also appealed to 'racism' as an explanatory category but racism was not conceptualized in both its institutional and experiential components, but instead as a set of values and sentiments held by individuals.

Accentuating the normative and moral dimensions of conflict and inequality was crucial to the TRC's nation-building mission. This meant that reconciliation could be more of the religious and redemptive variety where individuals could readily change their attitudes and join the rainbow nation, redeeming both. Explaining violence through reference to the social and political organization of conflict and inequality was more problematical, as this implied a more long-term and contentious program of socio-economic redistribution and transformation of South African state and societal institutions.

The language of civic nation-building came with historical baggage which in the hands of the Amnesty Committee expressed a classic liberal blindness to issues of race. Constitutionalism, in rejecting race and identity as a category of the 'political' and confining these to the realm of the 'private', created a political environment where race and ethnicity were sometimes dismissed as political motives for committing violations. The Amnesty Committee showed little awareness of how racial classification and racism actually worked in apartheid society, and therefore it could not recognize and apprehend the link between private racism and national party politics. In less legally constituted areas of its work, the TRC did venture onto culturalist terrain, but this was only in the narrowly defined area of *ubuntu* and populist Africanism. The TRC emerges here as a highly contradictory organization, which was over-legalistic in certain contexts (for example, when it was oblivious to the political aspects of race) and 'under-legalistic' in others (for example, when it re-oriented human rights to the imperatives of a multicultural Africanist nation-building project).

The project of nation-building was not the only factor determining which truths the TRC could tell. In the immediate post-apartheid era, there was a fundamental realignment in South African politics and a process of consolidation of the state by the ANC, which ruled alone after 1996. The unwillingness of the TRC to challenge the shifting political axis in national politics could be seen most clearly in the benign treatment of Chief Mangosuthu Buthelezi and absence of a full investigation into his responsibility for public violence.

When the TRC began its work, there was a government of National Unity, South African politics were more pluralistic and the ANC's control over state institutions was still tenuous. Nation-building and state-building were not reducible to a single process. In 1999, after the ANC had won its second election with a massive majority and the political opposition was fragmented and crushed, nation-building and state-building became more and more unified. The ANC has shown itself to be the most adept ruling party in Africa, and any analysis of the politics of truth-telling in South Africa has to grasp how the nation-building mission of the TRC came to fit into a wider project of state centralization by one party. Here, human rights institutions and discourses are embedded in political consolidation and the exigencies of institutional transformation, rather than expressing the ideals of transnational human rights covenants. In the hands of nationalists and state-builders in post-authoritarian countries, human rights talk has developed into something quite distinct from its international legal origins.

PART II

RECONCILIATION, RETRIBUTION AND REVENGE

CHAPTER 4

RECONCILIATION THROUGH TRUTH?

Reconciliation has come to occupy a special place in human rights talk in newly democratizing countries, particularly within transitional institutions such as truth commissions. Reconciliation is not a term with any legal standing, like 'proportionality' or 'gross human rights violation', which is one reason why many lawyers in South Africa object to its prevalence in transitional human rights talk. Like the term *ubuntu*, reconciliation has had a particular role to play in blending human rights talk into a new nation-building project after the demise of apartheid. In the transitional era, reconciliation discourse mitigated the crisis of legitimacy caused by granting amnesty to torturers and entering into a power-sharing arrangement with former apartheid leaders.

Indemnity from criminal prosecution for human rights violators was the price paid by opposition parties in El Salvador, Guatemala, Chile, Argentina, Uruguay and South Africa to persuade authoritarian regimes to relinquish their death grip on society and state. Each transition has ushered in more democratic governments, yet at the cost of not pursuing entrenched terror networks through the courts. While exalting a new 'culture of human rights' and rational rule of law, new political leaders wrap their complicity within the sophistry of reconciliation talk. Reconciliation was the Trojan horse used to smuggle an unpleasant aspect of the past (that is, impunity) into the present political order, to transform political compromises into transcendental moral principles. Reconciliation talk structures a field of discourse in order to render commonsensical and acceptable the abjuring of legal retribution against past offenders. It creates a moral imperative which portrays retributive justice as blood-lust and 'wild justice' and as an affront to democratization and the new constitutional order.

The South African Truth and Reconciliation Commission made much more of reconciliation talk than any truth commission before it. All others had a less ideological commitment to reconciliation since they left it largely to church leaders and politicians, and amnesty was administered by the courts (if at all, in the case of blanket amnesties). The moral precepts within reconciliation talk became a defining feature of the South African peace process. The ubiquity of reconciliation meant that it became the epicenter of competing interpretations and strategies both inside and outside the TRC.

This chapter examines exactly how reconciliation became defined and disseminated by the TRC. The dominant formulation of the term linked reconciliation with notions of confession, forgiveness, sacrifice, redemption and liberation. Orthodox versions of reconciliation were forged within TRC committees, memos and internal policy documents, and were conveyed to the population primarily through the Human Rights Violations (HRV) hearings.

For two years, in the historical moment that the fledgling 'new South Africa' was born, the TRC's hearings became national rituals of reconciliation, forgiveness and truth-telling. Reconciliation is a quasi-religious term that became a guiding principle for new rituals of civic nationalism. As in the writings on ritual of the nineteenth-century sociologist Emile Durkheim (1915), HRV hearings were emotionally intense public ceremonies which generated collective moral values and sought to inculcate them in all who participated, including those who watched the hearings on television each night. Like all rituals, they were met with a complex mixture of compliance, acceptance, indignation and resistance.

Through documenting and analyzing the competing normative discourses around reconciliation, we can come to understand how the TRC's values and classifications both diverged and overlapped with wider, popular values and norms. What were the effects of the values and classifications constructed through TRC rituals on social thinking and normative practice in wider South African society? TRC hearings provided a channel to the mass ANC-supporting constituency for new state values by conjoining them to religious narratives, but how successful were they in establishing a new dominant ideological framework based upon rights talk?

DEFINING RECONCILIATION

Reconciliation was not fully defined in the initial state documents establishing the TRC, and its meanings proliferated and transformed during the life of the Commission. As noted in chapter 1, the legal framework for amnesty was first established in the postscript of the 1993 Interim Constitution entitled 'National Unity and Reconciliation'. This created the constitutional mandate for amnesty as the main form of national reconciliation. The passage in the epilogue with the most relevance for our discussion reads:

> The pursuit of national unity, the well-being of all South African citizens and peace require reconciliation between the people of South Africa and the reconstruction of society.
>
> The adoption of this Constitution lays the secure foundation for the people of South Africa to transcend the divisions and strife of the past, which generated gross violations of human rights, the transgressions of humanitarian principles in violent conflicts and a legacy of hatred, fear, guilt and revenge.
>
> These can now be addressed on the basis that there is a need for understanding but not for vengeance, a need for reparation but not for retaliation, a need for *ubuntu* but not for victimization.

This passage answers some key questions for implementation, such as; who is reconciliation to be between? We are told in the first paragraph 'the people of South Africa', as opposed to, say, between state institutions and citizens, or between South Africa and its past history. For what ends is reconciliation to be sought? For the pursuit of national unity, the well-being of all South African citizens and peace. The next question is, then, through what mechanisms is reconciliation to be achieved? The postscript offers one sentence of guidance:

> In order to advance such reconciliation and reconstruction, amnesty shall be granted in respect of acts, omissions and offences associated with political objectives and committed in the course of the conflicts of the past.

According to the Interim Constitution of 1993, the only function which the TRC absolutely had to fulfil in pursuit of reconciliation was to grant amnesty in a spirit of *ubuntu* and understanding, for politically-motivated acts committed within a specific time period. There was no other mention of any other functions which the TRC was later to undertake, for instance, making recommendations to the State President regarding reparations to victims, or holding human rights violations hearings. For the purposes of the peace negotiations and the final political settlement to the conflict, the amnesty provisions were the only indispensable and necessary part of the process of 'national unity and reconciliation'. The rest was superfluous to a political compromise between the National Party and the ANC which led to power-sharing and the short-lived Government of National Unity (1994–6). In the critical period of negotiations during 1993, the most basic, minimal understanding of reconciliation which NP and ANC negotiators could agree on was this: that reconciliation meant amnesty for violators of human rights.

This is significant not only in terms of our understanding of the place of the TRC within the peace process, but also insofar as it contrasts with the more elaborate versions of reconciliation which would appear once South Africa's political transition was underway. The National Unity and Reconciliation Act (henceforward, the Act) of July 1995, which established the TRC, did not make clear specifically what definition of reconciliation would be used, or who precisely would be reconciled, but it indicated the four main means through which the objectives of 'national unity and reconciliation' would be achieved. These were, in abridged form: 1) establishing as complete a picture as possible of the causes, nature and extent of the gross violations during the period under consideration through investigations and hearings; 2) facilitating the granting of amnesty to those that meet the legal requirements; 3) establishing the fate and whereabouts of victims and recommending reparations; and 4) compiling a report providing a comprehensive account of the findings of the Commission.[1]

At the very end of chapter 2, almost as an afterthought, the Act left open the possibility of mediation between individuals in a section titled 'Principles to govern the general actions of Commission when dealing with victims'. The final sentence referred to 'informal mechanisms for the resolution of disputes, including mediation, arbitration and any procedure provided for by customary law and practice shall be applied, where appropriate to facilitate reconciliation and redress for victims'.[2] This passage was the only one in the Act which dealt with interactions between the TRC and informal institutions of adjudication and mediation. The Act explicitly relegated the dispute-resolving functions of the Commission to a secondary status.

The subsequent chapters (3, 4 and 5) in the Act were wholly concerned with finding truth, granting amnesty and making recommendations regarding reparations. They detailed the structure and functions of each of the three committees, but reconciliation was not mentioned at all in these chapters. Nor were the informal mechanisms mentioned in chapter 2 included within their ambit, and it was left unclear which of the three committees would implement such measures. Nowhere in these chapters did it say that the function of the TRC should be to reconcile anyone (such as victims and offenders). Instead reconciliation was to be a secondary outcome which flowed from the other, more important, activities of investigation and indemnification for offenders.

Partly due to the ambiguities and silences on reconciliation in the Act, which were themselves the legacy of unresolved questions from the peace negotiations, no single idea or practice was established early on in the life of the Commission. This was, however, not unique to defining reconciliation but was part of the general difficulties which the TRC was having in defining policy. A full year into the life of the TRC, Commissioners had still not defined what was considered a 'gross human rights violation' or who was a 'victim'. Questions such as, 'Do forced removals and detention without trial fall under the category of severe ill treatment?' and 'Who is the victim – just the person against whom the offence was committed, or their spouse, or the whole family?' continued to be asked in frustrated closed-door Commission meetings and remained unresolved.

Defining exactly what was meant by reconciliation remained one of the great incomplete tasks of the TRC. This stemmed from a number of factors including the pragmatic realization on the part of Commissioners that if they defined a key objective, then they could be held accountable for not achieving it, and it was obvious to Commissioners that attempts at reconciling individuals would achieve only mixed results. In the context of a largely critical media, unleashing such a messy and unmanageable process would be leaving a hostage to fortune. In addition, reconciliation, like all central unifying metaphors, would function best as a kind of social glue when it was left indeterminate. Different groups with dissimilar agendas could then appeal to reconciliation to advance their own objectives.

Yet perhaps the most significant obstruction to a single definition was related to internal TRC dynamics and the number of disparate political traditions within the Commission. The two main fault lines of contestation concerned admissions of guilt and remorse by 'the white community' or 'Afrikaners', and over the question of whether all human rights violations were morally equivalent, as expressed in the Act. The Act did not give any grounds to distinguish between the actions of, say, a security policeman and an ANC activist, and this caused great ideological difficulties for those involved in the anti-apartheid movement.

The intense debate around these issues was illustrated at a workshop on reconciliation at the Johannesburg offices of the TRC in February, 1997. Former Democratic Party politician and TRC Commissioner Wynand Malan sparked off a debate on race and remorse with a broadside directed against TRC Chair, Desmond Tutu:

> Reconciliation shouldn't be based on repentance and remorse … it is just a capacity to co-exist as individuals. It shouldn't be based upon Christian ideas. We should guard against stereotyping collectives, for instance when Archbishop Tutu says, 'If only the Afrikaner would apologize, then we'd see the goodwill of society'. But who is the Afrikaner? Can I apologize for all Afrikaners? I don't think so. The concept of guilt does not exist in traditional societies, only responsibility. (Author's notes)

His stance was opposed moments later by TRC Executive Secretary Paul van Zyl, who favored admissions of guilt and remorse:

> We must go beyond a mere recognition of responsibility to admit guilt as well. Perpetrators must not only say 'I ordered it' or 'I did it', but they must also say, 'It was wrong'. (Author's notes)

The demand for whites to accept collective culpability was made strongly by Debra Matshoba, a representative of a victims' support group from Soweto:

> One would like to see white people as a group admit that they are guilty – not just the bandits, but the white people who put the National Party in power. Without the National Party, we wouldn't have had poverty, Bantu education, and detentions. Those votes created [Col. Eugene] de Kock. The victims go to the hearings and you feel better, but the next day you go to work and it is still dominated by white people. The TRC cannot achieve its goals unless white people's attitudes change. You people must admit that you still like to be called *baas*.[3] (Author's notes)

Rabbi Hendler resisted this hardening of positions, pointing out that it was impossible to force guilt onto people. However, his voice was drowned by subsequent speakers who demanded that whites collectively express remorse, repent and request forgiveness for wrong-doing. To a large degree, however, the participants were debating a moot point: there was no legal mechanism within the TRC to require an admission of remorse, which was left up to each individual perpetrator. The 'must' in van Zyl's plea amounted to a moral imperative and nothing more.

The debate on reconciliation quickly turned into a heated discussion about whether racial groups were collective actors and, if so, could bear collective guilt and responsibility. Participants argued over what whites should or should not do to make amends, whether some blacks had benefited also from apartheid, and whether whites were behind all 'black-on-black' killings. A TRC psychologist present, Thulani Grenville-Grey, put his head in his hands, looked up resignedly and shook his head. 'It all became too polarized around race … yet again', he said to me in a disappointed tone afterwards. Only weeks earlier, the unity of the Commission had been severely compromised by public accusations by Commissioner Hlengiwe Mkhize that it was run by a 'white liberal clique'.[4] The irony is plain, of course, that the institution perhaps most dedicated to non-racial nation-building in the new South Africa was itself often paralyzed by racially polarized disagreements.

However, the controversy did not stop there, as the workshop then launched into a heated discussion of the second most divisive issue within the Commission: the 'just war' debate. Kadar Asmal, the most eloquent proponent of the 'just war' thesis, expounds this view thus:

> While there were scattered infringements of the ideals of the African National Congress by those resisting apartheid and its war machine, they were aberrations in no way commensurate with the atrocity that was apartheid. There was no moral similarity between the goals, instincts, basic values, or even the tactics, of those who fought to end apartheid, when measured against the values and conduct of those who struggled to uphold it. Not once did the ANC target any apartheid leader for assassination; the apartheid system systematically targeted its opponents.[5] (Asmal et al. 1997:6)

Asmal's view commanded majority support in the TRC, and would be endorsed in the final *Report*, with the caveat that although a just war was fought against apartheid, unjust means were sometimes used by liberation cadres. In calling upon the classic Augustinian distinction between *jus ad bellum* and *jus in bello*, the TRC drew (as it so often did) from Christian theology to formulate its moral position. Yet during the life of the Commission, there was not clarity and consistency in the just war debate. The official view, expressed by Desmond Tutu and TRC manager Alex Boraine, was faithful to the Act, which did not provide a basis for atrocities committed by the former apartheid government to be treated any differently than atrocities committed by those in the liberation struggle. The official view during the life of the TRC was that it was not investigating apartheid as a total political system, it was investigating the individual gross human rights violations which took place between certain dates.

The issue as to whether anti-apartheid activists should apply for amnesty for political crimes forced the Commission to reject the just war thesis in public press releases. In November 1996, public support for the just war view by key ANC figures such as Mpumulanga Premier Matthews Phosa and Justice Minister 'Dullah' (Abdullah) Omar[6] led to an open clash with the Commission. Matthews Phosa in particular came very close to saying that ANC fighters did not need to apply for amnesty since their war was a just one. Desmond Tutu replied forcefully: 'The Truth Commission legislation is quite clear: it does not make provision for moral distinctions and that is something the ANC must be aware of. You have to ask for amnesty ... To talk about a just war is to introduce irrelevancies' (*Star* 4 November 1996).

The just war debate triggered the greatest crisis in the whole life of the TRC. Tutu went so far as to threaten to resign if the ANC did not formally reverse its policy. After protracted talks, he struck an agreement with the then ANC secretary-general, Cheryl Carolus, that ANC policy would formally authorize amnesty applications from party activists (*Star* 11 November 1996). Yet issues of collective responsibility and the moral equivalence of all human rights violations remained unresolved within the Commission up until the publication of the final *Report*.

Participants left the workshop unreconciled, holding views just as polarized as before, a process which was to be repeated in committee meetings for the duration of the TRC's existence. Indeed, the TRC held another workshop on reconciliation a little over a year later, in March 1998, as the Commission was winding up its activities. With the issue of defining reconciliation still quite unresolved, the press release on the workshop admitted that, 'While the process of truth-telling and verifying the truth in the work of the Truth and Reconciliation Commission has been fairly straightforward, the notion of reconciliation presents some serious challenges.'[7]

From this organizational and conceptual morass emerged three main narratives on reconciliation, each with its own approach to vengeance, rationality, forgiveness and the past. These I have termed, from most elite and orthodox to most populist: the legal-procedural, the mandarin-intellectual and the religious-redemptive. These were not often held in their pure form by any single person or committee but instead were articulated in a mixed form, in particular the religious narrative which, being the most populist, plagiarized extensively from surrounding idioms.

Each narrative bears a certain relationship with sectional interest groups within the TRC. The first two narratives were more single-mindedly adhered to by lawyers and intellectuals respectively, as both groups are generally more prone to doctrinal orthodoxy. The third was more the idiom of members of the Commission who were politicians, those who had religious backgrounds, and those from the 'caring professions' (social workers, psychologists and such).

THE LEGAL-PROCEDURAL NARRATIVE

This approach to reconciliation was closest to the mandate of the Act and was dominant among TRC lawyers and, especially within the Amnesty Committee of the TRC, constituted mostly of judges. This was a legal positivist, procedural view of reconciliation, which emerged as a result of the application of legal principles contained within the Act. It was concerned with creating fairness as a result of the direct application of statutes to individual cases of gross human rights violations. It was by self-definition immune to attempts to impose surrounding values and political judgments on the actions of the TRC. For instance, it was unconcerned if a perpetrator did not express guilt at an amnesty hearing. If he fulfilled the essential legal criteria as laid down in the Act, then he must be granted indemnity. Just war arguments emphasizing the moral differences of actions likewise had no bearing upon how a case was treated.

During an interview, Amnesty Committee Judge Bernard Ngoepe stated the legal-procedural view clearly to me. I began by asking him how his work on the Amnesty Committee facilitated reconciliation and Ngoepe replied:

> I personally don't worry about it [reconciliation]. I consider it insofar as it would enable me to make a correct interpretation. When you interpret a statute, you try to establish an interpretation of that statute which may be obscure due to clumsy wording. That the Act was directed towards reconciliation helps us to interpret a particular section. We try to achieve that objective in our interpretation.
>
> AUTHOR: So how does the Amnesty Committee contribute to reconciliation?
>
> NGOEPE: If it gives a judgement which it believes to be correct and consistent. If you are consistent in your decisions, you're going to end up denying amnesty to a left-winger and giving it to someone on the right and vice versa. (Personal interview, 17 December 1996)

Reconciliation here was a broad value which facilitated a judicial interpretation in the 'spirit' of the Act. Judge Ngoepe seemed unsettled by my persistent questioning on reconciliation, and he clearly did not see it as central to his activities. He asserted, after a while, that it had been a mistake to incorporate the Amnesty Committee into the institutional structure of the TRC. Instead, amnesty should have been a legal mechanism integrated into the criminal justice system and unencumbered by all the politicking and high rhetoric of reconciliation. His parting advice to me was, 'When speaking of the TRC, do not include the Amnesty Committee'.

Reconciliation did not really figure as a key concept in the hearings and operations of the Amnesty Committee. This was ironic considering that in the 1993 Constitution, amnesty was the main (indeed the sole) instrument for achieving reconciliation. In over six weeks of amnesty hearings I attended, the word 'reconciliation' was never mentioned by any member of the Amnesty Committee. The legislation had already written reconciliation, remorse and forgiveness out of the practices and decisions of the Amnesty Committee, since the Act did not stipulate that offenders apologize, show remorse, or request forgiveness as requirements for receiving amnesty. This structuring of the field of the sayable by the Act led to a discursive invisibility of reconciliation in amnesty hearings.

Occasionally, an applicant (usually a security policeman) appealed to the notion of reconciliation as part of a desperate plea for clemency. This was done in a specific way which furnished yet another spin on reconciliation. For instance, Security Branch Brigadier Jack Cronje interpreted reconciliation through the historical lens of Afrikaner nationalism by referring to the failed reconciliation between oppressed Afrikaners and the English after the South African War (1899–1902). When applicants did express remorse, this was more of an add on for media purposes rather than a central part of their legal case for amnesty. For the Amnesty Committee, reconciliation was immaterial in its decisions. Amnesty could be granted even though an applicant still expressed pride in his actions, and even though he had neither requested forgiveness, nor been granted it by the victims or their families.

What were some of the implications of this legal reading of reconciliation? The Amnesty Committee's statutes and practices coincided with those of common law insofar as the victims' experiences were not considered central to the process. When granting amnesty, the 'feelings of the family' were placed to one side, vengeance was renounced on their behalf and the law's right to punish – the basis of the social contract – was withdrawn. This relinquishing of law's historic responsibility to punish offenders on behalf of citizens was the main reason why the Amnesty Committee was silent on the question of reconciliation. Since 'reconciliation through amnesty' would have sounded absurd to all concerned, it was best to make as few claims as possible in this regard. Criminal law conventionally defines itself in terms of its antonym (vengeance, mob violence, 'wild justice' and so on), but can only do so by upholding its view of itself as dispensing rational, dispassionate retribution. In renouncing punishment, the TRC judges, bereft of their punitive function, were left with only legality itself. Pure proceduralism served as the organizing principle for the legalists' paradigm of reconciliation.

THE MANDARIN-INTELLECTUAL NARRATIVE

Another policy on reconciliation emerged from an alliance between dominant individuals on the Human Rights Violations Committee (HRVC, which provided most intellectual leadership of the three committees) and the Research Unit. It was not, as we shall see, particularly prevalent at the level of TRC practice in Human Rights Violations hearings, what socio-legal scholars might call the 'living law' of the TRC.

The mandarin-intellectual approach explicitly rejected an individually-oriented[8] notion of reconciliation and leant towards a more abstract focus on the nation, as Wilhelm Verwoerd from the TRC Research Unit summarized: 'The Human Rights Violations Committee is working with victims, with individuals, but I'm not sure that the TRC can contribute at this individual level. We cannot undertake an extensive survivor-offender mediation program. This would need to be undertaken by the criminal justice system' (personal interview, Cape Town, 17 December 1996).

An anti-individual bias in favor of a more transcendent and collective nation-building endeavor was highlighted in a discernible shift from the 'people' to the 'nation' as the focus of who or what was to be reconciled. As originally stated in the postscript of the Interim Constitution of 1993, it was the 'people of South Africa' who were to be reconciled. Within mandarin thinking, the focus became the 'nation of South Africa' itself. The nation, in this view, has a single psyche, a collective conscience, which is the repository of a collective memory.

This official TRC view on 'reconciliation' was formulated in late 1996 by the Research Unit Director, Charles Villa-Vicencio, who argued that the Commission should adopt an abstract reading of the concept. Instead of promoting reconciliation at the level of individuals (say, victims and perpetrators), or social groups (classes, races), the TRC should enhance reconciliation at the level of the South African nation. This view was illustrated in a press release for the March 1998 conference on reconciliation at the TRC offices in Cape Town which framed the terms of discussion by asking, 'How can we reconcile a nation that still bears the scars of a divided society?'

What does 'reconciling a nation' mean in this formulation: how can a nation be reconciled? Academic historian and Human Rights Violation Committee member Russell Ally indicated that the nation must be reconciled with its own collective past:[9]

> Some people in the Reparations and Rehabilitation Committee think we have to facilitate victim–offender mediation, so that reconciliation happens at the individual level. I take a more global view of the state of the nation. By being politically independent, by listening to all sides of the conflict, we can deal with our past and move away from bitterness. We must reconcile *with our past* as opposed to promoting reconciliation between individuals. It is too much to ask victims to forgive. They may get some satisfaction from knowing the truth of what happened and who ordered what. But it's their right to hate the perpetrators.

> From the Reparations Committee the view is 'Have you hugged a perpetrator yet today?' (Personal interview, Johannesburg, 28 October 1996)

TRC mandarins such as Ally took a more open approach to individuals' feelings of vengeance and hatred, accepting that they would continue to exist. This did not undermine the process in their eyes, however, since reconciliation operated at a more abstract, transcendental and national level. Yet like the legal-procedural view, the mechanisms of reconciliation are to be found in rationality, procedure, and an abstract national history project. Within the mandarin-intellectual ideal type, reconciliation emerged through listening to everyone on all sides without bias, and discovering the truth through investigations and making findings. The motto of the TRC, found on every poster pasted across the country, was 'Reconciliation through Truth' and 'truth' here was a catalyst for reconciling the non-racial and constitutionally-defined nation of the present with the racially exclusive nation of the past.

Intellectuals such as Ally or Villa-Vicencio (another academic) maintained that they were taking the long view, and that reconciliation would not come in a matter of a few years, but more like a decade. The TRC, through its disclosure of the truth about specific human rights violations would facilitate the basis for peaceful co-existence, which would provide the substrate from which forgiveness and national reconciliation may later grow.

This view required a great deal of faith in the effect of unadulterated truth upon the citizenry. Lingering doubts were aired in the press release for the March 1998 TRC conference on reconciliation: 'The second, and crucial question, relates to whether the reams of data produced by the Truth Commission from victims, and perpetrators, will, on their own, help us to realize the vision of a commonly shared identity as a nation.'

The transcendental definition had the virtue of being intellectually coherent, precise and fair, and closely related to the Act. Yet this view was not widely adopted outside the narrow confines of certain sections of the Commission and a small community of academics and lawyers. Nevertheless, it was significant insofar as it scuppered any major program of active TRC engagement with local-level adjudication and mediation organizations, from conflict-resolution NGOs involved in victim-offender mediation to urban and rural community courts, or *lekgotla*. There was a certain amount of pressure inside and outside the Commission to engage in victim-offender mediation in the first year of the Commission, but by the end of the first six months this was no longer a remote possibility as the mandarins' opposition to individualized mechanisms of reconciliation won out.

THE RELIGIOUS-REDEMPTIVE NARRATIVE

> For me, the concepts of confession, repentance, cleansing, regeneration, reparation, restoration and forgiveness are inseparable parts of the whole context of reconciliation and liberation. Frank Chikane, Secretary General of the South African Council of Churches 1987–1994 (quoted in Boraine 1995:101)

> [T]he true justification of religious practices does not lie in the apparent ends they pursue, but rather in the invisible action which they exercise over the mind.
>
> Emile Durkheim (1915:403)

The difference between the religious-redemptive narrative of reconciliation and the two approaches we have just considered is very much like the distinction made by socio-legal scholars between the formal law of statutes, and the 'living law' found in the day-to-day functioning of the police and the courts. In contrast to the proceduralist assumptions of the two prior paradigms, the religious-redemptive narrative pursued a substantive notion of reconciliation as a common good, defined by confession, forgiveness and redemption, and the exclusion of vengeance.

This variance between formal policies and concrete dealings with the public was most acutely expressed at the Human Rights Violations (HRV) hearings. In these hearings, Human Rights Committee members encountered individual narratives on violence and they were challenged to present a version of reconciliation with mass appeal. The redemptive view of reconciliation was advocated most strongly by TRC Chair Desmond Tutu and members of the Reparations and Rehabilitation Committee (many of whom are health care professionals).

The religious-redemptive narrative sought not just the reconciliation of 'the nation', but also reconciliation between individuals within the nation. Yet because there was no mass TRC-sponsored program of mediation, the HRV hearings became a symbolic substitute for it. As mentioned in chapter 1, the emphasis on moral unity and group cohesion is a feature of liminal rituals and institutions and arises in the absence of secular and political mechanisms to deal with and properly resolve conflict. HRV hearings replaced a serious project of harnessing local informal mechanisms such as counselling, victim-offender mediation and township or customary courts to the TRC process. Detached from wider adjudicative and mediation mechanisms within civil society, the HRV hearings became rituals of healing which enacted symbolic reconciliation between victims, but lacked the capacity to follow up individual cases afterwards.

During these hearings, the first step towards symbolic reconciliation involved revealing truth through testimonies, with echoes of a Christian act of confession. Perceiving truth as confession allowed Commissioners to expand beyond the forensic legal consciousness of Infocomm and the Amnesty Committee and adopt a more global approach. In contrast to the legal-procedural approach, the redemptive project embraced the social truths presented in victims' testimonies. In the HRV hearings, the TRC came closest to a social approach to truth which integrated people's narratives, myths and experiences. This was important for the hegemonic project of the TRC in a transitional South Africa: by not being hemmed in by legal protocol, the TRC could be more effective than the courts in capturing social truths and implanting popular narratives within its own framing of truth, reconciliation and nation-building.

In the religious-redemptive paradigm, the act of truth-telling contained a healing power which transformed bitterness and revenge. A section in Volume 5 of the final *Report* illustrates how the HRV hearings were like a born-again Christian revivalist meeting. One African man stated after testifying: 'I feel that what has been making me sick all the time is the fact that I couldn't tell my story. But now it feels like I got my sight back by coming here and telling you the story' (5:352).

Despite the plastering of banners proclaiming 'Reconciliation Through Truth' around the town halls of the country, the main function of HRV hearings was to encourage emotional 'catharsis' rather than to unearth information which could be of use to the investigative unit. Commissioner Fazel Randera confirmed this when he stated, 'In the end we are going to be looking at the statements and evidence from the investigative unit for our findings, not at the hearings, which are only a window on a period'.[10] As we saw in chapter 2, the objectives of making findings and writing the truth in the final *Report* were largely unrelated to the hearings. Hearings were important for the media image of the Commission and transmitting the principles of nation-building, but they had no value in creating knowledge about the past.

The wider notion of truth as authentic testimony and confession thrived in the HRV hearings and was sanctioned by Christian discourses on suffering, forgiveness and redemption. As seen in the Chikane quote above, reconciliation was conjoined with a liberation narrative, where suffering itself is contextualized and given meaning in terms of sacrifice for the liberation. This discourse, in providing new meaning for suffering and death, created heroes and martyrs in a new mythology of the state. Being memorialized was the victim's recompense for suffering, vitiating the need for retaliation or retribution. The liberation narrative focused on individuals and wrote them into the wider story of liberation of the nation. This is where the TRC was to be most effective in the conversion (replete with its religious connotations) of the individual to a nation-building project.

The best way to illustrate how this conjoining of individual and TRC narratives worked in practice is to examine the dynamics of the HRV hearings held across the country in 1996 and 1997. In the hearings, HRVC members laid a universal redemptive template across individual victims' testimonies, with predictable chronological stages. There was a progressive structure built into the stages, which began by concentrating on each testimony and then moved from the individual towards the collective and the nation, and finally returned to the individual in order to facilitate reconciliation and forgiveness.

Recognizing and collectivizing suffering

The first stage involved Commissioners expressing appreciation of the evidence, sympathy for the witness and granting value to the testimony. From the idiosyncratic individual circumstances the Commissioners quickly moved to the universal aspects of suffering under apartheid. When Peter Moletsane recounted at the Klerksdorp hearing how he was tortured in police custody in 1986 when he protested against the killing of his uncle (23 September 1996), Desmond Tutu responded, 'Your pain is our pain. We were tortured, we were harassed, we suffered, we were oppressed.'[11]

Commissioners' responses drew together Christian and psychotherapeutic approaches to suffering which sought to transcend individuals' preoccupation with pain. Individuals often stressed the singularity and specificity of their suffering in a way that precluded any wider meaning. In contrast, the Commissioners told people in TRC hearings that 'you do not suffer alone, your suffering is not unique but is shared by others'. In the quote above, Tutu was engaging in high rhetoric, in a similar way to President John F Kennedy when he said 'I am a Berliner'. In saying 'we were tortured etc.', Tutu was not claiming that he had been actually tortured like Moletsane. Instead, Tutu was constructing a new political identity, that of a 'national victim', a new South African self which included the dimensions of suffering and oppression. Thus, individual suffering, which ultimately is unique, was brought into a public space where it could be collectivized and shared by all, and merged into a wider narrative of national redemption. At ritualized HRV hearings, suffering was lifted out of the mundane world of individuals and their profane everyday pain, and was made sacred. In Belinda Bozzoli's words, this led to 'a new form of sequestration of the experiences' (1998:193) of ordinary township residents and an attaching of those experiences to a sacred image of the nation.

The moral equalizing of suffering

In the HRV hearings, Commissioners repeatedly asserted that all pain was equal, regardless of class or racial categorization or religious or political affiliation. Whites, blacks, ANC comrades and Inkatha members and others all felt the same pain. No moral distinction was drawn on the basis of what actions a person was engaged in at the time: whether they were informing to the police or placing explosives for the Azanian People's Liberation Army (APLA). That they suffered was enough.

Post-war regimes often adopt a strategy of moral equalizing to avoid publicly identifying with one side in the conflict. Eric Santner describes a public ceremony of reconciliation in Bitburg, Germany, in 1985 where the ruling Christian Democrats under Helmut Kohl brought President Ronald Reagan to a cemetery where both perpetrators and victims of the Nazi regime were buried. At the ceremony, Kohl and Reagan laid wreaths together, and Santner understands this as a 'sentimental equalization of all victims of war', which was part of a wider rehabilitation of the SS within a narrative of 'Western' resistance to Bolshevism (1992:144).

Public rituals such as the TRC hearings in South Africa (like the Bitburg memorial service) constitute part of a set of complex mnemonic readjustments designed to signpost momentous events in a revised narrative of apartheid, and in so doing to expunge the ideological motivations for the conflict. Post-conflict states practice such historical revisionism in order to depoliticize the past – this is usually what is meant by 'laying the past to rest'. This strategy is often met with resistance by those who maintain their commitment to (anti-apartheid, or anti-fascist in the case of Germany) political principles.

Another type of moral equalization could be found in the case of Susan van der Merwe, who told how her husband, an Afrikaner farmer, had been killed by MK guerrillas whom he picked up hitchhiking along the border with Botswana. His vehicle was found but his body remained missing, hidden somewhere in the scrub brush of the desert. Archbishop Tutu responded to the story by saying:

> I hope that you feel that people in the audience sympathize with you. Our first witness this morning [a black man, Gardiner Majova, whose son had disappeared in 1985] also spoke of getting the remains of a body back. It is wonderful for the country to experience that – black or white – we all feel the same pain. (Klerksdorp, 23 September 1996)

As we have seen earlier in this chapter, this view was contentious within the TRC itself, as many clearly saw a moral distinction between actions which were part of a 'just war' against apartheid and those which were not, or which buttressed the apartheid system. Within this view, an Afrikaner farmer may have been seen as a legitimate target in the armed struggle against a system of white economic domination of the rural economy. The moral equivalence view also contradicted the Commissioners' own tendency to contextualize and valorize suffering in terms of its contribution to the 'liberation'. As we will see in more detail later, the Commissioners juggled two contradictory positions: one which upheld the ideal of neutrality and balance, and the other, prevalent in the HRV hearings, which gave special place to suffering incurred in the struggle against apartheid.

Commissioners were frequently swayed from their neutral position by audiences which showed up at HRV hearings to applaud those who had fought apartheid. Comrades of the ANC Youth League would often play to the crowd, using the HRV hearings as a platform to proudly recount their suffering in a just war against apartheid. Madibo Seakgoa, for instance, testified that during his incarceration:

> A man came in and gave me 200 Rand and some cigarettes and biltong and asked me to write the names of the leaders of the struggle and those who gave me my orders. I wrote the names Nelson Mandela, Oliver Tambo and Joe Slovo and I underlined them several times [appreciative cheers]. He then kicked me in my private parts and hit my head on the wall. I have been hospitalized numerous times in the last 3 years from nervous stress and bad health. I would like for the TRC to pay for all past and future medication because I took part in the justified liberation struggle against a minority government ... I am a disciplined member of the most glorious political organization on the African continent [audience roars its approval]. (Klerksdorp, 23 September 1996)

Commissioners' attempts to accord a moral equivalence to all suffering often met with resistance from partisan audiences at HRV hearings in and around Johannesburg, which were largely sympathetic to the ANC, and hostile to the state security forces and the Inkatha Freedom Party. Audiences often jeered and laughed during testimonies by IFP members and those who were seen as collaborators with apartheid.

The Tembisa hearings in November 1997 were a case in point. They gave a great deal of emphasis to the nefarious activities of an IFP gang called the 'Toasters' based at Vusimuzi hostel, which terrorized the ANC-sympathizing township in 1991–2. The gang's name came from its preferred method of dispensing with its victims, which was to douse them with gasoline and burn them alive. The gang of young men, themselves originally ANC comrades from Umthembeka section of the township, was heavily armed with AK-47s and according to many witnesses counted on police support during their forays into the township to attack ANC comrades and others. They were led by a certain Peter 'Yster' Zulu, who was eventually killed in 1992. His mother Thoko Zulu, a domestic worker, testified at the HRV hearings, crying as she told how ANC comrades dug up his coffin after the funeral. They removed Zulu's corpse, tied it to a fence and then burned it. The police tried to extinguish the corpse and took it to the police station for protection.

The audience collapsed in mirth on hearing Zulu's account. Disorder broke out as people laughed and talked. A man behind me shouted triumphantly, 'Ah! And then *Yster* was toasted!' Completely unprompted, a young Tembisa man sitting next to me leaned over and enthused, 'We were so happy the day Yster died!' Commissioners were visibly horrified at the audience's patent enjoyment of a grisly act of revenge. The chair, Hlengiwe Mkhize, sternly reprimanded the unruly crowd for mocking the gang leader's mother. Another Commissioner, Joyce Seroke, asked rhetorically, and to little effect, 'Don't Yster's parents need comforting too?'

Liberation and sacrifice

> The political theater enacted in funeral rites of a fallen hero becomes an occasion to make a statement about his position in history, the invincibility of the 'struggle' ... and the inevitability of the ultimate price that has to be paid for freedom.
>
> Mamphela Ramphele (1996: 107)

> You have to understand. These people are heroes!
>
> TRC Commissioner Tom Manthata (Personal communication at HRV hearing, 16 September 1996)

During this stage, Commissioners abandoned any pretence to moral neutrality in order to embrace the just war thesis, to place suffering into the context of the liberation struggle and to grant meaning to trauma and loss. The observation that the religious-redemptive narrative positioned itself within the just war approach to the struggle against apartheid should perhaps come as no surprise, since Norman reminds us that the just war tradition originally developed within Christian morality (1995:117).

As within liberation theology in Latin America, religious narratives on suffering and deliverance and political narratives on liberation were fused together creatively by politically inclined clergy. Individual narratives were linked to wider political narratives, providing meaning for death by building a heroic figure of self-sacrifice in a new mythology of the nation-state. Meaning was attached to death by a process of teleologizing – of mapping onto the experiences of the dead and the survivors a narrative of destiny which portrays an inexorable progression towards liberation. This teleologizing of loss and pain is a common feature of 'survivor's syndrome', and has been documented for the Holocaust (Bettelheim 1952) and Argentina (Suarez-Orozco 1991).

The message was that people had died not in vain, but for the liberation of the nation. Commissioners often referred to victims as 'heroes'. The history of the new South Africa is a history of suffering which was necessary for the liberation and redemption of the nation. A clear link was forged between religious interpretations of suffering emphasizing sacrifice and martyrdom and a more secular liberation narrative, with its imagery of national heroes.

The unifying symbol which brought these two narratives together in a particularly powerful way was the figure of Steven Biko. In the amnesty testimony of security policeman Gideon Nieuwoudt (who was denied amnesty) it emerged that Biko had been chained to a gate in the crucifix position before he died of head injuries, turning him into a symbol of the Black Christ of the African Nation (*Guardian* 31 March 1998). With his scruffy beard, intense eyes and the burning radical idealism of youth, he endures as an Ernesto 'Che' Guevara figure, a secular saint of the African oppressed. If Mandela is the Father of the liberation struggle, then Biko is its beloved Son, whose life was cruelly cut short, just at a time when his message was strongest, and when he was welding together charterist and black consciousness strands of the liberation struggle. Biko symbolizes the unfulfilled expectations of the 1970s and is untarnished by the excesses of the 1980s and the disappointments of the 1990s. The bitterness of the present seems to continue to gravitate around Biko's image of youth, intelligence, hope, and a promise which was never realized.

Benedict Anderson (1991) has drawn our attention to how nations are imagined through their war dead, with cenotaphs and tombs of the unknown soldier, which are filled with the ghostly imaginings of the nation. On certain days, nations mark a simultaneous event to memorialize their war dead. Similarly, HRV hearings often ended with the Chair asking the audience to stand and observe one minute's silence for fallen heroes. In February 1997 at the Duduza HRV hearings it was in commemoration of a young woman necklaced by ANC comrades after the '0-hand grenades' incident and later found to be innocent of collaborating with the security police. This memorializing of sacrifice for the nation has been institutionalized in South Africa with a Day of Reconciliation on 16 December. Ironically this is also the day on which the ANC celebrates the beginning of the armed struggle in 1961, and Afrikaner nationalists celebrate the 'Day of the Covenant' in memory of the defeat of 12,000 Zulu warriors at the 'Battle of Blood River' in

1838. This date, which is annually contested by competing nationalists, was the date on which the TRC started its work in 1995.

The TRC drew its imagery from a previous history of political funerals during the anti-apartheid struggle to interweave narratives of liberation and Christian sacrifice and redemption. In the 1980s in particular, funerals of activists became a form of political theater where anti-apartheid groups sought to make as much capital as possible out of the death of fallen comrades. With their coffins lined up in rows, and surrounding by dancing and singing activists, mass funerals became incredibly important stages to display to the outside world the brutal nature of apartheid. The apartheid state was fully aware of this, and this is why it carried out a 'war of vanishment', where opponents simply 'disappeared' so that nothing physical remained to be imbued with political capital. Similarly, court cases or inquests in the 1980s re-enacted the drama of fierce repression and fatal resistance. In drawing heavily on this history and placing it in a more sober town hall environment, the TRC became a cross between a 1990s court inquest and a 1980s anti-apartheid mass funeral.

Mamphela Ramphele (1996) has written how political funerals in the apartheid years created a category of 'political widowhood', where the widow became the custodian of the collective memory of the fallen hero. During the apartheid years, this category was granted selectively as only a few out of the thousands of widows were chosen for special status. In the immediate post-apartheid era, the TRC generalized the category of political widowhood to include many of those previously excluded. Political widowhood was extrapolated out from a few central ANC and PAC figures to include all those in society. The TRC generalized and democratized political widowhood. Each mother coming before the TRC became a 'mother of the nation' (whereas before the designation was reserved for those such as Winnie Mandela), the nation being defined by a history of suffering and sacrifice. A new history of state brutality required an expanded category of fallen national heroes, represented by an enlarged community of political widows. In the post-apartheid context, they embodied the symbolic contrast between the old brutal state and the new benevolent regime.

The embedding of an individual's account in an allegory of liberation began immediately after the testimony. The first question by the Commissioner leading the cross-examination was almost always about the context of the township or area at the particular time, not the individual event or unique circumstances of the victim. In this way, individual events were sutured to a context of chaos, resistance, rioting against the police, and rent and school boycotts and therefore they became integrated into a wider liberation narrative.

'Sacrifice' provided the main symbolism for grafting individual pain onto wider narratives. In the following quotes, the image of sacrifice looms large: Desmond Tutu told Peter Moletsane: 'You are one who is still young, who sacrificed himself for the fruits of liberation which we have now, which our children were fighting for' (Klerksdorp, 23 September 1996). Denzil Potgieter said to trade unionist Sam Senatle, testifying about torture in police custody, 'It is important to remember the price that was paid for what is being enjoyed by people now. Thank you for reminding us of the sacrifice of young people for the democracy we have today' (Klerksdorp, 26 September 1996).

The liberation-redemption narrative was applied to witnesses in a uniform manner, whether it was obviously relevant and appropriate (as in the cases above, involving a comrade and a trade unionist respectively) or not. Occasionally, it was employed by Commissioners even if the victim rejected a political role and was unwilling to locate their own suffering in a wider liberation context. It was as if Commissioners got round the difficult question of judging whose actions were heroic sacrifices and whose acts were trivial by glorifying all who came to the hearings as a hero. Such was the case of Sello Mothusi (Klerksdorp, 26 September 1996), who was shot by police on 4 March 1986. In his testimony to the TRC, Mothusi stated, 'I went to the shop to buy things for my mother ... I was not involved in any politics'. However, the Commissioners' line of questioning relentlessly pushed Mothusi towards the events of that day in Kanana township, in order to link his story with that of United Democratic Front comrades fighting police at the barricades. During rioting that same day, four comrades had been shot dead in the street by police. At the Klerksdorp hearings, Sello became the living representative of their sacrifice. He himself was a reluctant hero, wanting no part of the dead boys' glory, and he stressed how he had 'done nothing wrong' and become unwittingly caught up in events. To the Commissioners' annoyance, he doggedly kept to his story that he knew nothing.

Ramphele has also described how families became an incidental part of the theater of 1980s political funerals when many were dragged unwittingly into highly politicized funerals (1996:106–107). Families were too insignificant to get in the way of the political capital which could be made before a national and international audience. Likewise, it appeared that Commissioners could not cope with accounts that did not fit their redemptive template. Commissioner Hlengiwe Mkhize replied to the testimony of the mother of 'Yster', the leader of the Toasters gang in Tembisa:

> Some people who gave statements were frightened to speak at hearings. We ask the leaders to encourage people who gave

> statements to come forward and not be frightened, so people like you struggling for freedom should be recognized.

Now to my mind, the idea that the Toasters gang was 'struggling for freedom' during the apartheid era calls for a stretching of the imagination bordering on the surreal. Rather, the Toasters were a hardened criminal gang 'struggling' only for their own freedom to rape, pillage and murder. The gang first associated itself with the ANC, and then changed allegiance to the IFP, and it did not hold any cogent political position for any length of time. The Toasters collaborated with apartheid police and participated in a fratricidal and murderous war in the townships. Bringing the Toasters gang into the history of 'the struggle' demonstrates the arbitrary connection between individuals' histories and the fundamental ideological assumptions of the TRC. Some personal stories fit quite well into the universal template of the TRC, but others did not at all. What is clear is that the liberation narrative was the only historical framework that was used to recognize and valorize manifestations of suffering.

However, one can detect something else going on in Mkhize's response, which allows her statement to make more sense. She could instead have been asserting that Thoko Zulu, in coming forward and participating in the TRC hearings, despite the jeers of the audience, was somehow participating in the present and ongoing liberation of the country. Even though she had lived with her son, Yster, in the IFP-dominated hostel while he sowed terror during the final years of apartheid, her actions now redeemed her and made her a partner in the new nation-building project. The political redemption of an old enemy is portrayed by the TRC as carrying forward the struggles of the 1980s into the new constitutional order. Redemption and images of renewal, as Victor Turner has stated, are regular characteristics of rituals of transition, and seek to imprint a new moral unity and sense of group cohesiveness upon the participants (1967:99). Harnessing the legitimacy of the anti-apartheid struggle to the transitional TRC structure was ultimately part of an overall project of entrenching a new ANC-led bureaucratic authority in the townships.

The fairly indiscriminate use of the liberation narrative also allowed the TRC Commissioners to get around the problem raised by the 'just war' debate discussed earlier. The Act did not provide a basis for making any moral distinctions between cases. Each case had to be treated equally. Yet many individual Commissioners and much of their township audiences adhered to the just war argument which distinguishes between different types of violence and regards them as either repressive or liberating. In the end, everyone was treated equally by bringing all accounts into the liberation narrative. Therefore, although the TRC was resistant at times to the just war argument because it wanted amnesty applications from anti-apartheid activists, in its encounters with the public at hearings, it relied upon a just war framework to classify and give meaning to suffering.

Redemption through forsaking revenge

> Forgiveness will follow confession and healing will happen, and so contribute to national unity and reconciliation.
>
> TRC Chair, Desmond Tutu, on the first day of hearings in the Eastern Cape (in Tutu 1999:91).

In this final stage, the spiritual recompense for the loss of a family member was accentuated in the hope that it would preclude any acts of retaliation. The experience of coming before the TRC would 'heal wounds' and smooth over resentments. Once individual suffering was valorized and linked to a national process of liberation, it was possible to urge victims to forgive perpetrators and abandon any desire for retaliation.

For the first six months of the Human Rights Violations hearings around the country, Commissioners specifically pressed those testifying to forgive the perpetrators then and there. After hearing each testimony, they asked as a matter of course, 'Do you forgive the offender?' This question was seen as fairly outrageous by numerous observers (including this author) and just as many victims, and was occasionally met with such a hostile response that it eventually had to be abandoned. However, at subsequent HRV hearings, victims were more subtly pressed by Commissioners to testify, to forgive and to reconcile. Throughout the entire amnesty process, victims were asked as a matter of routine whether they opposed the application and whether they forgave the applicant.

The TRC took a highly individualized notion of reconciliation, assuming that individuals had the power to forgive on behalf of whole families and communities. This provoked anger in some, but compliant acceptance from just as many others. The TRC's use of Christian discourses on forgiveness often swayed religiously-inclined individuals and, for some, the act of testifying in public created a loyalty to the TRC's version of national reconciliation.

What was striking about the TRC hearings was the way in which Commissioners never missed an opportunity to praise victims who relinquished a desire for vengeance. Desmond Tutu made clear his views on retaliation in his response to two instances of murder where the body was not found. To Susan van der Merwe referred to earlier, the widow of a white farmer who had lived in relative penury after her husband's disappearance, Tutu said: 'It is good to see that you are not bearing any grudges. You state that your story of pain is but a drop in the ocean, but it is still pain that happened to you. I hope that God will anoint your wounds with the Holy Spirit and heal them' (Klerksdorp, 23 September 1996).

In the case of Gardiner Majova, whose son had gone missing in 1985 and who was himself tortured by the police, Tutu praised his passive forbearance:

> Thank God for people like you – that you haven't gone mad. All you ask for are the remains of your child so you can give him a proper burial. You don't speak of anger or a desire for revenge. We pray that God will strengthen you and help the TRC find the Truth and find your son so you can give him a decent burial. (Klerksdorp, 23 September 1996)

For Tutu (1999), forgiveness is not conditional upon the wrongdoer expressing remorse or asking for forgiveness, but is a duty incumbent upon all victims. There are no unforgivable perpetrators, no persons who cannot be redeemed, and this redeption also 'liberates the victim'.[12] The hearings were structured in such a way that any expression of a desire for revenge by victims would seem out of place. Virtues of forgiveness and reconciliation were so loudly and roundly applauded that emotions of vengeance, hatred and bitterness were rendered unacceptable, an ugly intrusion on a peaceful, healing process. When such emotions did inevitably emerge at hearings, Commissioners were poorly prepared to deal with them. Commissioner Mkhize described at a TRC workshop on reconciliation (27 February 1997) one well-publicized episode at the hearings in Alexandra township:

> There was a woman called Margaret Madalane who saw her son Bongani shot dead by the police during the Six Day War in 1986. She was screaming and hysterical. She said she wanted to get a job as a domestic worker so she could get rat poison and kill white children. She intimidated us as Commissioners. We were writing notes to each other, asking who will reply to her and what will they say. It was Hugh Lewin's [a white journalist] turn to reply. He received a note from [Commissioner] Yasmin Sooka saying, 'Don't feel guilty, you paid your price during apartheid'. The woman was rushed to hospital with high blood pressure. (HRV hearings 29 October 1996)

Hearings were seen as having a near-miraculous capacity to transform bitterness. Commissioners at press or public meetings were often given to recounting individual cases where this took place. Hlengiwe Mkhize provided a paradigmatic statement expressing this view:

> There was an 83-year-old man from Alexandra township called Thladi. He had spent 12 years on Robben Island and was very bitter. In his statement he said that if he went to heaven and met his jailers there, then he would ask to leave. He testified at the Alexandra Human Rights Violations hearings and became less bitter. He was reconciled and died a few months later. (TRC workshop on Reconciliation, February 1997)

For some, however, the construction of the TRC hearings as rituals of healing over-simplified the complex psychological processes at work. In the words of one psychologist who worked closely with the Commission, Brandon Hamber,

> The word catharsis gets used too often within the TRC. There is a perception that as long as a person is crying then healing must be taking place. But for the majority, crying is only the first step and there is no follow-up after the hearings. In fact, the adrenalin of giving testimonies on national television masked psychological problems which then surfaced later. (Personal interview, 30 September 1996)

THICK AND THIN RECONCILIATION

The main priority of the Chilean and Argentinian truth commissions was to reveal truths about the authoritarian past, and particularly to determine the fate of the thousands of disappeared. In contrast, the South African Truth and Reconciliation was much more ambitious. More than any other truth commission before it, the TRC sought reconciliation as the basis of nation-building. That the TRC took a liberal interpretation of its mandate was due primarily to the personal force and charisma of former Archbishop Desmond Tutu. More than any other national figure, Tutu was able to combine three key narratives in his public statements – Christian morality, the liberation narrative of the 1980s and the reconciliation narrative of the 1990s. Due to his influence, the TRC initially made substantial promises to reconcile individuals and social groups.

Over the life of the Commission there was a gradual progression towards a 'national reconciliation' perspective among Commissioners themselves, from what I shall term 'thick' (religious) to 'thin' (secular, national) reconciliation. Nevertheless, Desmond Tutu continued to advocate in his public statements most of the elements of 'thick' reconciliation: confession, forgiveness, sacrifice and redemption. This is important in assessing the wider impact of TRC values in South African society, and it is the impact of the religious-redemptive version of reconciliation that I shall evaluate. To what degree did 'thick' reconciliation talk advance the cause of nation-building and diminish the desire for vengeance?

Intellectual and legal versions of national reconciliation were too abstract, cerebral and bloodless to create a new hegemony within the media and to appeal to most South Africans. They were elaborated and held by the Commission's intellectuals, and found favor only within a narrow band of people in government, educational institutions, and among human rights professionals. The religious-redemptive approach was the only one with any purchase in society, and the one which supporters gravitated towards and opponents resisted. It was the only version of reconciliation with any pretensions to reshaping popular legal and political consciousness. The focus in the next three chapters is upon the variegated impact in the townships of this attempt at constructing a post-apartheid dominant ideology.

CHAPTER 5

RECONCILIATION IN SOCIETY: RELIGIOUS VALUES AND PROCEDURAL PRAGMATISM

LEGAL PLURALISM AND HUMAN RIGHTS IN SOUTH AFRICA

The next three chapters evaluate how the religious-redemptive model of reconciliation was received by its intended audience in African townships. Based in ethnographic methods and extensive interviews in the Johannesburg area, they attempt to answer the questions: How does human rights talk interact with everyday moralities and understandings of justice? Do national leaders' calls for reconciliation have any purchase in areas traumatized by political violence? By examining these issues in particular locales, we can get a sense of how successful post-apartheid regimes have been in inculcating a 'culture of human rights'.

Over the past fifteen years, there has been a lively dialogue between anthropologists and colonial historians regarding the relationship between state law and informal morality and justice. A key and contested notion in this debate has been 'legal pluralism'; this is a descriptive term and analytical concept which attempts to address the existence of more than one legal system in a single political unit. In general, anthropologists have found the term useful, whereas historians of colonialism have objected to it. These three chapters ask whether the idea of legal pluralism is valuable for thinking about legal consciousness in the unique historical phase of the dismantling of apartheid.

Legal pluralism originated in anti-positivist legal philosophy in the early twentieth century as a reaction to an exclusionary state centralism which regarded only state law as law.[1] In reality, argued pluralists, state law was far from absolute, and in many contexts was not particularly central in the normative ordering of society. In opposition to a unitary view of the legal order, the anthropologist Bronislav Malinowski (1926) asserted that social norms in non-state societies perform the same regulatory functions as legal norms. He therefore raised uncodified social rules to the status of 'law' and advanced the important insight that law does not have absolute privilege in dealing with conflict.[2]

Legal pluralists such as Jane Collier (1975) and Sally Engle Merry (1988) reinforced Malinowski's stance by conceptualizing legal and social norms as equivalent and mutually constitutive. Judicial rules and extra-state norms (found in customary or 'community' courts, for example) are both 'law' on the grounds that both are codes of social thought expressing moralities and social identities.[3] The legal and the non-legal relate to each other as interacting normative discourses. There is no inherent *categorical* hierarchy between them, although the state usually enjoys an institutionalized dominance over private moralities.

More recently, this approach has found favor within post-modernist jurisprudence which challenges legal positivist claims of doctrinal unity and complete domination of surrounding social conventions. Both legal pluralism and post-modernist jurisprudence disaggregate law and power, drawing power and discipline out of state legal institutions and locating them in society. For the Derridean legal scholar Margaret Davies our understanding of 'law' is not to be confined to the highly selective and limited conception of positive law. Echoing the distant anthropological voices of Karl Llewellen and Adamson Hoebel in *The Cheyenne Way* (1941), Davies writes that, 'law is everywhere – in our metaphysics, our social environment, our ways of perceiving the world, the structure of our psyche, language, the descriptive regularities of science and so on' (1996:7). Legal pluralism and post-modernist legal theory converge on a number of premises, and primarily upon Clifford Geertz's assertion that 'law is culture' (1983).

However, the emphasis on the importance and autonomy of social norms rather than positivized rules often entailed a neglect of the colonial state in the writings of mid-century legal anthropologists of Africa.[4] Legal anthropology in the colonial context often saw state law and informal law as co-existing but unconnected spheres of authority and adjudication, which employed different procedures embedded in distinct moralities. Discussions of the relationship between state and informal law often portrayed the two systems as static and isolated, thus fueling parallel debates about universalism and cultural relativism in the area of human rights.

In Southern African legal anthropology, an isolationist perspective is adopted in Comaroff and Roberts' influential book *Rules and Processes* (1981). This characterized 'Tswana law' as a forum for individual negotiation that is separate from the interventions of colonial and post-colonial legal regimes. Although the authors have since moved on to look in greater depth at the place of 'customary law' within colonial policy (Roberts 1991), others have maintained a view of it as autonomous at the level of local communities and culture, rather than by colonial and post-colonial states. Gulbrandsen (1996:125), for one, argues that the colonial encounter did not erode the local political-juridical bodies of the Northern Tswana of the Bechuanaland Protectorate (now

Botswana), which were able to safeguard a 'genuinely Tswana normative repertoire'. The stress in Gulbrandsen's study is upon the preservation of 'cultural integrity' and the 'autonomy of Tswana jurisprudence' according to culturally specific ideas (p.128), to the detriment of a thoroughgoing analysis of the transformation of customary law by successive states.

The anthropological consensus on legal pluralism was directly challenged in the mid-1980s by legal centralist critiques which argued that collapsing legal and social norms into the same category mistakenly turns all social norms and values into 'law'. This move makes defining law problematical in that every norm is defined as legal. Legal pluralism, it is argued by legal theorists such as Brian Tamanaha (1993), loses sight of how the rules of state law are constructed through quite different processes: positivised, written legal rules are generated by specialists within rationalized bureaucratic structures. Moreover, Tamanaha correctly points out that legal anthropologists never formulated a cross-cultural definition of law that did not somehow rely upon the state.[5]

The primacy that anthropologists tend to grant to Africans' juridical autonomy has been subjected to recent critiques by colonial historians, who generally take the view that customary law was utterly transformed by, controlled and integrated within the administrative apparatus of the colonial state.[6] Instead of legal pluralism in Africa, there was only 'a single, interactive colonial legal system' (Mann and Roberts 1991:9). The most influential and consistent advocate of the centralist approach to African legal history has been Martin Chanock (1985, 1991), whose work focusses primarily on the place of the legal regime in the policies of colonial states. He asserts that legal ideology has been a central part of the domination of society by the state. In his materialist reading, colonial and customary law were welded into a single instrument of dispossession and were part of a wider administrative policy of creating and maintaining a particular type of peasantry (Chanock 1991:71). Rather than being the product of immutable tradition, 'custom' was manufactured as a legitimating device for maintaining the status quo after dispossession by reinforcing the position of the chieftaincy. Pluralism is but a legal fiction, a part of the ideology of British indirect rule in African and Indian colonial territories. According to Chanock, 'An indigenous system of land tenure did not exist under colonial conditions, but its shadow was summoned into existence by both colonial and post-colonial states, essentially to retard the establishment of freehold rights for Africans' (1991:81).

This is a cogent and persuasive argument which anthropologists are advised to heed. However, we are not forced to choose between the insights of legal pluralists and those of legal centralists, who have been moving closer to each other's position to look at the interplay between state law and local ideas and institutions of justice. Because of the way the question has been formulated (What is the relationship between law and society?), neither tradition is wholly indispensable. Legal pluralism provides an important descriptive model of society as made up of a diversity of modes of conflict resolution, shattering the myth of state law's unchallenged empire.[7] At the same time, the centralist argument has identified a logical contradiction: when the domains of the legal and non-legal are fused,[8] the category of law becomes meaningless, as it includes everything from table manners to national constitutions and transnational covenants of rights. Further, centralists remind us of Max Weber's maxim that law is a semi-autonomous discourse created by bureaucratic officials for the purposes of legal domination.[9] Law's norms are positivized ones, often far removed from, though not wholly unrelated to, the lived norms of experience.

It is possible to take a more synthetic view of the creative tension between anthropologists and colonial historians and build up a version of legal pluralism that is useful for thinking about the interactions between new human rights ideas and local morality and justice in African communities. Recent studies have conceptualized the relationship between state and non-state legalities in increasingly sophisticated ways. There has been excellent work by social historians on the interactions between Africans and European colonial administrators, each pursuing their own interests, with the result being a 'complex patchwork of overlapping legal jurisdictions' (Mann and Roberts 1991:16).

The work of anthropologist Sally Falk Moore (1978, 1986) provides a useful point of departure, as she maintains a legal pluralist perspective while keeping the state firmly within the scope of her analysis. In Moore's view, customary law is the product of historical competition between local African power holders and central colonial rulers, each trying to maintain and expand their domains of control and regulation. Law is imposed upon 'semi-autonomous social fields' with uneven and indeterminate consequences. We must not over-estimate the power of law to exert its will, as the connection between native courts on Kilimanjaro and the British colonial high court was often 'nominal rather than operational' (1986:150).

Moore takes us away from a static view of plural legal systems to look at the historical transformations of regulatory practices, and her work oscillates between small-scale events (individual court cases) and large-scale social processes such as colonialism, and decolonization. Moore largely accepts Chanock's portrayal of the profound transformation of customary law by colonial rule, yet her more interactionist focus upon the Habermasian 'lifeworld', and more specifically upon the kinship basis of Chagga society, means that she allows room for local strategizing in pursuit of greater political autonomy. She concludes in one essay that 'local law cases reflect the local history of African peoples rather than the history of the Europeans who ruled them' (1991:125).

Yet there is still some work to do on the notion of legal pluralism in order to replace the stark dualism of pluralism versus centralism. Instead of adopting over-systematizing theories which construct 'law' and 'society' as two total and coherent cultural systems with distinct logics,[11] we could redefine the subject matter and analyze how adjudicative contexts are transformed over time by the social actions of individuals and collectivities within a wider context of state regulation and discipline. In any locale there is a variety of institutions and competing value orientations which have emerged through a long process of piecemeal aggregation, rupture, and upheaval and they continue to be transformed by social action.

In a revised view of legal pluralism, the question to be answered is how social actors (encompassing both individuals and collectivities) have contested the direction of social change in the area of justice and what the effects of this are for state formation and the legitimizing of new forms of authority. This is a legal pluralism of action, transformation, and interaction between legal orders in the wider context of state hegemonic projects. In post-apartheid South Africa this involves looking at how TRC Commissioners, magistrates, township court officials, Anglican clergy and others combine human rights talk, religious notions of redemption and reconciliation, and popular ideas of punishment and revenge, in an effort to control the direction of social change, or what the French sociologist Alain Touraine (1971; 1995:219, 368) refers to as 'historicity'. new theory lookup!

Touraine, it must be acknowledged, defines historicity in different ways, but I am using it in the sense of a portrayal of social life as a set of relations between the social actors who contest the bearing which social change takes. The struggle over historicity in the area of ethics in post-apartheid South Africa presents itself as a struggle over how to deal with the political crimes of the apartheid past and how to construct discontinuities with the past and in so doing to reconfigure legal authority in the present.

The advantage of Touraine's sociology is that it moves us away from a static view of 'society' towards an examination of the remarkably rapid movement in the production of norms such as human rights. This rapid change in social values is linked to the rise of modernity:

> Modernity rejects the idea of society. It destroys it and replaces it with that of social change ... The reason why ... I constantly focus

> my remarks on the idea of *historicity*, is that social life can no longer be described as a social system whose values, norms and forms of organization are established and defended by the State and other agencies of social control, and that it must be understood as action and movement. Social life is therefore a set of social relations between the actors of social change [emphasis in original]. (1995:219)

Applying this to South Africa, we can see that legal institutions, be they township assemblies, magistrates' courts or human rights commissions, are simultaneously subjected to *centralizing* and *pluralizing* forms of social action and knowledge production. Modern states continually attempt to rationalize and institutionalize their legal dominion, and yet encounter resistance in a context of legal pluralism. These countervailing tendencies, emanating from informal justice and popular legal consciousness, are a contradiction at the heart of modernity. Weber's analysis of the emergence of legal authority asserted that the character of national law is:

> [s]tructured by the competition between central rulers trying to maintain the maximum of power over their subjects and the local power-holders trying to carve out their own domains of arbitrary power over their dependants and limit the central government's claims on them. (Humphreys 1985:246)

At different historical moments, one set of strategies may exercise dominance over another and become hegemonic. In the mid-1980s, as the internal anti-apartheid movement led by the United Democratic Front reached its crescendo and 'popular courts' punitively enforced counter-hegemonic values and political strategies, the dominant tendencies in the area of justice were fragmenting, decentering and pluralizing.[12]

Since the post-apartheid elections of 1994, the main direction of legal change has been towards greater centralization as state officials attempt to restore the legitimacy of legal institutions. Government officials, such as the Minister of Justice Dullah Omar, have sought to integrate certain non-state structures (armed units of the liberation movements and Inkatha Freedom Party) into the criminal justice system, and to exclude others, such as township courts. Part of my general thesis about the South African Truth and Reconciliation Commission is that it represented one effort on the part of the new government to formulate a moral leadership and to establish a unified and uncontested administrative authority. This is a common strategy of regimes emerging from authoritarianism, as they seek to unify a fragmented legal structure inherited from the *ancien régime*. The notion of reconciliation found in human rights talk is the discursive linchpin in the centralizing project of post-apartheid governance. Human rights talk performs a vital hegemonic role in the democratizing countries of Africa and Latin America; one which compels the population away from punitive retribution by characterizing it as illegitimate 'mob justice'.[13]

The new values of a rights culture are formulated primarily by intellectuals and lawyers representing a new political elite which has sought to superimpose them upon a number of semi-autonomous social fields. These values engender new discursive and institutional sites of struggle and their impact is uneven and emergent, raising questions for research such as: Has the centralizing project as pursued through the TRC altered the terms of the debate on post-apartheid justice, and, if so, how? How can we more precisely conceptualize the specific continuities and discontinuities between normative codes? In what areas of social life are human rights ideas and practices resisted, when are they appropriated, and when are they simply ignored?

In post-apartheid South Africa there are various competing discourses and systems of values around justice and reconciliation. Christian discourses on forgiveness advocated by TRC officials often swayed individuals at hearings, but they also clashed with the retributive notions of justice routinely applied in local township and chiefs' courts. In thinking about how to understand the complex reception of the TRC's redemptive concept of reconciliation, I assert that there were three forms of connection and disconnection between the TRC and its constituencies. Along the continuum from acceptance to resistance, they are:

1. *adductive affinities:* the close associations between the TRC's understanding of reconciliation as forgiveness and the religious values of victims and local churches. Dominant values are successfully conveyed to the intended audience. The positive responses of victims to the idea of national reconciliation can be understood in terms of both the ritualized aspects of hearings and pre-existing value associations between human rights and religious discourses.

2. *procedural pragmatism:* victims pursue their own agendas through TRC mechanisms, without there being any necessary loyalty to the dominant ideology of human rights and reconciliation. Hearings became an arena for pre-existing processes of dispute resolution (primarily between victims, rather than victims and perpetrators) to progress further. Victims' reconciliation was the result of the creation of a forum outside local structures where victims could communicate more directly, rather than a commitment to the wider TRC goals or an ideology of reconciliation or nation-building.

relational discontinuities: these express resistance to key elements of the dominant value system. Human rights talk diverges from ideas of justice prevalent in gangs and local courts, which emphasize vengeance and punishment rather than reconciliation. If reconciliation is the key category of the new state's centralizing project, then vengeance is the main concept around which pluralizing notions of justice coalesce.

These categories are not discrete and mutually exclusive: ironically, the threat of punishment through 'community' institutions often delivers the kinds of results which human rights commissions seek, namely co-existence between former community pariahs and their neighbors in the townships.

ADDUCTIVE AFFINITIES

> 21 September 1996: Street theatre sponsored by the South African Council of Churches at the Central Methodist Church during a meeting of the survivors' organization the Khulumani Support Group.
>
> *A black minister presents a white Afrikaner policeman to his congregation. The policeman confesses to the daughter and widow of a dead man that he was present at the torturing and murder. The policeman says, 'I'm sorry. I was afraid. I would like to seek to reconcile with you'. The women react angrily and the mother shouts 'You are a bastard and you deserve to die'. The minister puts himself between the two to protect the white policeman. An old man, a relative also of the deceased, enters and quotes Genesis. He says that he forgives the policeman, 'I forgive but I won't forget. I want to build a new South Africa.' The black pastor says, 'You have set an example for the others', and he sends the victims to a trauma counselor.*

The concept of adductive affinities is inspired by Max Weber's notion of 'elective affinities', developed in *The Protestant Ethic and the Spirit of Capitalism* (1976) to explain why capitalism emerged in Calvinist Europe rather than India or China. In arguing that there was a special affinity between capitalist values and Calvinist asceticism, Weber focussed attention on the reciprocal effects resulting from a resonance or coherence between systems of values in different social fields. In the case of South Africa I am arguing that there was a special affinity between a religious ethic of reconciliation and a political ethic of human rights. In adapting Weber, I use 'adductive' affinities in order to denote an association which may be conscious or unconscious. Weber's term 'elective' lends too much weight to conscious agency and individual choice. The meshing of human rights and religious discourses and organizations reinforces the arguments of centralists which emphasize how law dominates other moral and legal frameworks in society, bending them to its rule-bound will.

Post-1994 South Africa has been characterized by a discernible correspondence between the state's nation-building discourse on reconciliation and the social doctrine and pastoral activities of the politically progressive wings of mainstream Protestant (for example, Anglican and Methodist) and Catholic churches. This section of the religious community has been a fountainhead of symbolism for the TRC's own conceptualization of reconciliation. It also provided the main societal infrastructure for the TRC.

The ethical concepts of the TRC were taken from theological doctrines, which in some cases led to a new practical orientation towards past conflicts. Both TRC and Christian ethics encouraged the confession of past wrongs, saw the forsaking of retribution as a healing and redemptive act, and both made forgiveness near-compulsory. Moreover in TRC hearings, a religious ethic was often conjoined with a politicized liberation narrative which sought to draw the individual closer to the restorative justice approach of the Commission. This weaving together of religion, liberation and reconciliation was central to the wider hegemonic project of the first post-apartheid regime, which sought to incorporate individuals into a wider nation-building project by enmeshing their narratives within a new mythology of the nation-state.

As we saw in the previous chapter, part of the influence of religious narratives lay in how the TRC's values were transmitted to participants through the collective effervescence of ritualized meetings. Ritual action became the mechanism through which an idealized image of reconciliation was implanted in the hearts and minds of participants. TRC hearings positioned individuals and their private narratives within a public narrative structure which made them aware of themselves as particular types of subjects, such as 'victims'. These subjects occupied certain types of roles within public narratives of suffering, oppression, liberation and redemption. The creation of new identities ('victim', 'perpetrator') engendered new types of attitudes and dispositions (forgiveness, repentance), which could, in certain instances, bind individuals to the TRC's own reconciliation project. This drew upon a context of existing affinities but also forged new dispositions in the hearings themselves. The important thing here was the ability of the ritualized hearings to create loyalties and identities which had not existed before.

Belinda Bozzoli (1998) has advanced a similar perspective in her article on the HRV hearings in Alexandra township, using a distinction between the sacred and profane derived from Emile Durkheim in his opus, *The Elementary Forms of the Religious Life* (1915). Bozzoli draws attention to the extensive religious symbolism present in the HRV hearing: from the creation of a sacred space using flowers and candles, to the ceremonial trappings of the event; funereal choral singing, prayers, and the treatment of the audience as the congregation. The HRV hearings were a negative 'piacular rite' which separated the sacred from the profane, the individual from the collective, and during hearings individual beliefs were replaced by collective representations. Through constructing myths, individuals bridge the gap between themselves and the objects of their cult (in this case, God, the 'community' and the new South African nation) and in this way, argued Durkheim, law helps to instil a new civic ethic. The creating of public and private myths during the rite allows expiation and healing.

Bozzoli provides important insights into the mechanisms by which ritualized TRC hearings supplanted private attitudes towards justice and forgiveness with collective representations. As we will see in more detail later, TRC rituals shared many features with private memorial services. Complementary to this ritual process were important organizational links, and pre-existing affinities between human rights values and wider societal moralities. In order to get the full picture, we cannot grant the entire emphasis, as Durkheim might have, to how ritual action creates and inculcates values in participating individuals. Explanations of the TRC's successes in promulgating its version of reconciliation cannot focus solely upon its ritualized symbolism, but must also analyze its place within wider moralities and social institutions. We must look at the relationship between the TRC and religious organizations and value systems and ask how the parameters for the TRC's action were shaped by those societal moralities, and how in turn they transformed them.

The TRC's organizational structure was intertwined with a number of societal institutions, but none like the church sector. The use of the same networks of personnel by both institutions led to an overlapping of structures and the joint (or parallel) transmission of the idea of national reconciliation to individual victims. The TRC relied more on the churches than NGOs, such as the Center for the Study of Violence and Reconciliation, as it saw the former as more authentic representatives of 'the community'. As Commissioner Tom Manthata told me,

> The community is the most effective with its own mechanisms for healing and reintegration. If the communities hadn't had their own mechanisms, then people would have gone mad. We're not going to start anything new, just build upon that which is already in the communities. The NGOs from Braamfontein divide communities. Only the leaders show up. (Personal interview, 26 September 1996)

Because of the overlap of TRC and religious personnel in statement-taking, religious values were conveyed to victims even before the hearings. The majority of statements taken in the Johannesburg area were written down by religious activists or in church settings, and this was probably true across the whole of the country and for all statements (more than 21,000) taken by the Commission. Statement-takers were crucial in the construction of the raw material for the TRC nation-building narrative. They were the interface between the TRC and thousands of deponents, as they were the first line of interaction between the Commission and society. All victims encountered a statement-taker in presenting their testimony before the Commission, but only a small, select minority would have the chance to testify (the ratio in the hearings around Johannesburg was about one public testimony for every four statements).

During my interviews with statement-takers, it was apparent that they integrated the TRC's message on reconciliation into victims' statements as they took down the oral testimony. This pre-structuring of the narrative even before hearings commenced illustrates how, from the very beginning, the TRC shifted the moral debate away from retribution and towards a view of justice as emanating from truth and reparations. The Reverend Ollie Mahopo was the head coordinator of all statement-takers in the four provinces controlled from the Johannesburg office. It was his job to train statement-takers in Gauteng and surrounding provinces, and to oversee their work. Mahopo is a pastor whose previous post was in the regional office of the South African Council of Churches (SACC), overseeing the welfare of political detainees and their families. His work at the TRC was but an extension of the SACC in his view: 'For me it's a ministry here – a continuation of my past work as a reverend' (personal interview, Johannesburg, 16 October 1996).

From the pastoral arm of the SACC to a key first link in the investigative structure of a truth commission is not a likely progression unless one is aware of how important the religious model was to the TRC. Although the TRC did not have the SACC's parish infrastructure, it represented the SACC's organization of pastoral care to the victims of political violence through its recommendations for urgent interim reparations. In the minds of victims, the two occupied the same symbolic space, as victims appealed to the TRC and the churches for the same charitable and pastoral services.[14]

For Mahopo, reconciliation had an important religious underpinning which he encouraged in victims, much as a pastor would to his congregation: 'Reconciliation is a divine principle. I must counsel people and encourage them to see that we are for reconciliation and not revenge. Reconciliation, not prosecution, is the ultimate objective.'

But what if a person demands prosecution in their statement? Mahopo replied, 'When we are counseling a person, we sell the ideas that we are not for revenge but reconciliation. Not prosecution, but reconciliation is our ultimate objective.' (Personal interview, Johannesburg, 16 October 1996)

Two of the Vaal's most active statement-takers were also Christian stalwarts.[15] One of them, Thabiso Mohasoa of Sebokeng's Zone 7, is an International Pentecostal Church activist. He proudly wears a badge designating his religious identity on his suit jacket. A former teacher, Thabiso Mohasoa is urbane and eloquent, but he has few work opportunities because of a permanent injury to his leg. With time on his hands, he threw himself into working on behalf of the TRC. He saw his mission as to facilitate reconciliation between blacks in the townships, rather than between blacks and whites. Perhaps strangely for someone committed to writing down oral histories of past political violence, he felt that: 'Reconciliation means to forget what happened. We need to say that was the apartheid system, and to understand how we were oppressed. Now we are all people who belong to the same country.' When asked how he responded to a victim's feelings of revenge during statement writing, Mohasoa described how he steered a victim's perspective in order to (in his words) 'uplift reconciliation':

> I had understood those feelings before. I understood retaliation. If people don't experience life outside of South Africa then they don't know any better. Life in South Africa means fighting one another and retaliating. If he does it to me, I will do it to him and to his grandchild and then I will be satisfied … when taking a statement people would be aggressive, saying, 'I want these perpetrators to be hanged.' But the TRC will be a failure if people send negative ideas to it. (Personal interview, Vereeniging, 9 October 1996)

Beyond the overlapping networks of TRC statement-takers and church activists, there was an institutional fusion of churches and TRC structures in the Vaal. Religious groups were the only local organizations in the Vaal explicitly working with the TRC towards the goal of reconciliation; not businesses, or health institutions, or educational establishments, just churches.

Before the HRV hearings in Sebokeng in August 1996, a group of churches led a prayer service in Sebokeng's notoriously violent Zone 7 to encourage victims to testify. Local township clergy helped the TRC to identify victims, their members took the vast bulk of the statements and advised in the selection of cases to come to public hearings. After the hearings Commissioner Fazel Randera called the Reverend Peter 'Gift'

Moerane,[16] a Methodist minister in Sharpeville and a leading religious figure in the area, to discuss the intimidation of witnesses, and the expressions of anger and revenge which had surfaced during the testimonies. Alleged perpetrators of political violence such as Nhlanhla Cindi (accused of several drive-by shootings in 1993) appeared at the Sebokeng hearings. Cindi's presence terrified his victims, such as Sanna Nhlapo, who refused to testify publicly. After the hearings, the house of one victim who had testified was attacked in a drive-by shooting. Commissioner Randera said to Moerane, 'For the first time in the history of the TRC we have underestimated the extent of the anger in an area. What can the churches do to rescue the situation, to help the communities to heal?' (Personal interview, 16 January 1997.)

The result was a three-day TRC workshop on Reconciliation in the Vaal in November 1996, held in St Peter's Lodge, an Anglican conference center. The workshop brought together TRC Commissioners such as Randera, the police commissioner based in Vereeniging, the police's public relations officer and chaplain, as well as ministers from many of the Vaal's local churches. White churches, representing a highly conservative constituency, did not cooperate with the TRC in any way whatsoever, so none of their representatives were present. Representatives from political parties were also absent. What the meeting assembled, therefore, were truth commissioners, police public relations officials and black churchmen, as opposed to key political actors in the Vaal – the white elite and its political parties.

In the end, the representatives produced a program for reconciliation in the Vaal which recommended the dismantling of the IFP's KwaMadala hostel and the return of hostel-dwellers back to the township with assurances of their protection. It encouraged police perpetrators to confess to crimes and finally it asked white churches to approach people in the townships to seek reconciliation. None of this has since occurred and only three low-ranking policemen in the whole Vaal applied for amnesty for relatively minor violations. However, further initiatives also emerged. The Vaal Council of Churches began running counseling training workshops to train church activists to deal with the legacy of political violence; this became the only trauma counseling available to the thousands of victims in the area.

In addition to direct organizational links, the work of the TRC was indirectly reinforced by the conflict-resolving agendas of local ministers. A key actor in the Vaal was an Irish priest fluent in Sesotho called Father Patrick Noonan. The priest-activist had been at Nyolohelo Catholic Church in Zone 12 of Sebokeng since the early 1970s. He had radical political sympathies and was known affectionately by the local ANC youth as 'Comrade Patrick'. Father Noonan was a firebrand in the

1980s when the Vaal was made ungovernable by rent and school boycotts, barricades on street corners, and the necklacing of alleged apartheid collaborators. But after 1994, his mission became to pursue reconciliation through forgiveness. Father Noonan saw the TRC as an extension of religious activities and values, but he privileged the churches' local efforts to create 'reconciliation':

> The TRC is like a national confession. There is an injection of morality and ethics and that is good. People are being reworked into better human relations ... but the TRC is a side show. Life goes on. People marry, divorce, baptize their infants ... The majority of victims have never gone to counseling, but those that do go mostly through the parishes. That was my program of renewal. (Personal interview, Sebokeng, 30 September 1996)

Father Noonan's views on reconciliation had a significant impact on individual members of his congregation. Cecilia Ncube has had to cope with the murder of her husband David, killed in the Night Vigil massacre on 11–12 January 1991. David and Cecilia had been attending the night vigil for their nephew Christopher Nangalembe at 11427, Zone 7, Sebokeng. Christopher, a member of the ANC Youth League and a Peace Committee monitor, had been killed after bringing his childhood friend Victor Khetisi Kheswa to a court run by the comrades.

Victor Kheswa, a local Zone 7 hoodlum, had been judged by the comrades for stealing cars and abducting a young girl, whom he raped and later killed. The comrades shot him in the leg with his own gun and locked him into the trunk of a car and drove him to where he was to be executed. Being a car thief, Kheswa escaped from the trunk and fled to Kwamadala hostel which was controlled by the Inkatha Freedom Party. Kheswa exacted his revenge by kidnapping Christopher on Saturday the 5 January 1991, while he was doing his rounds as a carpenter. Kheswa strangled Christopher with wire and left his body in the dump near Boipatong. Cecilia left Christopher's night vigil at 10 pm on Friday the 11th and went back to her house across the street. She was awakened at 1am when members of Kheswa's gang [Kheswa himself was in hospital with a gunshot wound in the stomach], allegedly accompanied by Third Force police agents, attacked the gathering of mourners with hand grenades and AK-47s. Cecilia reported, 'I heard shooting big sounds, like a bomb or hand grenade and then sirens'. Press reports at the time placed the death toll at between 36 and 42. Over a hundred were wounded. The case against Kheswa and his gang members collapsed after it was found that the confessions had been extracted by police under torture.

After the Night Vigil massacre, Kheswa became a regional legend, referred to as the 'Vaal Monster'. He went on to terrorize Vaal residents for another two years and in that time over 200 deaths were attributed to him and his gang. Finally, Kheswa was found dead on the road to Sasolburg on 17 June 1993 while he was in police custody. Several members of his gang similarly died in questionable circumstances; both Kheswa and another gang member were accidentally run over by cars carrying Vaal police Sergeant Pedro Peens, Kheswa's police handler. Many observers allege that members of the IFP-aligned gang were killed off one-by-one by their police handlers when they threatened to expose their Third Force links with the police.

Instead of being consumed by a desire for revenge, however, Cecilia Ncube now embraces the new ethos of reconciliation in the country and credits Father Patrick Noonan for guiding her:

> He is the man who gave me the strength to forgive these people. They didn't know what they were doing. That is how I survived. I just forgave and moved on. I was on a local renewal committee and I had to be strong. From Father Patrick I learned that I couldn't bear a grudge and just had to forgive. (Personal interview, Sebokeng, 30 September 1996)

She distanced herself from the other relatives of those killed in the Night Vigil massacre who combined to form the organization 'Vaal Victims of Violence'. One leader of the group is a member of the Pan Africanist Congress (PAC), an African nationalist political party which was consistently hostile to the TRC's amnesty provisions. Cecilia commented on the service of unveiling the stone memorial to those killed, 'the other victims were still sick. They were aggressive and violent and calling for revenge. I am a teacher and understand better. They are just ordinary people.'

That year, Father Noonan performed a Catholic memorial mass for Cecilia's husband in her house. Only the family was present, and the event was captured on video in an elaborately produced home movie, with opening titles and a sequence of photos of their marriage. In more communal acts of forgiveness and reconciliation, Father Noonan held a service with the names of victims of violence in Sebokeng on the altar, in an act which presaged the TRC's plans for memorials and 'symbolic reparations'. On 16 December 1996 (National Day of Reconciliation) Father Noonan held a 'Reconciliation Service', bringing together his congregation, members of the Khulumani Support group and a black police choir in starched white shirts and black bow ties, led by police public relations officer Captain Thabang Letlala (a member of the Task Team of the Vaal Council of Churches).

There is a close affective affinity between the ritualized TRC hearings and those rituals of memorial performed privately by people in their houses or local churches. It is tempting to say that the TRC hearings were like a private memorial service writ large. The associations between TRC hearings and private memorials became apparent to me when I attended a family's memorial to their activist son in Soweto in 1996. The graveside in Avalon cemetery became a sacred space marked out with prayers and candles. Photos were taken under the hot midday sun. The family and friends held their fists high and sang the ANC liberation song and South African national anthem, *Nkosi Sikelel' iAfrika*, which was also sung at the beginning and end of HRV hearings.

Both private religious rituals and TRC hearings combined private narratives and public symbols, fusing images of the nation and a martyred hero into the object of a family cult. Much like during the testimonies of victims at TRC hearings, the father at the Avalon graveside cleared his throat and made a short speech about the young man, how he was an ANC activist and how he came to be shot on 9 September 1990. He got many of the dates and details wrong, and was politely corrected by his wife, as in many TRC hearings, where fathers often took on the public role of representing the family, but did not (compared to the women) have a precise knowledge of domestic history. After the graveside memorial service, the mourners returned to the family's house for a meal, a practice which the TRC adopted, with Commissioners eating lunch with the victims on the day of their testimony.

In addition to their role in promulgating the values of reconciliation as forgiveness and their symbolic duties, church ministers continue to mediate in ongoing armed conflicts arising from the apartheid era. The Reverend Peter 'Gift' Moerane visits militarized youth of both the ANC and IFP, attempting to negotiate an end to their cycle of violent revenge killings. He is one of the very few non-political party leaders in the community with any real authority among militant youths in Sharpeville. Similarly, Father Noonan used his credibility with ANC youth to try to stop revenge attacks.

I have reviewed the situation in black townships primarily, but I should point out that churches dominated reconciliation issues in white areas as well. Any initiatives from white areas were almost always led by churches and most took a similar form. It was a common practice of repentant whites in the 1994–8 period to build churches in poor black areas and undertake 'mission work'. This often reproduced the patterns of patron–client relationships of the nineteenth century and early twentieth century, as well as mirroring the historical process of colonization through missionizing. Instances include the Reverend Henri Meyer's NG Kerk congregation who spent their holidays building a church and doing mission work in Venda. Former SADF officer and now Pastor Craig Botha of the Western Cape led his congregation in building the Jubilee Community Church in Khayelitsha, where members of the white community go to the township to join in the services.

Given South Africa's crime statistics (it is one of the most violent countries in the world) the ministers are generally fighting a losing battle. Nevertheless, the clergy claimed some notable successes in reconciling victims (though not perpetrators and victims) in the Vaal. Father Patrick was a significant part of the transformation of Duma Khumalo from an angry former political prisoner to a leader of victims in the area and Khulumani Support Group fieldworker. Duma Khumalo's story, in brief, was that he was sentenced to death with five others in 1986 for the murder of black councilor Mr Dlamini, which he always claimed he never committed. The 'Sharpeville Six' became a *cause célèbre*, a case which was taken to the United Nations and became an international symbol of the lack of justice for blacks in South Africa (Parker and Makhesi-Parker 1998). Released in 1993 after seven years on death row, Duma demanded a retrial, but was ignored. He could not gain employment, having been arrested in the middle of his teacher training, and became depressed. He staged a sit-in at Sharpeville police station for 27 days in November 1995. In December the police took him to meet with the chief prosecutor and magistrate in Vereeniging, who said that he had no legal case to hear, as there was no new evidence.

On 5 January 1996, Duma hid an axe in his coat, entered the Vereeniging court while it was in session, and went berserk. Duma is a powerful and imposing figure with his shaved head, over 6 feet tall and weighing over 200 pounds. The prosecutor cowered under his desk, put his hands in the air and shrieked, 'Don't kill me!' Others fled screaming; he swung the axe at desks, chairs, furniture, and the court's PA system. Duma did not attack anyone, and when armed police arrived he put his axe down calmly and put his hands in the air. In minutes, he had caused pandemonium, created a large pile of expensive teak firewood and wreaked about $15,000 worth of damage.

Duma spent three weeks in detention and his bail was paid by Father Patrick. He received a one-year suspended sentence with correctional supervision after a Johannesburg psychologist testified that further incarceration after already so long in prison would be highly detrimental to his mental health. 'Everyone thought that I was that crazy man Duma', he told me, 'but I just wanted justice after losing seven years of my life.' Afterwards, Duma encountered the Khulumani Support Group which arranged for psychological counseling at their trauma clinic. Duma turned his energies towards organizing victims in the Vaal to lobby the TRC, which was about to begin hearings in early 1996. He called meetings, took statements and toured Europe on behalf of victims of South African political violence. Duma was the main agent of his own personal transformation, but Father Patrick's influence and the opportunities for survivors created by the TRC had an impact on his new orientation.

Having seen some of the processes operating at the local level, we can begin to understand better why the TRC's version of reconciliation exerted a sway over some victims. This influence was partly the result of the ritualized nature of the hearings, and also the pre-existing value dispositions of participants, born out of their experiences in their communities and immediate social networks. The religious background of individuals were often crucial in determining whether they were responsive to the TRC's message.

RECONCILIATION THROUGH AMNESTY?

The first celebrated national case of reconciliation between a victim and the police occurred in October 1996 at the amnesty hearings of five security policemen from the Northern Transvaal Security Branch who applied for, and eventually received, amnesty from prosecution for 40 counts of murder and dozens of other crimes, including attempted murder and torture.[17] This was one of the first batch of public amnesty hearings which brought victims and police perpetrators together into the same forum. Since it was only a few months into the program, the media had been full of the HRV public hearings featuring only victims. Now victims were finally being brought into the amnesty hearings for a legal purpose – to verify if perpetrators were making full disclosure, to watch their own lawyers cross-examine the applicants and to reply to the standard question posed by Commissioners, 'Are you willing to forgive?'

All victims at this amnesty hearing bar one were unwilling to grant forgiveness there and then. Some, such as Jerry Thibedi, withheld it as he did not see forgiveness as the prerogative of a single individual and stated he would first have to consult his family and his party, the ANC. Thibedi had been the target of a bomb attack on 22 October 1987, when Captain Hechter and Warrant Officer van Vuuren threw a home-made bomb through the window of his shack in Makopane.[18] The shack was so flimsy and full of holes that the bomb demolished the house but did not harm anyone inside it. The mothers of ten young ANC comrades from Mamelodi (the 'Nietverdiend 10'), who were drugged by apartheid security police operatives and pushed off a cliff in a van to their deaths, bitterly opposed amnesty. One mother, Martha Makolane said: 'I will never forgive them. I want to see them dead like our children' (*Star* 4 November 1996).

At the hearings on the same day in October 1996, only one person was able to shake hands with the hit men in a dramatic act of reconciliation, TRC-style. It was no coincidence that he is a priest and theologian at the Institute of Contextual Theology. Practically all those who I heard say they were willing to forgive at a public amnesty or HRV hearing invoked their Christian identity as their motivation. The Reverend Smangaliso Mkhatshwa[19] is a Catholic priest and activist in Durban who was targeted for 'elimination' by the state security apparatus in the 1980s. Various bizarre plots were hatched to kill him, including one to force Mandrax tablets down his throat and make it look like a drug overdose. In the end Mkhatshwa survived abduction, torture, imprisonment, banning and three assassination attempts.

On the orders of the then security police chief, General Basie Smit, one such attempt involved Warrant Officer Paul van Vuuren attempting to shoot Mkhatshwa with a .308 rifle fitted with telescope and silencer as he disembarked at Durban airport. Fortunately for Mkhatshwa, a female passenger was in the line of fire and no shot was attempted. After testifying, Captain Jacques Hechter, the security policeman who organized the assassination attempts, walked over to Mkhatshwa and put out his hand. Mkhatshwa accepted it and agreed to meet Hechter afterwards to discuss reparations for Mkhatshwa's community in 'the spirit of reconciliation'.

At the amnesty hearings the next day, the Reverend Mkhatshwa explained his actions:

> ... when Capt. Hechter stood up and stretched out his hand I had ambivalent feelings. The first feeling was one of uncertainty, of hesitation but also of deep skepticism, for the simple reason that the last time I think when Capt. Hechter and I met, he had a gun in his hand pointed at my forehead. In the same time, because of my deep-felt belief as a Christian, but because also of the policy of the Government of National Unity, the main emphasis on reconciliation and building a new nation, my second sentiments immediately said to me to stretch out your hand and meet Capt. Hechter.[20]

Being a priest and a national political figure, Mkhatshwa was a member of the dominant elite and could articulate and endorse the TRC mission of reconciliation and nation-building. He stated, 'The reconciliation between him and me could be an example for the rest of the nation' (*Sowetan* 30 October 1996). He invited the former policemen to come to his church in Shoshunguwe and say that they were genuinely sorry for what happened there, and pay for school fees of the children of victims of violations.

From the experiences in the Vaal and elsewhere, we get a picture of the TRC as having close affinities to religious values and institutions; sharing personnel and organizational structures, ritual symbolism and values of forgiveness and reconciliation. The association between human rights talk and religious doctrine remains one of the best explanations for the TRC's ability to convert many to the new dominant human rights ideology.

As Chanock has demonstrated, this involvement in legal consciousness on the part of Christian missionaries is nothing new (1985: 79–84). During the colonial period, missionaries sought to shape African attitudes to legal transgression by introducing ideas about individual and humanist rights, and about Christian guilt and sin. As in previous historical periods, then, the post-apartheid centralization of justice required a shift in the popular legal consciousness in order to reduce the plurality of legal and moral systems in society. Organized religion proved a reliable ideological accessory to state centralizing strategies.

Some observers have assumed that the TRC's audiences went away convinced of the need for reconciliation and nation-building, but I would argue that this worked only for a certain group of people. Other local actors pursued different agendas and different notions of justice which were less shaped by Christian values, throwing into relief the limitations of religion in resolving political conflicts.

PROCEDURAL PRAGMATISM

In assessing the impact of human rights talk, we should not grant too much weight to the power of ideology and to shared values, but should remain aware of the diversity of agendas and motivations for social action. These motivations are often instrumental and do not imply acceptance of the ideology of reconciliation, and involve what I have termed a 'procedural pragmatism'. South African citizens may have engaged with human rights talk and institutions not because of shared values, but, rather, because they wanted to pursue a personal agenda and pragmatically decided to pursue it through TRC procedures.

The decision to approach the TRC often resulted from a particular need of victims to clear their name, and to use a public forum to do so, rather than from a deep commitment to reconciliation and nation-building. The lesson from the Musi case recounted next is one which a number of legal anthropologists such as Merry (1990) and Conley and O'Barr (1990) have been drawing clearly: that people become involved in legal processes for a variety of reasons which may be very distinct from what the law itself thinks it is doing. Their involvement does not necessarily mean a deep loyalty or affinity to nation-building or a new language of rights.

Many litigants see the mechanisms of law as useful instruments towards particular ends, but their motivation for participation may diverge significantly from those of the officials administering them. Conley and O'Barr, for instance, demonstrate how many litigants narrate their side of a dispute in terms of social relationships rather than the rule-oriented thought processes of court specialists such as judges, lawyers, and clerks. Moreover, relationship-oriented litigants may have 'theories of evidence, proof, causation, blame and responsibility which differ markedly from the official legal versions' (1990:176).

The following discussion tells the story of an encounter between individuals at a Human Rights Violations hearing which appeared to illustrate perfectly the TRC's own ideal of reconciliation. It was a case which Johannesburg Commissioners and Chair Desmond Tutu (1999:192) would refer to on a number of occasions as the apogee of the TRC's reconciliation process. The testimony of Zandisile 'Zando' John Musi was heard on an unseasonably cold, overcast morning in November at the West Rand hearings held in the imposing gray buildings of Laretong Hospital. Zandisile Musi, accompanied by his older brother, Mbulelo Musi, was subdued as he recounted in Xhosa the events of 15 February 1982.

In 1982, Zandisile Musi was 19 years old and at secondary school in Kagiso. This was a time of politicization of the township and country. The Kagiso Residents Organization and the Congress of South African Students (COSAS) had just been formed. With his close childhood friend, Fanyana Nhlapo, Zando Musi participated in COSAS activities and Young Christian Workers at the Faith Mission Church in Kagiso where the Reverend Frank Chikane was minister. There he met Eustice 'Bimbo' Madikela and Peter 'Ntshingo' Matabane. Like thousands of other young men after the Soweto uprising of 1976, they decided to join the armed wing of the liberation movement. In January 1982, they expressed their desire to leave the country and receive military training with Mfalapitsa Ephraim Tlhomedi, a friend of Zando's older brother Mbulelo who was himself in exile with the ANC.

Ephraim discouraged Zandisile and his three friends from going abroad, saying that the ANC needed structures within the country, and he would train them himself to carry out operations. Ephraim said they should wait for him at Leratong Hospital at 8 pm. The four young comrades lied to their families, saying that they were going into Johannesburg to a Millie Jackson concert at the Coliseum. They even went so far as to buy tickets, but Ntshingo's mother was suspicious. She confiscated his ticket and refused him permission to go. In the end she relented to his pleas.

At 8 pm Ephraim picked up the four young men in an inconspicuous white van (or 'Kombi' as they're called in South Africa) like those used by taxi drivers in the townships. Behind the wheel of the Kombi was a black man they had not met before, with a large scar across his face. The youths were taken to the West Rand mine shaft, where 'Scar-face' remained in the car. Ephraim led them all into the shaft. Inside, he took out an F1 hand-grenade and a Makarov pistol. He showed them how the pistol worked and then fitted the detonator onto the grenade and showed them how to pull the pin. He left the hand-grenade with Ntshingo and departed in a hurry, saying he was going to retrieve more grenades.

Zandisile noticed a box in the corner which he thought looked curious. He walked over to it and there was a huge explosion. The last thing he remembered was feeling himself flying up, then falling and crashing down. He was in and out of consciousness the whole night, trapped under bricks. He called for his friends and only Fanyana answered. The other two had been killed instantly. Zando held hands with Fanyana who was still talking despite having a large hole in his chest. Zando assumed that the explosion must have been Ntshingo's fault as he was holding the grenade.

The police came at about 9 am and took Zandisile to Leratong hospital. Fanyana had died in the night. Zando's leg was broken, his ears were bleeding and he could hardly see. He has been partially deaf since then. He was given first aid and then taken by police out to a field where a policeman stuck a gun in his mouth and asked who had taken him to the West Rand mine shaft. He said nothing, protecting Ephraim and 'Scarface'. Zando was then taken to Krugersdorp police station, where the police interrogated him further, beat him and stood on his broken leg. He was charged with possession of explosives and after two months in detention, he was given bail of 500 Rand. His grandparents paid and Zando was taken straight to hospital to have his leg set properly. He was eventually acquitted because a white official from Krugersdorp prison had heard Zando's screams and testified that the police had tortured him. In 1985 Zandisile was arrested once again under the State of Emergency and sentenced in 1987 under the Explosives Act. He was sent to Robben Island until his release in December 1990.

Slowly, Zandisile had been able to piece together what had happened that night in February 1982. After he was released from jail, he telephoned his older brother, Mbulelo, who was in exile in Zambia. Zandisile told him what had happened. His brother said that Ephraim was 'working for the Boers'. But only in early 1996 had he learned more of the story from a South African Broadcasting Company (SABC) journalist, Reggie Morobe, who was making a documentary on reconciliation. The driver with Ephraim, 'Scar-face', was the *askari* Joe Mamasela (at this point a shudder went through the crowd at the HRV hearing, as whenever Mamasela's name was mentioned). The young comrades had been tricked by double agents or *askaris*, former ANC combatants who had been 'turned' by the security forces.

The case was similar to a famous earlier incident in Duduza in 1985, where Joe Mamasela had given 'zero hand grenades' to young comrades which were primed to explode as soon as the ring was pulled. In Duduza on the East Rand, victims were ignorant of the shadowy role which the security police *askari* Joe Mamasela played. A young woman, Maki Skhosana, was necklaced by an angry crowd who suspected her of being a police informer. Shortly thereafter, President P W Botha declared a state of emergency on 20 July 1985.

In the same way, people in the township of Kagiso were suspicious of the deaths of three youths in the West Rand mine shaft. Suspicion focused on Zandisile, as he was the only survivor. It emerged in the hearing that relations were strained between Musi and the families of the three dead comrades:

> MS J SEROKE: After you had recovered from the explosion, and you had gone back home, how did your friends' parents respond and react towards you?
> MR Z MUSI: I did not come across them that often. I only saw them, because I felt guilty. I perceived that things were not going too well between the families.
> MS J SEROKE: Were they blaming you for having taken their children or were they suspecting that you were part of the plot?
> MR Z MUSI: I fetched Fanyana from home, I am the one who fetched him. That's what they said as well. That I took Fanyana from home and the next thing he is dead.

After the explosion, the families of the comrades did not visit Zandisile Musi in hospital but they did attend his trial. Zando felt that they blamed him and he was plagued by guilt since he had been the group's leader and had put his three friends in touch with Ephraim.

> PROF MEIRING: Then the very last question is: you said in the course of your testimony that the feelings between the families are sometimes not too good. Do you think that today in coming to the Truth Commission will help to heal the relationship between the families?

> MR Z MUSI: Yes, I would really appreciate it if the Truth Commission would help in the reconciliation of these families.

At the very end of his testimony, when asked what he wanted from the TRC, Zandisile replied:

> My request is that it be known that Fanyana and Ntshingo and Bimbo have contributed to the freedom we have to this day. They died being aware that there will be a qualitative change in our country. They have died as heroes of South Africa. Could their families perhaps get some form of compensation?

There followed the testimonies of the three sisters of the fallen comrades. They were all still living in Kagiso, as was Musi. Common to all of their testimonies was a lack of awareness of the political activities of their brothers, and previous suspicion of Zandisile Musi's role in their brothers' deaths.

> MS EMILY GUMEDE (sister to Fanyana Nhlapo): It was painful as Zando came to get my brother, he knows everything. But now we're satisfied as Zando has opened his mouth and said everything.

It turned out that the TRC hearings were the culmination of a process which Musi had already begun in the township. He had begun to approach the families once he and others involved had learned of the identity of Joe Mamasela through the investigations of Reggie Morobe.

> MS SELEBE (sister to 'Bimbo' Madikela): I didn't know Zando or his friends. I hated him after the incident. I met Zando this April (1996) after Reggie Morobe from SABC came and told me about the case. Zando knocked on my door and I said that if it wasn't for you then my brother would be alive now. He pleaded with me and said 'I want to apologize to you'. I found it in my heart to sit down and listen. If I had a gun, I would kill my brother's killers now if they walked through that door. I feel bitterness. I have forgiven Zando now and pity him for what he's endured. I blamed Zando but have forgiven him and take him as my own brother.
> PROF MEIRING: Zando has asked for a meeting between all the families. Do you want us to arrange mediation?

All parties agreed, and Joyce Seroke summed up the session,

> When we say that this is the Truth and Reconciliation Commission, then we mean that it is only the truth which can lead to reconciliation. Thank you all for saying that you have forgiven Zando. How must he have felt all this time with this pain in his

> heart? Reconciliation should not end in this hall, but carry on in the communities. I hope in Kagiso that Zando would be accepted in the community now. Everyone should know that he was not responsible.

BEHIND THE SCENES IN KAGISO

It was uncommon that 'reconciliation' was as obvious at a hearing as in the West Rand mine shaft incident. This case exemplifies better than any other what the TRC itself thought it was doing to facilitate reconciliation in the country: victims told their stories, the truth came out, and people openly forgave each other after years of resentment. Reconciliation was conspicuously there for all to see.

Yet if one looked at what was going on between victims before and after the hearings, one got a different sense of the complexities involved in reconciliation. In particular, there was a variance between the TRC's interpretation of events and the actual degree to which victims identified with the values of the Commission. In late 1998, I interviewed Zandisile Musi and other members of the families in Kagiso a number of times, individually and in groups, and started to get a picture of where the TRC fitted into their long process of reconciliation. Zando is now in his mid-thirties, married with two sons and working as a taxi driver in Kagiso. His brother Mbulelo, in whose footsteps he had wanted to follow as a teenager, is Deputy Director of Communications of the Gauteng Provincial Legislature. Musi's family has prospered under the new ANC regime, but Zando still feels his life has been ruined. When asked why he went to the TRC, Musi replied:

> I wanted my case to be known and what happened to me. To appear before the TRC would help to remedy the misery of my life. I wanted the families [of the other victims] and the world to know ... I had avoided them. I had always blamed myself for what happened and didn't know how to start with them. The TRC was an avenue that could make it possible to convey that.

The attendance of some family members of the deceased had only been made possible by developments earlier on that year. Chilled relations between Musi and the families of the three dead comrades began to thaw in early 1996 due to the intervention of the SABC television journalist, Reggie Morobe. Musi admits he 'only kept in touch with Ntshingo's family and visited them when I got out of prison – I didn't see the other families as they had a negative view of me. Because of Reggie, we rounded up the families and he explained the whole incident.' Morobe was hoping to film a meeting between the families and the perpetrator, Ephraim, for his documentary on reconciliation for the SABC current affairs program 'Newsline'. Without Morobe's new evidence and independent confirmation of Zando's story, there might not have been any 'reconciliation' at the hearings at all.

The timing of events was fortuitous for Zando Musi. When asked whether he felt that he had been forgiven by the other families before, during or after the hearing, he replied: 'Before – I could see they had forgiven me before we went to the TRC.' I continued, 'So the TRC was a public expression of what had already happened privately?' Musi commented:

> Yes. And it continued afterwards, even though the TRC said they'd arrange mediation between the families but they didn't. There was no further communication. But afterwards we all had a meeting here at my brother's house over a weekend. We just sat here and talked and talked.

Yet interviews with relatives of the three dead comrades showed that they were not fully convinced, and that perhaps the TRC hearings had played a more important role. Ntombi Emily Zanele, the younger sister of Fanyana Nhlapo, said:

> Zando came to explain to us what had happened in 1996, but our family didn't understand. After the TRC hearings, we saw that Zando was telling the truth. We listened, but others did not. Myself and my aunt were the only ones to attend and we told our family about the hearings, but they didn't want to understand. They were suspicious of Zando and think he got money and used it for himself.

I then asked, 'Do you think Zando has finally cleared his name in Kagiso?' and Emily Zanele replied, 'No … the community blames Zando. They say, "How was it that you survived and they died?"'

A lingering suspicion did not prevent Zandisile Musi from redoubling his efforts to help the families through the TRC process. He obtained TRC forms requesting reparations, took them to the families and helped them fill them out. He aided them in obtaining death certificates and the required evidence. Their main intention was to buy tombstones for the three comrades buried in Kagiso cemetery. After more than fifteen years, Musi and the families, through the hearings and reparations process, joined together in a ritual of memorial and reparation to the three dead victims.

The families were buoyed along more by Zandisile's energy than any national imperatives. They did not go to the TRC hearings because they were committed to the TRC as an institution, or the national process of reconciliation, or nation-building, but for Musi alone. Maide, the sister of Bimbo Madikela, made this plain:

> I just want to forget about it, you know. I just want to get on with my life. I was very negative, I didn't think we could do anything about it, I didn't think we could have a court case. I am working in the day and studying for a degree at night. I want to be left alone but it keeps coming up again and again … The only reason I went to the hearings was for Zando.

Other families similarly wanted to be left alone, and some found that the hearings caused more damage than 'healing'. This was certainly the case for the family of Ntshingo. His younger sister, Tsolo Lebhake, said:

> We really did not want to know. There had been no communication with Zando until he came by with Reggie [Morobe] and told his story. My mother died of heartbreak just before the TRC hearings. I attended the hearings with my father. We were the only two from our family. The hearings just made us feel worse. My father died just afterwards. He was always talking about his son, even in his sleep.

If we delve deeper into the morality and sense of justice held by Musi and the three victims' families, it is clear that the values of the TRC were not a motivating factor in their attendance. Further, having attended the hearings, these values were not successfully transmitted to all participants. Thus I must recognize that earlier comments on the TRC as a ritual, where a framework derived from Durkheim was used to explain how the new values of reconciliation are transferred to the audience, may have limited applicability. Aspects of the HRV hearings are highly ritualized in order to create new identities and to engender new dispositions of forgiveness, but we must take into account not only how values are transmitted, but also how they are received. This was apparent when I asked Zandisile, 'Did you share the same idea about reconciliation as the TRC?' and he replied, 'What was the concept of reconciliation of the TRC? I don't know.'

Participation in the TRC hearings had not, in this case, led to victims forgiving perpetrators and forsaking revenge. On 31 October 1998, the TRC final *Report* was publicly released and I obtained a copy quickly. It was beyond the reach of the majority of South Africans: at 770 Rand, it cost more than many earned in a month. The next day in Kagiso, Zandisile and I flicked through the pages of the volumes together. It took us a while, as there is no index to the *Report* which is some 3,500 pages long. Finally we found his case in volume 3 on pages 582–583. Zandisile learned for the first time who had applied for amnesty for the murders and what the findings of the Commission were. The findings were quite dramatic since they were based upon revelations made in amnesty applications:

> The Commission finds a number of Security Branch operatives responsible for this operation and, in particular, Brigadier Willem Schoon, the Head of the Security Branch, who authorized the operation that led to the commission of gross human rights violations. The Commission finds further that Mr Christian Siebert Rorich, Mr Abraham Grobbelaar, Mr Joe Mamasela and Mr Ephraim Mfalapitsa were responsible for carrying out the operation, for the deaths of the three COSAS members and the gross violation of human rights.
>
> The Commission finds the former state, the Minister of Police, the Commissioner of Police and the Head of the Security Branch responsible for the gross violation of human rights. The Commission finds that, through their actions, the former state is vicariously responsible for criminal conduct in that it secured these deaths through extra-judicial means.

For over a decade, Musi had only ever been aware of Mfalapitsa and Mamasela, and he learned for the first time about the involvement of three white Security Branch police officers. According to law, he should have been informed in writing by the TRC that amnesty applications had been made in his case, but the TRC had not fulfilled this obligation. Zandisile's immediate response was to say, 'Those people did not apply for amnesty for reconciliation, only because they knew what would happen. They would be prosecuted.' Then he asked me who I thought he should sue; the individuals who had applied for amnesty or the Ministry of Safety and Security as the institution held criminally responsible. Legal retribution, not reconciliation, was uppermost in his mind.

The animosity and bitterness of the relatives of the dead comrades was even greater than that of Musi. In Reggie Morobe's 'Newsline' documentary shown in 1997, he asked the sisters if they wanted to meet Ephraim. Bimbo's sister, Maide, said: 'It is still unbelievable for me that he died. I am still angry. If I see Ephraim, then I would have to kill him. I hate that person.' Morobe questioned, 'How long will you carry that anger?' and Maide replied, 'Until justice is done. There is no death sentence now, but he should be given a life sentence. But I would prefer a death sentence.' Ntishingo's sister, Tsolo, left even less room for forgiveness: 'If you bring Ephraim in front of me, then I will kill him with my own hands. I won't forgive him. I am prepared to carry this burden until I die.'

There are a number of theoretical implications which we can draw out of my interviews in Kagiso regarding participants' reception of the TRC's message. These generally run counter to over-systemic approaches to 'discourse' or 'hegemony' which tend to ignore the intentionality of social actors and which emphasize how individuals' experiences are produced and managed by dominant institutions and discourses. My approach draws its inspiration from thinking on ideology in the Weberian tradition, and, in particular, on the writings of Abercrombie, Hill and Turner (1980, 1990). In 1980, these three wrote *The Dominant Ideology Thesis*, followed by the edited volume *Dominant Ideologies* (1990), both of which challenge the powerful influence in the social sciences of Gramsci and the concept of 'hegemony' in the analysis of ideology. In the 1970s, many Marxists adopted a very strong, coherent and totalizing view of hegemony in order to explain why the industrial classes of capitalist societies seemed to accept the core assumptions of capitalism and did not seek to overturn the conditions producing alienation and exploitation. Their answer focused on how capitalism could generate hegemony, or a coherent 'worldview' by means of dominant state and social institutions, and through it generate loyalties to basic principles of the capitalist order.

By the late 1970s, Althusserian and Gramscian Marxists alike had become so enthralled with the power of a 'dominant ideology' that subordinated classes almost seemed enslaved at the level of ideas rather than of material relations. There was very little attempt by Marxists to empirically verify whether the dominant ideology did indeed 'interpellate' subordinate social classes: that is, to see if at the level of transmission and reception, ideology worked as it was theoretically expected to work. Further, many Marxists had not yet discovered everyday 'resistance' (which was not to come until the mid-1980s in the writings of James C. Scott). There was little room, therefore, for understanding how people might exercise relatively autonomous agency outside of, or in opposition to, the dominant ideology, and create subjectivities which were not solely produced by overarching ideologies or discourses. This criticism applies more to European and North American Marxists than to those in South Africa, where there was an established group around the History Workshop which drew upon the writings of E P Thompson to examine diverse forms of resistance and counter-hegemony in African society.

The *Dominant Ideology Thesis* came in the interregnum between 'hegemony' and 'resistance' and provided an important counterpoint for understanding how people pragmatically participate in political and economic processes, but do not necessarily take on the values of dominant societal and state institutions. Abercrombie et al. argued that the dominant value system is not consistent, and that major parts of the ideology of property, accumulation, profit and managerialism are rejected by industrial classes. The deviation of values is so great that one may speak of a 'dual consciousness' between social classes, at the same time that workers pragmatically continue to perform their roles and therefore participate in the reproduction of capitalist society.

Contrary to the view that consensus results from common values, Weberians argued that the system could function with a kind of pragmatic, un-ideological acquiescence on the part of the majority, that is to say, without the working class necessarily believing in it. This argument is even more relevant two decades later as the globalization of a neo-liberal political-economy has fragmented national identities and reduced the ability of states to orchestrate social consensus and cohesion.[22] Social regulation emerges more from the dull compulsion of global economic integration than from the relatively uniform ideological conditions found in the mid-century mass industrial societies of western Europe and North America.

A Weberian analysis is appropriate for thinking about the Musi case and the TRC in South Africa. Involvement in the TRC was often pragmatic rather than deeply ideological. People may pragmatically perform roles and take part in HRV hearings and reparations procedures, but did not necessarily accept the core human rights assumptions of the institution. They may have their own values (for example, on the death penalty, or reconciliation) to such an extent that we might speak of a 'dual consciousness' in the area of justice. The strategy adopted by the Kagiso families reinforces state centralist strategies insofar as they are participating in state-sanctioned procedures, rather than taking violent revenge themselves or trying to drag perpetrators before a local township court. Yet their attitude of seeking reconciliation amongst themselves while harboring a desire for vengeance (sometimes legally retributive, sometimes just plain murderous) against the black *askaris* and their police superiors undermines the homogenizing project of human rights-based nation-building.

Victims participated in TRC procedures for their own reasons, some of which meshed with the institutions and language of human rights, whereas others diverged sharply. This divergence seems to be working less at the level of conscious resistance (which is why I am invoking Abercrombie et al. rather than James C Scott) than a sheer lack of awareness of (and even interest in) the values which victims were supposed to subscribe to. While it is clear that there is a hegemonic project around human rights which the TRC pursued in tandem with other state institutions, it is not at all clear that the reception of the main targeted constituency (urban, ANC-supporting blacks) conforms to the intended pattern. On television or at the town hall, it might all seem to work nicely, but listening to what victims say outside hearings during in-depth interviews can take us to an unexpected place that is between or, perhaps, beyond either acceptance or resistance.

If many urban blacks attending TRC hearings are only pragmatically acquiescent, and many others (as we will see in the next two chapters) actively resist the dominant human rights ideology, then what was the point of the TRC's hegemonic project? Again, neo-Weberian sociology comes up with some interesting and unexpected answers. Ideology does have important effects, but these are primarily upon the dominant rather than the subordinate classes. Hill writes: 'What has been important for the stability of capitalism is the coherence of the dominant class itself, and ideology has played a major role in securing this' (1990:2). According to this view, human rights ideology in South Africa was not so much directed towards building a culture of human rights among the masses as it was about holding together a fragile elite coalition in the first years after apartheid.

So perhaps I have been looking in the wrong place all along for the main effects of the TRC's human rights talk. I should have entertained more seriously my suspicions that the TRC was a strategy to forge greater coherence between an established white economic elite and an emergent black political elite. Instead of driving around the hot, dusty and dangerous townships of Johannesburg, I should have been in air-conditioned company boardrooms, in newly racially-representative law firms, racially-integrated private schools, and (now I'm getting carried away at the prospect) the fashionable 'Old Eds' Health and Racquet Club in exclusive Houghton. Alas, having fallen for the TRC's assertions early on that the process was meant primarily for the victims of apartheid, this was a project that I would have to leave to other researchers.

RECONCILIATION FOR WHOM?

In Kagiso, we saw reconciliation of a particularly limited type: between victims' families – urban blacks of similar background and socio-economic status, who share political inclinations (largely ANC supporters) and still live in the same township. In some ways, it was a strange scenario at the TRC hearings, where victims were apologizing to other victims for the suffering they did not directly cause, where truth was revealed, but by those who did not need to express any remorse or accept any blame.

'Reconciliation through Truth' was never likely to achieve more than the restoration of social relationships *between victims*, where suspicion and stigma had been wrongfully attached to one person or family. Hugo van der Merwe's research on the HRV hearings in Duduza in 1997 came up with similar findings.[23] The family of a necklaced woman, Maki Skhosana, told the story of how she had been wrongfully accused of working for the police. The sister felt relieved that Maki's innocence had been acknowledged and the stigma which had hung over the family had been removed. One TRC Commissioner offered to bring together Maki's family and her killers (former comrades from the township), though nothing came of this in the end. The family felt that Maki's innocence had been established in the hearings although there were still unresolved tensions between the family and the local people who had initiated the necklacing.

Reconciliation between victims and perpetrators required a little more than the HRV hearings were able to provide. In the Musi case, there was no contact, much less reconciliation, between Musi and the policemen who stood on his broken leg, nor the officer who stuck a gun in his mouth, nor the security police operative Joe Mamasela, nor Ephraim Mfalapitsa, who is still in the West Rand region, reputedly working as a pastor in Rustenburg, nor the three white Security Branch policemen named in the report: Rorich, Grobbelaar and Schoon. Part of the reason for this lay in the fact that the TRC's divided structure kept perpetrators and victims apart: the HRV hearings were for the victims and the amnesty hearings were solely for the perpetrators.

At amnesty hearings, victims were in contact with perpetrators only indirectly, through judges and their lawyers' cross-examinations. As in a court of law, they were themselves sometimes subjected to hostile cross-examining from the applicants' lawyers. Unlike in a court of law, the victims' experiences were unimportant in both judicial decisions and sentencing. There was no arena where victims and perpetrators formally came together and interacted directly and at length. I never heard of a case where Commissioners arranged mediation between victims and killers where the latter were security force operatives. Despite their generosity at the Kagiso hearings, and the willingness of the families, the Commissioners did not arrange mediation between Musi and the families of the three fallen comrades; they had no further contact with the Commission after that cold November day. Bringing together victims and perpetrators was problematic for the legal proceduralists in the Commission, who were interested in impartially applying the principles laid down in the Act to individual amnesty applications, not in messy acts of mediation. Mediation for the redemptive reconcilers would have necessarily meant confronting very real feelings of vengeance, which the TRC was ill-prepared to cope with.

It could be argued that the TRC's place in reconciling victims with each other, as in the Musi case, is in itself a significant achievement.

Indeed, this view has a resonance with the needs and desires of actual victims, a majority of whom were more concerned with coming to terms with local people who assisted the police, rather than 'reconciling' with security policemen and their superiors. It is the former group of people who they see on a regular basis, with whom they share social and perhaps kin networks. Many township residents thought the TRC was primarily for resolving conflicts between blacks rather than between whites, blacks and others. As councilor Simon Mofokeng told me, 'The whites in the Vaal are not part of the process of reconciliation. They have withdrawn and see themselves as far away from the TRC, as if it is for blacks, not for them' (personal interview, 2 February 1997).

This was largely how most whites saw it too, and the TRC final *Report* excoriated whites for their disposition: 'The white community often seemed either indifferent or plainly hostile to the work of the Commission' (5:196). Finally, one of the more enduring images from Antjie Krog's book, *Country of My Skull*, is where blacks are in a HRV hearing, revisiting the scarcely believable traumas of the apartheid era, while local whites are having a picnic and enjoying a cricket game right outside the hall.

Victims and their families often expressed the desire to confront perpetrators, to feel empowered by standing up to those who had victimized them, to challenge them about their actions, and to demand an explanation. This occurred in the Kagiso case, where Dianah Lebokeng (older sister of Ntshingo Matabane) finished her testimony thus:

> My question I would like to put to Mamasela is: How could he kill those children? And my question to Ephraim is: How can he preach to his congregation after killing those boys?

None of the three TRC narratives on reconciliation considered in the previous chapter (intellectual, legal-procedural and religious-redemptive) could respond to the demand for some form of victim–offender mediation, or even, as in the Musi case, victim–victim mediation. Instead the dominant TRC approach sought to isolate victims' stories and universalize their individual suffering, to treat all suffering as morally equal, to valorize it by placing it within a wider discourse on liberation and, crucially, to excise vengeance from individual narratives. This approach was effective in certain cases, but as we will see in more detail in the next chapter, it often clashed with a widespread desire for vengeance which was the main impediment to human rights talk and nation-building in the country.

CHAPTER 6

VENGEANCE, REVENGE AND RETRIBUTION

> ANTONY:
> And Caesar's spirit, ranging for revenge,
> With Ate by his side, come hot from hell,
> Shall in these confines, with a monarch's voice,
> Cry 'Havoc!' and let slip the dogs of war,
> That this foul deed shall smell above the earth
> With carrion men, groaning for burial.
>
> ALL THE PLEBEIANS:
> Revenge! About! Seek! Burn! Fire! Kill! Slay!
> Let not a traitor live!
>
> Shakespeare (*Julius Caesar* III, i; III, ii)

> The spirit of revenge: my friends, that up to now, has been mankind's chief concern; and where there was suffering, there was always supposed to be punishment.
>
> Friedrich Nietzsche (*Thus Spoke Zarathustra*, 1969:162)

So far this book has examined how the reconciliation of human rights talk becomes meaningful for some members of its targeted audience; this chapter and the next explore ideas and practices of retribution and revenge. The high visibility of a revenge ethic in South Africa created a counterpoint to the TRC's vision of national redemption and forgiveness, and highlighted the disjunctures between formal and informal justice which I characterize as *relational discontinuities*. During acts of violent punishment on the streets and in cases heard in township courts, local actors draw distinctions between humanitarian and Christian values of forgiveness, reconciliation and redemption on the one hand, and vengeful notions of punishment on the other. At the level of local justice practices, this results in a rejection of the TRC's project in favor of more punitive and vengeful responses to 'resolving' past conflicts and violations under apartheid. The deviation between state versions of human rights and aspects of popular legal consciousness is so great that Weberian approaches to ideology are justified to refer to a 'dual consciousness' of state and informal understandings of justice.

In drawing attention to discontinuities, we must be careful not to fall into the pattern of a traditional legal pluralism which portrayed legal systems as separate and hermetically sealed. Organizational disjunctures between state institutions (magistrates' courts and the TRC) and township courts are not the result of isolated, 'traditional' legal cultures. Rather, these discontinuities are 'relational' and historical, as divisions go back at least to the end of the nineteenth century and the creation of a dual legal system. They result not from the isolation of rule systems from one another, but from the ways in which state law both conjures up and creates local legality, and how local courts and armed gangs develop semi-autonomously within the interstices of state legality.[1]

Discontinuities between different legal forms emerge from enclaves where the state does not hold a total monopoly on either the right to adjudicate or to carry out punitive sanctions. In the legally plural context of post-apartheid South Africa, there are constant jurisdictional disputes between different forms of interconnected legal authority, including the bureaucratic legality of the state justice system, the patrimonial authority of township courts, the coercive authority of armed gangs, and the humanitarian-religious authority of human rights commissions such as the TRC, the Human Rights Commission and the Gender Commission.

Where there are confrontations over the right to punish or forgive offenders, we see how these forms of authority are locked into close, symbiotic relationships and overlap and influence one another. Competition over different versions of justice occurs primarily (though not exclusively) in attempts to control the construction of the 'community'. At the HRV hearings, the TRC was engaged in the very redefinition of the community itself, by conflating its narrative on the reconciliation of the unified nation to local witnesses' narratives of community and the liberation struggle. In the selection and presentation of the oral histories of testimonies, the ritualized hearings sanctioned particular narratives on the experience of the community of the abusive apartheid era, and promoted collective rather than individual truths. Bozzoli observed this process in the Alexandra hearings, where witnesses before the TRC were presented as witnesses for the community, rather than for themselves:

> Key speakers were included in the hearings, not as witnesses to specific abuses, but as 'community representatives' ... The commission was there to hear not just the individual witnesses – who in a purely legal setting would be individuals before the law – but an entity thought of as 'the community', of which the witnesses

> were representative in some way. The 'community' again came to resemble the 'congregation': the truth will be spoken from and about it, as well as from and about individuals who were 'part' of it. (1998:173)

As detailed in a previous chapter, the TRC linked the community narrative of the liberation struggle to other more forgiving and religious notions of community. Bozzoli argues that the myth-making ritual in Alexandra fused together the community, the TRC, God and the nation (ibid.). The TRC combined images of community, God, nation and African-ness in the notion of *ubuntu*, where the community becomes a site of common humanity and sympathy, of benign brotherly love, with a soft pan-Africanist hue.

Only barely expressed at the HRV hearings, but thriving in the townships themselves, were politically oppositional discourses on community advocated in local community courts, and by young comrades of the ANC Youth League (ANCYL) and the political parties of African nationalism (especially the Pan Africanist Congress, or PAC, and the Azanian People's Organization, AZAPO). Their formulations of community were characterized less by reconciliation and *ubuntu* than by the pursuit of vengeance and *lex talionis*. 'Justice' here is less concerned with restoration of social bonds than it is with the punishment of wrongdoers who have violated correct values as defined by the community. A main source of authority for black nationalists and local court officials came from their ability to channel widespread discourses on revenge and to exact retribution for their followers. According to these actors, the community is a site of the expression of popular sovereignty rather than individual human rights. For them, the 'will of the community' is harsh, determined and unyielding in its quest for punitive justice, and sees reconciliation TRC-style as a weak and liberal diversion from true justice and liberation for Africans.

REVENGE IN MODERN LEGAL THOUGHT

> The end of punishing is not revenge, and discharge of choler; but correction, either of the offender or of other, by his example.
>
> Thomas Hobbes (*Leviathan*, 1985: 389)

In the early modern period, as expressed in Shakespeare's *Julius Caesar*, violent revenge and the unpredictable wrath of the commoners were openly recognized as a principal motivator of political and legal behavior. Since the Enlightenment, the dominant tendency has been to deny that the state's punishing of wrongdoers is a type of revenge, and to assert that the law has other aims, namely reparation, restraint and correction, and other methods, namely due process and proportional punishment.[2] State law has been constructed through the rejection of its ideological opposite, and its perennial dark penumbra is violence without due process. The origins of the liberal state lie in its calming of wild justice and the assuming of the right to punish, which consenting citizens relinquish.

Since the late eighteenth century very few legal and political writers have lent any credibility to popular languages of vengeance. According to Michael Ignatieff (1998:188), revenge is commonly regarded as a low and unworthy emotion because its deep hold on people is rarely understood (Stuckless and Goranson 1994). Ignatieff recognizes that revenge is a profound moral desire to keep faith with the dead, to honor their memory by taking up their cause where they left off. To this end, revenge keeps faith between generations and the violence that follows is a ritual form of respect for the community's dead; for Ignatieff therein lies the legitimacy of revenge.

Friedrich Nietzsche has been one of the few writers to accord revenge a kind of respect and dignity. He recognizes its universality and undeniable force and argues that it cannot be suppressed without consequences.[3] In Nietzsche's category of *ressentiment*,[4] he asserts that the emphasis on mercy in the Judeo-Christian tradition was a veiled reaction to the repressed desire for vengeance on the part of the oppressed. In *Thus Spoke Zarathustra* (1969:162), he rejected a Christian notion of redemption as based upon the impossibility of returning to the past to mend the wrongs committed. The desire for revenge wells up from this impossibility, and the legal punishment of state law is but a mask for profound feelings of revenge: 'Punishment is what revenge calls itself: it feigns a good conscience for itself with a lie' (ibid.). These ideas were later picked up by Max Weber who wrote that, 'the moralistic quest serves as a device for compensating a conscious or unconscious desire for vengeance' (1965:110).

Weber and Nietzsche's comments on Christianity and punishment contain an important recognition of the link between formal state legality and the desire of many victims for revenge, and they point us towards understanding how a moralizing quest for reconciliation by churches and human rights commissions can suppress punitive understandings of justice. Unfortunately, Nietzsche clothes these insights in a needlessly eternal garb, which requires qualification by more historical approaches. Austin Sarat has offered a more sociological view that explains the rise of vengeance in the USA as a response to the deepening divide between legal values and social values (1997:175). In his formulation, a lack of shared public values in the neo-liberal 1990s precipitated a crisis in the state legal order and fomented the desire for vengeful responses to criminality, such as the death penalty.

Sarat's thesis is appropriate for South Africa insofar as it too is characterized by a lack of shared public values and a crisis of legitimacy in legal institutions. In addition, it draws our attention to the ANC government's efforts to centralize authority and re-establish the rule of law in the post-apartheid order. The post-1994 regime has not been able to recover from the crisis of the legal order and the increasing fragmentation (or pluralization) of justice during the last ten years of apartheid. This crisis has been exacerbated by rocketing crime figures in both townships and white suburbs, thus widening the chasm between vengeance in the townships and the saccharin-coated invocations of reconciliation by the TRC. According to the South African Institute of Race Relations 1997–8 *Survey*, between 1975 and 1997, incidents of assault increased by 69 per cent, murder by 184 per cent, rape by 252 per cent and robbery by 223 per cent (1998:30). Meanwhile, convictions for serious offences plummeted by 40 per cent from 373,590 in 1991–2 to 218,394 in 1995–6.[5]

Thus, vengeance is not a free-floating discourse *à la* Nietzsche, but is the direct consequence of the failure of state institutions to regulate social conflict. In South Africa, it arises from past state brutality, and present socio-economic inequality and impunity. Revenge does not flourish on its own and according to its own rules, but thrives where more institutionalized forms of retribution (be they state or informal) are lacking.

Township justice historically emerged in the interstices of the state system, controlled and constrained by the fragile and contested authority of state law. To fully understand the position of vengeance in informal courts, we must also look at its place in state jurisprudence. In so doing, we get an insight into the ambiguous nature of the relationship between state retribution and 'popular' vengeance, and an awareness of the (often occluded) connections between state and informal law. We ought to be aware of these connections, if only to understand the widespread acceptance in South Africa of retribution and vengeance. This view of justice is shared by both formal and informal courts, and could be a possible route to re-legitimizing the post-apartheid legal order. Human rights (in the sense of both human rights talk and international treaties) could play a role in democratization if they were closely associated with ending impunity and prosecutions of those offenders most responsible for past wrongdoing.

Instead, as we have seen, human rights have been reconceptualized as restorative justice and forgiveness, ideas which have only a tenuous hold in townships affected by criminal and political violence. Furthermore, advocates of amnesties and truth commissions have emphasized the connections between revenge and retribution in order to close down legal avenues of dealing with past atrocities, and to justify a shift towards victim-oriented restorative justice. Advocates of the amnesty and TRC point out that revenge and retribution arise from the same ignoble emotions of 'getting even' and making the wrongdoer 'pay his dues' and are therefore deemed morally unacceptable (Tutu 1999). We are then offered the stark rhetorical choice between a pyrrhic vengeance and national amnesia. On the basis of evidence presented in this chapter, my conclusion is that the TRC's version of human rights as reconciliation did little to challenge the prevalence of revenge in the townships because it could not meaningfully engage with a punitive view of justice. Further, it could be argued that the TRC's amnesty for human rights offenders exacerbated an already existing situation of judicial impunity and a trend towards violent retribution. As David Crocker has written:

> It is not unreasonable to believe that amnesty-forgiveness in fact has undermined peaceful coexistence in South Africa or at least that fair prosecution-punishment would have promoted it just as well or better. When some victims, bystanders and even perpetrators believe that heinous killers do not deserve to go scot free, let alone return to their former places of social privilege, then amnesty-forgiveness may deepen polarization rather than reduce it. (2000:13)

In order to advance the idea that protecting human rights requires a measure of retributive justice for offenders, we need to recognize that there are some significant ways in which retribution and revenge differ from one another. Robert Nozick (1981:366–368) outlines five elements that distinguish revenge from retribution:[6]

1 Retribution is done for a wrong, whereas revenge may be carried out for a slight or perceived slight and not for a wrong.
2 Retribution sets an upper limit on punishment according to the seriousness of the wrong (what lawyers call 'proportionality'), whereas revenge sets no such limits.
3 Revenge is personal whereas agents of retribution need have no personal tie to the victim of the wrong for whom they exact retribution.
4 Revenge involves a specific emotional tone-pleasure in the suffering of the punished, whereas retribution either involves no such emotional tone, or involves a different one – such as pleasure at justice being done.
5 Revenge has no element of generality, as the agent of revenge is not committed to punishing a similar act done to anyone, only those

> done to a particular group (say, his family, or all those designated 'Serbs'). In contrast, retribution is committed to general principles mandating similar punishment in similar circumstances.

Nozick's contrasts are accurate empirically in a variety of settings and allow us to acknowledge the similarities between revenge and retribution without equating them to one another. Nozick, for instance, is willing to concede that people can be moved by mixed motives, or that a stated desire for retribution can mask revenge (368–369). Victims' vengeful motives enter into the process of compensation, as for some the suffering of the wrongdoer is a type of compensation for the wrong in itself. Nozick states (p. 368) that revenge and retribution share a 'common structure' and both are acts of communicative behavior, even if what is being communicated might be different.

My own use of vengeance, revenge and retribution largely follows Nozick's distinctions but is also based upon organizational attributes and a distinction between language and acts:

> *Vengeance* refers to a language and an emotion (like Nietzsche's *ressentiment*) of reciprocal punishment and suffering of the offender as compensation for wrongdoing or perceived harm;
>
> *Revenge* applies to the unchecked violent acts of individuals and armed gangs motivated by the desire for vengeance with no element of proportionality; and
>
> *Retribution*, although often motivated by a desire for revenge, pertains to the type of justice as punishment dispensed by more institutionalized types of mediation and adjudication, found in township courts and magistrates' courts and characterized by the elements outlined in Nozick's framework above.

Vengeance is present in both revenge acts and retributive justice, but enacted differently in each, with greater due process and accountability and proportionality in the latter, even if it is the due process and harsh punishment favored by patrimonial authority. My aim is to explore a language and set of emotions of vengeance within both revenge and retribution, while recognizing that the two differ in significant organizational and conceptual respects.

Distinguishing between vengeance, revenge and retribution in the manner outlined above allows us to reflect in a more complex manner on actual connections and disconnections between different levels of legal authority in the townships, and between township structures and the national criminal justice system. This is part of my program to go beyond over-generalizing approaches towards 'state' and 'society' in order to look at how these categories themselves are fragmented and how different forms of authority relate to one another in different ways, according to the strategies adopted by social actors.

As we will see later in this chapter, revenge is most often found in the township of Sharpeville in the Vaal (see Map 3), the historic home of 'wild justice' in South Africa; where the justice of the lynch mob was made infamous by the murder of councilor Jacob Dlamini in 1984, which sparked the final round of resistance to apartheid. Post-1994, Sharpeville remained the home of armed gangs exercising the law of the AK-47 in the context of an utter deficit of state legitimacy. Legality and authority were extremely fragmented, existing at the level of the block or even the street, where gangs fought to maintain power through sheer violence alone. Sharpeville is iconic of many other places around South Africa, such as the East Rand townships of Katorus, the midlands of Kwazulu-Natal and the Cape Flats, where local discourses of vengeance and practices of revenge perpetuate the discontinuities between local justice on the one hand, and organized external authority found in state law and human rights on the other.

Sharpeville's revenge ethic contrasts with the retributive justice structures found in the neighboring township of Boipatong. In Boipatong, there is a local court which, through its establishing of basic rules and mechanisms for retribution (rather than uncontrolled revenge), has moved closer to the punitive apparatus of state law, but remains antagonistic to human rights talk. Since 1994, the denizens of Boipatong have shifted from revenge to a more measured retribution by implementing procedures in a local court accountable to the authority of the 'community'. However flawed the due process of Boipatong's local court, and however much punishment gives vent to emotions of vengeance, it has at least shifted the adjudication of conflict a certain distance along the continuum from revenge towards retribution. Unlike their Sharpeville counterparts, Boipatong residents have established a legal mechanism which has enjoyed a certain (albeit contested) legitimacy within the township, in contrast to the extreme fragmentation of Sharpeville. In Boipatong, justice is what defines the 'community' and its internal power structures in relation to external structures of law (the police, the magistrates' court, the TRC and so on). There is a disciplining of passion and the application of a measured punishment; even if it takes the form of a harsh public beating, it reins in the impetus for violent murder which rampages without encumbrance in neighboring Sharpeville. Crucially in Boipatong, the township court has entered into a close working relationship with the police, which seems impossible in the Hobbesian context of Sharpeville.

Despite the distinction I have drawn between vengeful Sharpeville and retributive Boipatong, it is wrong to suppose that the categories of revenge and retribution are watertight in practice, or that there is a neat teleological progression between the two.[7] The permeable boundary is continually transgressed in practice; institutions of retribution feed off the unrefined emotion of vengeance, channeling it into conventional procedures, but never quite breaking with the expectation of due punishment for wrongs and suffering for the offender. Sentencing judges and members of informal courts usually maintain contact with the raw power of vengeance as they are aware that this forms the basis of their legitimacy. Every informal and state court of law in South Africa, albeit in different ways, not only relies upon the construction of these categories but at the same time blurs their limits. An awareness of this ambiguity forms the basis of my analysis of the relationship between informal and formal legal institutions and allows us to better understand the disposition of some township residents towards both human rights commissions and state law.

NATIONAL DEBATES ON VENGEANCE

The Mandela United Football Club

> My family want the Government to reinstate the death penalty so that those who committed these murders can be hanged if found guilty ... We are not talking about vengeance here but justice.
>
> Chris Ribeiro (son of Dr Fabian and Florence Ribeiro, murdered in Mamelodi on 1 December 1986). (*Sowetan* 25 October 1996)

To fully understand the consequences of the TRC's language of reconciliation for popular legal consciousness and practices, we have to look at the ways in which the TRC and other national human rights institutions such as the Constitutional Court dealt with manifestations of an ethic of vengeance. During the life of the TRC, there was resistance to the principles of amnesty and reconciliation in the courts and in the public sphere. The leaders of this unyielding tendency were labeled opponents of national reconciliation, and were decried in the national press as anti-social wreckers of the new nation-building project. By refusing to succumb to the post-1994 combining of human rights talk, reconciliation and *ubuntu* nationalism, those advocating punishment for offenders were portrayed as detrimental to the well-being of the rainbow nation.

However, relatives of high-profile apartheid victims such as Chris Ribeiro expressed a version of justice as retribution which must be taken seriously. Even if the individuals or organizations representing these views are now considered a minority voice, this voice is perhaps not as marginal as some may assume. One of the main symbols of black anger and vengeance, Winnie Madikizela-Mandela (*Mail and Guardian* 23 December 1997), was politically rehabilitated in 1999 under the aegis of Nelson Mandela's successor, President Thabo Mbeki. This is no doubt due to the fact that she, unlike Mbeki, possesses significant charisma and is idolized in politicized urban communities.

Winnie Madikizela-Mandela never quite made the transition from the 1980s to the 1990s, from the Mother-of-the-Nation-yet-to-Become to the Mother-of-the-Nation-that-has-now-Come-to-Be. Indeed she became demonized in the press as the 'Mugger of the Nation'. In the special TRC hearings in late 1997 (*Mail and Guardian* 28 November 1997), Madikizela-Mandela became the symbol of a historical disjuncture, the ANC's own break with the past, the excesses of the 1980s struggle, and the new national historicity. In contrast, Desmond Tutu was elevated as the symbol of reconciliation and the continuity between humanitarian motives in the past and present.

Despite her public vilification, Madikizela-Mandela continues to be the national voice of black vengeance, someone who articulates widespread emotions of anger at the continued racialization of privilege in the 'new' South Africa and the lack of economic betterment for the majority of black South Africans. Her ability to channel and articulate this resentment is the best explanation for her continued popularity in urban townships, despite her unsavory links with the activities of the notoriously violent so-called 'Mandela United Football Club' and her 1991 criminal conviction for kidnapping Stompie Seipei before his murder at the hands of her agents. Winnie Madikizela-Mandela is still *the* national figure articulating a perspective that keeps alive the aspirations of a liberation narrative of the 1980s. Her politics opposes the sharp break with the past asserted by government, and institutions such as the TRC, and instead asserts a continuity between the present and a past of racial injustice and economic exclusion. She rejects reconciliation and instead nurtures the desire for a Robert Mugabe-style seizure of the political and economic resources still held by a white elite.

For nine days, the TRC's special hearings on the Mandela United Football Club in Johannesburg exposed Mandela's nefarious activities in graphic detail.[8] They placed clear blue water between the present order based upon a culture of human rights and the excesses of the struggle in the 1980s. They were an indictment, more than any other activity carried out by the TRC, of the acts of revenge pursued by gangs of young ANC comrades who crossed the line from political cadres to thuggish gangsters, who murdered suspected police informers and, in the process, many innocents. As the political journalist David Beresford wrote, the theatre of the Mandela United hearings lay in the procession of Madikizela-Mandela's former comrades in arms, who took the stand to confront her and tell her the war was over, and now it was time to reconcile and rebuild (*Observer Review* 23 November 1997).

Most chilling was the testimony of Jerry Richardson, self-styled 'coach' of the Club, as he described the interrogation of Stompie Seipei:

> We started torturing the youths in the manner that the Boers [Afrikaners] used to torture freedom fighters. The first thing that I did to Stompie was to hold him with both sides, throw him up in the air and let him fall freely onto the ground. Mummy [Mrs Madikizela-Mandela] was sitting and watching us ... I killed Stompie on the instructions of Mummy. Mummy never killed anyone, but she used us to kill a lot of people. She does not even visit us in prison. She used us!

The hearings engaged very little with Mrs Madikizela-Mandela's politics in the 1980s, nor with the suspicion-filled and violent context of Soweto at the time. Instead, the hearings became a ritual of renunciation, an expression of the incredulity of a human rights and Christian morality towards a cycle of fear and brutal retaliation. And in return, Mrs Madikizela-Mandela stonewalled haughtily. In Desmond Tutu's account of the Mandela hearings, he wrote that 'Mrs Madikizela-Mandela, resplendent in her elegant designer outfits ... disdainfully dismissed almost all the testimony against her as "ridiculous" and "ludicrous". She hardly turned a hair' (1999:132). Madikizela-Mandela answered few questions directly, implicitly negating the right of hard-nosed investigator Piers Pigou to ask her anything at all. Her demeanor veered between indifference and sneering derision, which surfaced in various comments to the press.

The final *Report*'s summary of the special investigation concluded:

> Mrs Madikizela-Mandela's testimony before the Commission was characterized by a blanket denial of all allegations against her and of the attempts by the community leadership to defuse the situation arising from the abduction debacle ... The picture that she sought to paint of herself was that she was right and that everybody else was wrong ... She refused to take any responsibility for wrongdoing. (2:578)

In terms of sheer theater, the Mandela United hearings were the sorest test of the TRC's redemption mandate. Resistance, evasion and outright hostility was perhaps to be expected from former security policemen at amnesty hearings, but to have such a central figure from the anti-apartheid struggle reiterate her opposition to a new culture of forgiveness and confession was much more damaging to the TRC's mission to convert politicized urban blacks to its message. As it transpired, nearly every security policeman who appeared before the Commission was more contrite and respectful of the TRC's authority than Madikizela-Mandela. In the end, the hearings salvaged a small amount of credibility for the TRC, when Mrs Madikizela-Mandela made her first public (albeit halfhearted) apology to the families of Stompie Seipei and another one of her victims, Dr Abubaker Asvat, when she admitted that 'things went horribly wrong' (Tutu 1999:135).

In the Mandela United Football Club hearings, there was often a resounding clash between the language of liberation and the new discourse of human rights. The two sides were not listening to each other, and were engaged in a dance of mutual avoidance. However, the two philosophies did confront each other directly and perhaps more meaningfully in the most human rights-oriented section of the legal system, and on the turf where an ethic of vengeance was perhaps destined to lose – the Constitutional Court – the foremost court in the land.

The Constitutional Court decision on amnesty

> We are concerned that the Commissioners are critical of efforts to bring to book those who perpetrated crimes against humanity. They think justice is of less value than their reconciliation showbiz and avalanche of tears. Lybon Mabaso, AZAPO Gauteng chair, telling a Johannesburg news conference that the TRC defeated the ends of justice by preventing attorneys-general from pursuing apartheid-era human rights offenders.
>
> (*Mail and Guardian*, 23 December 1997)

At the national level, the most forceful opposition to the provisions for amnesty in the 1995 National Unity and Reconciliation Act came from the remnants of the Black Consciousness movement of the 1970s. In April 1996, just a week before the TRC began its first hearings in East London, the political party AZAPO and the families of several high-profile murder victims – Steve Biko, Griffiths Mxenge and the Ribeiros – came together to challenge formally the constitutionality of section 20(7) of the National Unity and Reconciliation Act which permitted the Amnesty Committee to grant amnesty according to criteria laid down in the Act.[9] As a result, neither the perpetrator, nor the state vicariously, could be criminally or civilly liable in respect of that act.

AZAPO et al. boldly instructed their lawyer, Cyril Morolo, to serve papers on President Nelson Mandela, Justice Minister Dullah Omar and Safety and Security Minister Sydney Mufumadi, demanding to see the amnesty application of Dirk Coetzee who had confessed to the murder of Griffiths Mxenge. They threatened the TRC with legal action if it proceeded with its program of public hearings. Although this legal challenge was motivated by black nationalists' vision of justice as retribution, it was couched in the language of law and rights. This is one reason why the AZAPO challenge was more significant in many ways than the hostile posturing of Madikizela-Mandela, who was visibly unable to move on from her 1986 rhetoric when she told a huge rally that the masses would liberate the country 'with necklaces and our little boxes of matches'.[10]

In contrast, AZAPO et al. ingeniously formulated their plea in the framework of constitutional rights and international human rights law, stating that amnesty revoked their constitutional right (enshrined in the Bill of Rights) to insist that wrongdoers should be properly prosecuted before a court of law and punished accordingly. The basis of the AZAPO challenge was twofold:

- That section 20(7) of the National Unity and Reconciliation Act contradicted section 22 of the 1993 Interim Constitution to 'have justiciable disputes settled by a court of law, or ... other independent or impartial forum'.[11]
- That it was not valid for the state to indemnify itself against civil claims. The state should be required to compensate victims or their dependents for serious losses suffered as a result of the criminal acts of employees of the state.

AZAPO's legal representative, Advocate Soggot, appealed to international law to support his case, referring to the provisions in the 1949 Geneva Conventions[12] which obliged parties to enact legislation necessary to provide effective penal sanctions for persons committing grave violations such as killing, torture or inhuman treatment or wilfully causing serious injury.

In a majority ruling rejecting AZAPO's claim, Constitutional Court Judge Ismail Mahomed stated that section 33(2) of the Constitution permitted the suspension of basic rights if this were sanctioned by the Constitution or if this were justified in terms of section 33(1) of the Constitution (the limitation section). The court held that the 'National Unity and Reconciliation' epilog to the Constitution limited the right of access to justice of victims. Mahomed claimed that amnesty was permitted because without it there would have been no political settlement to the armed conflict in the first place. In so doing, he conflated revenge with legal retribution:

> If the Constitution kept alive the prospect of continuous retaliation and revenge, the agreement of those threatened by its implementation might never have been forthcoming ... It was for this reason that those who negotiated the Constitution made a deliberate choice, preferring understanding over vengeance, reparation over retaliation, *ubuntu* over victimisation.[13]

Mahomed argued that without an amnesty provision, there would be no incentive for perpetrators to come forward and reveal the truth. Further, there was a lack of evidence, as offenders had systematically destroyed incriminating evidence:

> The alternative to the granting of immunity from criminal prosecution of offenders is to keep intact the abstract right to such a prosecution for particular persons without the evidence to sustain the prosecution successfully, to continue to keep the dependents of such victims in many cases substantially ignorant about what precisely happened to their loved ones, to leave their yearning for the truth effectively unassauged.[14]

In his decision, Mahomed wrote that the amnesty provisions of the National Unity and Reconciliation Act were compatible with international human rights norms and he stated that reparations for victims of state repression needed to be balanced against other state obligations for reconstruction, especially for education and housing and health care in poor areas. The judge recognized the inadequacies of the national legal system and the problems of access to justice for the majority, and he asserted that preserving an abstract right to prosecution would in the end keep the majority of victims who did not have financial resources to pursue a civil case ignorant of the circumstances of criminal acts (and hence, the fate of their loved ones).

Was Justice Mahomed's judgment justifiable in terms of international human rights conventions on amnesty? Before addressing this question, we must assess the relative weight granted by the Constitutional Court to international law, and this is found in Justice Mahomed's judgment where he stated that:

> International conventions and treaties do not become part of the municipal law of our country, enforceable at the instance of private individuals in our courts, until and unless they are incorporated into the municipal law by legislative enactment ... Section 231(3) of the Constitution makes it clear that when Parliament

> agrees to the ratification of or accession to an international agreement such agreement becomes part of the law of the country only if Parliament expressly so provides and the agreement is not inconsistent with the Constitution ... The court is directed only to 'have regard' to public international law if it is applicable to the protection of rights entrenched in the chapter.[15]

These passages illustrate the clear prioritizing of national law over international law and they assert the authority of the South African Constitution over all other treaties or agreements which governments may enter into. This is part of a general pattern, and domestic courts upholding amnesties in Latin America have also downplayed the applicability of international law. For one commentator, the South African Constitutional Court only acknowledged international law in a 'cursory fashion' (*Mail and Guardian* 20 September 1996) and others put it more acidly, saying that the Court 'seems to have reduced the legitimate function of international law in constitutional interpretation to a meaningless *post hoc* rationalization' (Roht-Arriaza and Gibson 1998:873).

In assessing the use that Justice Mahomed actually did make of international law, we must again recognize that international human rights is ambiguous on the question of amnesty and that by quoting selectively, one can construct an argument to either justify or negate a national amnesty.[16] In writing that the South African Constitution was compatible with international practice in relation to amnesty, Mahomed cited the precedents of Chile, El Salvador and Argentina, where amnesties were combined with truth commissions, and he referred to Article 6(5) of Protocol II to the Geneva Conventions which provides that:

> {a}t the end of hostilities, the authorities in power shall endeavour to grant the broadest possible amnesty to persons who participated in armed conflict, or those deprived of their liberty for reasons related to the armed conflict, whether they are interned or detained.[17]

Yet there is a great deal of contention around the interpretation of Protocol II, and the International Committee of the Red Cross has concluded that Article 6(5) is inapplicable to amnesties that extinguish all legal responsibility to those who have violated international law and may apply only to combatants acting against other combatants. Roht-Arriaza and Gibson argue that there is textual justification to assert that the reference in Article 6(5) to the 'broadest possible amnesty' does not completely extricate states from their duty to prosecute human rights violations but implies the broadest amnesty 'without infringing on other binding international treaties or customary international law' (1998:866).

The stand-off between the 'international retributionists' and the 'nationalist pragmatists' over what international law definitively states on the question of amnesty is likely to shift in coming years with the extension of the jurisdiction of the International Criminal Court (ICC). The Rome statute setting up the ICC defines the crimes within the jurisdiction of the court and at Article 7 defines 'crimes against humanity' to include, *inter alia*, racial persecution and 'the crime of apartheid'. Michael Sharf states that 'It would be inappropriate for an international criminal court to defer to a national amnesty in a situation where the amnesty violates obligations contained in the very international conventions that make up the court's subject matter jurisdiction' (1999:514), but Sharf recognizes that the ICC in practice is likely to discriminate between generalized and blanket amnesties, such as that granted by General Augusto Pinochet before giving up the Chilean Presidency, and amnesties such as those adopted in South Africa which introduce principles of accountability, individualization of responsibility and reparation for victims.

Sharf (1999) concludes that the establishment of the ICC will probably not bring an end to amnesty provisions being agreed in negotiated settlements to internal armed conflicts. However, he notes the 'schizophrenic nature of the negotiations at Rome [in 1998]' and acknowledges that there is room for greater jurisdictional authority in the future. The ICC might develop increasing autonomy to judge whether national amnesties contravene the 1949 Geneva Conventions or the 1948 Convention on the Prevention and Punishment of the Crime of Genocide[18] and under Article 16 it may decide not to terminate an investigation even if presented with a UN Security Council resolution to defer or halt proceedings.

Having reviewed the international aspects of the amnesty debate, we need to ask what kind of public legitimacy did the Constitutional Court judgment receive in South Africa itself? The decision was widely praised in the press, demonstrating how hegemonic the language of reconciliation had become by 1996, and how little space was left to argue, in the national public arena, for prosecutions and punishment of human rights offenders. As the legal observer at the *Mail and Guardian* wrote:

> It is not surprising that victims and their families feel short-changed: there will be few further prosecutions and probably no successful civil claims. Instead there will be amnesties for men who deserve, more than most, to hang for their crimes. This is an

> extraordinary end to the grim Eighties but, a rational one and the price paid for a negotiated settlement. (8 November 1996)

The Constitutional Court decision on amnesty was a watershed in South Africa's transition, where a reconciliatory version of human rights talk triumphed (within the constitutional framework, at least) over a retributive vision of human rights. Although it did not work out this way in local communities, the national debate on how to deal with a past of violence and injustice had been addressed once and for all. Yet there was a sliver of principled doubt from one Constitutional Court judge: Justice Didcott published a dissenting judgment, in which he conceded that the amnesty provisions contained in the National Unity and Reconciliation Act *did* clearly violate the right to justice, suggesting that 'the state may be intrinsically ineligible for such protection (i.e. indemnity) under section 61'. Yet he recognized the impossibility of the state's compensating adequately all the victims of apartheid. After a tortuous discussion of what may or may not constitute the 'essential content of a right', he ended up supporting the dismissal of the application. Despite Didcott's final retreat from the precipice, his dissension reminded the Court of the political nature of its judgment and the acute compromises that were being asked from individual citizens.

During the Constitutional Court hearings, the Mxenge, Biko and Ribeiro families, like Winnie Madikizela-Mandela who was referred to by journalist David Beresford as a harbinger of 'Black Mischief' (*Observer Review* 23 November 1997), were demonized by the TRC and ANC in the media for their legal challenge. The opponents of amnesty were seen as 'anti-reconciliation'. Their actions outraged Desmond Tutu who bitterly denounced them in a press hearing, saying, 'I hope they get their come-uppance. I am annoyed and very hurt for the many people I know who want to tell their stories.'[19]

The ANC went quite a way further in its rhetoric, bizarrely accusing the anti-amnesty coalition of being in the service of apartheid perpetrators and 'the interests of those who for decades sat in secret plotting some of the most heinous crimes the world has ever witnessed'.[20] This accusation of complicity is little short of astonishing given the elevated, almost sacred, position occupied by the Biko, Mxenge and Ribiero families in the anti-apartheid struggle. The ANC went on to appeal to them to join the nation in the onward march of transformation and 'the national drive for truth, reconciliation, development and peace'.[21] This was classic propaganda, where the interests and well-being of 'the nation' were allowed to define the common good.

Despite the extreme language of vilification and the failure of their legal challenge, the constitutional appeal of AZAPO et al. against the amnesty provisions was valuable in that it highlighted how victims were being asked to give up something (namely the chance to pursue justice and compensation as defined in common law) and that the abrogation of their rights needed addressing, especially through substantial reparations which, in the end, were not forthcoming.

INTIMATIONS OF VENGEANCE DURING TRC HEARINGS

When asked about the degree to which he felt 'reconciliation' had occurred in public hearings, Wilhelm Verwoerd, a philosopher in the TRC's Research Unit, replied:

> Because of the media, there is too much of a desire to show that you're delivering the goods, like when Tutu welcomed the Dutch Reformed Church with too open arms after they provided only a mild apology. The audience wants to see visible reconciliation working on the screen, but it doesn't work like that. (Personal interview, 17 December 1996)

Indeed, creating reconciliation was often more difficult in the actual hearings than it appeared on television. Testimonies during Human Rights Violations hearings often elicited more condemnation from the audience than they did sympathy. This usually depended on the identity and political affiliation of the speaker. In the townships in and around Johannesburg, audiences were partisan and largely pro-ANC, and I witnessed many cases where the audience mocked the suffering of victims.

As we saw in chapter 4, the crowd at the Tembisa hearings made sport of the weeping mother of a murdered IFP gang leader. During the Kagiso hearings, the crowd laughed and hooted with approval as Mr P Tlhapane, a former ANC comrade, bragged how he was 'like a cat that caught everything that came near me' when he murdered a white man driving through the township. Tlhapane claimed that he sold the man's car to 'feed the community' and sent money to the liberation struggle in exile. Raising a serious question mark over the TRC's motto of 'Reconciliation Through Truth', one could see that this mantra only worked where the truth was in accord with the political sympathies of the audience. Otherwise, the 'truth' of those testifying rekindled the anger of the past and a desire to further humiliate the speaker.

Public expressions of delight in the extreme suffering of 'the enemy' is not confined to the TRC process, but has been a feature of South African criminal trials. Nancy Scheper-Hughes, writing on the Amy Biehl case (the American student killed by a mob in a Cape township) recorded:

> During the first stages of the trial as witnesses came forward to describe in horrible detail Amy Biehl's final agony, her pleadings and moans while being stoned and stabbed, the young PAC supporters who packed the court's upper gallery laughed and cheered. (1995:149)

Yet the press seldom reported on this aspect of audience behavior at TRC hearings, and one hardly ever read interviews with members of the public attending hearings. There were a few exceptions to this, when the rejection by witnesses of the language of reconciliation was dramatic and theatrical, thus warranting press coverage. One of the first examples of this occurred on 28 November 1996, when two senior policemen testifying at a TRC special event hearing in Cape Town on the high-profile Gugulethu 7 case walked out when an angry woman threw a shoe at them (*Star* 28 November 1996). Prior to this outburst, the TRC had shown grisly police footage of the murders of seven alleged ANC guerrillas, who had been shot by police in an orchestrated ambush on 3 March 1986, to an audience of commissioners, policemen and victims' relatives. The families became very distressed and several broke down in tears. One of the mothers of the deceased threw her shoe at the policemen, hitting Leonard Knipe, chief officer of the violent crimes police unit, on the head. The shoe ricocheted off Knipe's head and then hit Johan Kleyn, a police station commander. The commission adjourned as the two policemen and a number of family members left the room. Here was another case where truth and reconciliation seemed very far apart indeed.

Events such as these did ultimately have an effect on the Commission's proceedings. For the first six months, Commissioners had been asking each victim appearing at an HRV hearing whether or not they forgave the perpetrator. Commissioners received so many outraged and angry responses to their entreaty for public forgiveness that they made a policy decision to desist from asking such questions directly. Yet, as we saw in chapter 4 on reconciliation during the HRV hearings, the pressure to forsake revenge always remained implicit and unwavering.

RELATIONAL DISCONTINUITIES

We now move from examining the national context and the TRC's hearings to looking at the vitally important relationships between TRC hearings and community-level social processes. The complexity of the relationship between what happened at the hearings and what transpired in communities affected by violence was made clear at the TRC Human Rights Violations hearings held in Sebokeng in August 1996.

A large part of the week-long hearings held at the teacher training college dealt with the atrocities committed by Inkatha Freedom Party members based at KwaMadala hostel at the ISCOR iron and steel plant across from Boipatong. The most widely known case involved the testimonies of the mothers of two youths, both now dead, who had led a factional dispute involving the death of over 40 in the Sebokeng 'Night Vigil Massacre' and subsequent retaliatory acts (discussed in chapter 5).

The TRC hearing was the first time that Ms Margaret Nangalembe, the mother of ANC comrade Christopher Nangalembe, and Anna Kheswa, the mother of Christopher's killer Victor Kheswa, had met since their sons' feud had begun five years earlier. They both gave their differing accounts, and at the urging of Commissioners, shook hands publicly in an act of seeming 'reconciliation'. Ms Kheswa, an IFP member living at the notorious KwaMadala hostel, expressed her desire to return to her house in Zone 7 of Sebokeng township, across the road from the Nangalembe household. Mandla Nangalembe (Christopher's brother) accepted this request and said that the Kheswas could return without any fear of hostility from them.

However, this ritual enactment of reconciliation – the shaking of hands between the mothers of militarized youth – has not advanced the national reconciliation project at the local level. No IFP members from KwaMadala have successfully returned to any of the townships from whence they fled in the 1990–1 period. On the contrary, IFP members such as Dennis Moerane of Sharpeville were summarily executed by armed ANC gangs when they tried to return to their homes. The inability to translate the national reconciliation project into local reconciliation resulted from the lack of any dispute-resolution mechanisms within the TRC framework to negotiate the return of former 'pariahs' to the community. In many areas of conflict, the TRC became a ritualized performance with little accompanying organization on the ground to actually implement its grand vision of reconciliation.

Moreover, there were few initiatives within the TRC to engage with the bodies who actually exercise political authority in the townships, that is, local justice institutions, armed vigilante groups and local political party branches. These were seen as too compromised by their previous role in the violence. Commissioners I interviewed were hostile to the rough justice of local courts, demonizing them as 'kangaroo courts' antithetical to human rights. The recommendations in Volume 5 (p.327) of the TRC *Report* condemned informal courts as 'repressive' and urged their disbanding. This is ironic since some Commissioners linked to the United Democratic Front actually promoted 'community courts' in the 1980s as organizations prefiguring revolutionary people's power. In the new culture of human rights, armed units of the anti-apartheid movement must be either incorporated within policing and military structures, or abandoned.

There was a correspondingly profound disdain towards the TRC on the part of local political actors. The ANC representative to the 1991–2 Peace Committees, 'Watch' Mothibedi, a powerful political broker in Sebokeng, scorned the Nangalembe–Kheswa reconciliation, stating

> Those two are only individuals. Their reconciliation has no further weight. Ms Nangalembe cannot forgive on behalf of the community. She was not the only one to have suffered. She cannot allow Ms Kheswa's return. Individuals cannot do it. The whole community has to decide ... This must be done by legitimate community institutions, not by the TRC who come in for one week and then say they've sorted everything out ... The TRC cannot go into the depth of the situation ... The Vaal is a very violent place and it will erupt again because no healing has taken place. (Personal interview, Sebokeng, 12 January 1997)

If the TRC organizational structures and the semi-religious discourse on human rights and reconciliation are not working, then how do former 'enemies of the community' negotiate their return? Who absolves them and negotiates on behalf of the 'community' and what are 'legitimate community institutions'? When does local mediation process work, and when does it fail? What does this then tell us about the relationship between transnational human rights, the laws of the nation-state and local forms of legality? This and the next chapter try to answer these questions by examining two neighboring Vaal townships which have pursued very different ways of dealing with their histories of political violence: Sharpeville and Boipatong.

A HISTORY OF VIOLENCE IN SHARPEVILLE SINCE 1990

> The Vaal is a political giant, but it has turned its young people into monsters. Reverend Peter 'Gift' Moerane, Assistant Minister, Sharpeville Methodist Church of St. Luke.
>
> (Personal interview, 16 January 1997)

Sharpeville occupies a special place in modern black resistance to apartheid in South Africa. In many ways, it is synonymous with the struggle, and encompasses all its successes, excesses, triumphs and disappointments. The TRC began its investigations into the past with the beginning of modern resistance to apartheid – the massacre on 21 March 1960 of 69 unarmed protestors who were demonstrating against pass book regulations outside Sharpeville police station. On 3 September 1984, the rebellion which engulfed Sharpeville and other Vaal townships ignited uprisings across the country. On that day, the ire of Vaal anti-apartheid activists was directed against the lowest tier of apartheid administration in the townships. The murder of councilor Jacob Dlamini of Sharpeville by an angry mob, who were so provoked by his shooting at them that they burnt him alive, led to the internationally famous trial of the 'Sharpeville Six'. The handing down of the death sentence (never carried out) came to be one of the greatest post-1948 miscarriages of justice, and to epitomize generally the arbitrary nature of justice for blacks under apartheid.[22]

Sharpeville was an icon of militancy in the apartheid era, but since 1994 it has become a symbol of a traumatized township out of step with the new political order. Its history is characterized by the inability of political parties, and particularly the ANC, to rein in criminality from within their own ranks and by a failure to sell the political compromises of the transition to a militarized and unemployed youth. Revenge continues to thrive in the township as a result of the liberation movement's use of hardened criminals to fight their battles in the 1980s and 1990s and the conflict of rival armed ANC structures which emerged after the unbanning of anti-apartheid organizations in 1990.[23]

In the 1980s, the anti-apartheid movement set up armed 'anti-crime' structures, and these structures, labeled Special Defense Units (SDUs), proliferated in 1990–91 after the unbanning. SDUs comprised primarily ANC Youth League members, the self-anointed 'Young Lions' of the liberation struggle. They operated in an extremely localized manner, each controlling perhaps only a street or two. Some gave themselves revolutionary names such as the Slovos, Samoras, Castros, and Cutas. Those who sought a less political and more of a gangster profile called themselves the Germans, the Italians and the Untouchables.

From 1990 onwards, SDUs were drawn into the bloody war with the Zulu nationalist Inkatha Freedom Party which was organized in the migrant hostels[24] and armed and trained by the state security forces. SDUs also became heavily reliant on criminal activities. In areas such as Sharpeville, where ANC control was feeble, these new structures broke out of the confines of party discipline and became involved in gun running, protection rackets and extortion. SDUs unleashed a random campaign of violence, against the state security forces and the IFP, and against other anti-apartheid organizations (for example, the PAC which is well established in Sharpeville, and other SDUs). Between May and October 1992, Sharpeville SDUs were held responsible for 36 murders, 84 robberies and 21 rapes in the small township alone (*City Press* 10 January 1993).

The ANC exacerbated an already explosive situation when it introduced yet another armed structure into the region, the military wing of the ANC, Umkhonto We Sizwe (MK).[25] In late 1990, approximately 200 exiled MK members returned to the Vaal, refused to integrate into joint controlling structures with the SDUs, and sought to take charge themselves of all armed groups in the area. This led to a series of confrontations with the existing SDUs, township courts and trades unions, and created a violent power struggle in the area that lasted long after 1994 and the formal disbanding of the structures. In Sebokeng, a protracted conflict escalated between the late Vaal MK leader Ernest Sotsu and National Union of Mineworkers (NUMSA) leader Jerry Ndamase and over a three-year period seven people were known to have been killed in revenge attacks.

In 1993, at the same time that internecine ANC conflicts were breaking out in other areas such as the East and West Rand, the war between SDUs and MK units in Sharpeville reached fever pitch. On 16 February, a deputation of four MK leaders representing about 50 MK combatants living in Sharpeville approached the local ANC Branch Chairperson, Siza Rani, and told him that all ANCYL members must disarm and Rani must account for all branch funds, which they accused him of stealing. If all weapons were not handed in by 19 February, MK would launch a full-scale offensive on Rani and the entire Youth League. On that day, Youth League activist Oupa Manete was shot dead and on 11 April, his close friend and ANCYL member Andries Makibinyane was also killed.

In July 1993, Oupa Manete's younger brother Lucky Manete set up the infamous 'Germans' gang to avenge his brother's death. The gang was made up of about 60 youths between the ages of 14 and 21, most of whom were ANCYL members from Matthew Goniwe section of Sharpeville. That same month, MK member Benny Scott was gunned down. Lucky Manete was arrested for the crime, but he was murdered in the Rivonia Tavern while out on bail, and allegations of MK responsibility abounded. As Lucky Manete's funeral procession passed through Molekwane section on 31 July, MK members from Slovo section opened fire on the mourners and several were injured. These events led to a state of all-out war between MK and the SDUs, and the whole of Sharpeville was polarized into camps supporting either the ANCYL/SDUs or MK.

There were further allegations that the police had fanned the flames of the internal ANC conflict, arming the Germans and ferrying them around Sharpeville at night in Casspir armed personnel carriers. There seems to be some credibility for this charge, which was endorsed by some human rights monitors in the area. Both the Germans and the police were waging war on MK, and therefore shared the same interests. On 31 October 1993, the Germans allegedly carried out a hand-grenade attack on a tavern in Slovo section controlled by MK, leaving two people dead and 23 injured. After the attack, fifteen of the Germans gang sought refuge at the Sharpeville police station as avenging MK members closed in on them.

The ANC regional offices made some attempts to control the situation, but their authority was so weak that little headway was made. In mid-late 1993, a series of 'reconciliation talks' between the ANCYL and MK were initiated. At one meeting, MK member Thabang Vilikazi confessed to killing Lucky Manete and the gathering ended in chaos and shooting. At another 'peace assembly' on 2 August, MK commander Joshua Khumalo stabbed a Youth League member in full view of the regional leadership. The violence raged throughout 1993 and 1994 as MK and Youth League members hunted each other down as night fell in the township.

The end of the apartheid era did not signal the end of a dynamic of violent revenge in the Vaal. After the 1994 elections and the supposed end of the all-out war with the IFP (at least on the Reef, but not in KwaZulu Natal), there was a patchy and disorganized effort by the ANC and formal government institutions to demobilize the SDUs. In 1994, the ANC Youth League of Gauteng publicly declared that Defense Units should disband forthwith. But the SDUs did not easily disappear. Instead, SDU members found themselves with few alternatives for economic advancement or political participation. Many felt that after a decade at the barricades, they had sacrificed their education, their youth and their lives to the liberation movement which then discarded them.

Since 1994, in the absence of political and economic opportunities, ANC para-militaries have become criminals as a means of economic survival. Sharpeville gangs still calling themselves Special Defense Units run protection rackets, promising security from other criminals and SDUs in return for regular payments from terrorized residents. The ANC repeatedly attempted to arrange a cease-fire between feuding factions, but could neither maintain or enforce it. As Piers Pigou, a human rights monitor for 'Peace Action' in the Vaal, put it:

> The SDUs were never offered economic alternatives. The guys with guns only get their status through guns – if they're taken away, then they're nothing. The ANC would send down its big names and get people to agree to a truce at the table and then go away and there is no follow through. The ANC had a good understanding of the dynamics of the violence, but just didn't know how to control it. (Personal interview, 29 January 1997)

The situation was not improved by public officials, such as Gauteng Provincial Minister for Safety and Security Jessie Duarte, making unfulfilled promises to SDUs that they would be incorporated into the police at a time when the police budget was being cut. On 23 July 1995, Soweto SDU members from Diepkloof marched on Orlando police station demanding to be integrated into the South African Police Service (SAPS) (McKenzie 1996:31). Their representatives declared, 'If it means turning to violence and wreak havoc in order for our grievances to be addressed, then we will do just that. We have done it before and we got listened to. Nothing can stop us from doing it again' (*Star* 24 July 1995). In some areas, such as the East Rand,[26] the incorporation of SDUs into the SAPS was more successful but it still only amounted to 10 per cent of the total: 900 former SDU members became paid reservist 'community constables' out of 9,000 (Thulare 1997:13). In the Vaal, the numbers were much lower.

When I interviewed Minister Jessie Duarte in 1995, she became frustrated by my questions about a Meadowlands (Soweto) SDU who had just that week shot dead a petty thief. She objected strongly to my use of the word 'lawlessness' to describe the situation:

> There is not lawlessness! Just in certain areas. We can still count the incidents. The problem in Meadowlands is that the SDU have not understood that it is a new dispensation. We will have to get tough with these types ... where there are SDUs we must say, 'You're not a private army, and need to disarm'. (Personal interview, 10 September 1995)

Given the havoc they could wreak, there was a remarkable absence of political will to deal with the demobilization of armed liberation movement combatants. In 1996, the Minister of Safety and Security, Stanley Mufumadi, drafted legislation to ban military groups but this was a paper exercise and attempts to demobilize paramilitary structures in Johannesburg townships and elsewhere often failed (*Business Day* 6 August 1996). In 1996, Gauteng Provincial Minister Duarte tried to deploy the 1961 Reserve Police Force Act to integrate SDU members into the permanent police force, but this was opposed by senior apartheid-era police officers. The conservative Colonel Swanepoel, who was in charge of creating a new tier of community constables out of former SDUs, objected to the proposed charge on the grounds that new staff were 'undereducated', not properly trained and some had criminal records. According to Thulare (1997:17) writing on the East Rand, this breakdown in relations between community constables and police managers led to parallel policing command structures, exacerbating lawlessness and a lack of accountability.

Other measures were tried in the Vaal: on 5 January 1997, Minister Duarte called a meeting at Masiza stadium of all the SDUs in the Vaal in an effort to disband the armed units. Local Vaal heads of Safety and Security, Lebohang Mahata and Alfred Maloisane, requested that SDUs (and especially those in the violent hostels) send elected representatives, but the time came and went and no one showed up. The political groundwork had not been done by either the local or national ANC leadership which found itself, not for the first time, unable to control its armed bases. Sharpeville Minister, Gift Moerane, summarized the situation thus:

> There was no political leadership to help the militarized youth after the [1994] elections. There is nothing for them so they started to reorganize as gangsters. Until the unbanning in 1990, we didn't know that we had gangsters in our townships, since they were in our popular organizations, defending the communities, killing in the name of the political organization. When the cloud of political violence went away, they reorganized as criminals with the names of political organizations. They started demanding to be integrated into the military and policing structures of the state. The leaders in the communities couldn't control them. They were afraid of them ... they'd kill you if you crossed them. (Personal interview, 16 January 1997)

RECONCILIATION IN RUINS: THE DEATH OF DENNIS MOERANE

When I began interviews in the Vaal in 1996, Sharpeville was characterized by few overarching mediation structures and an extreme territorialization of power between six armed groups calling themselves SDUs. Sharpeville was a 'no-go area' where no one organization, and certainly not the ANC, had complete control. The only certainty in places like Sharpeville was the language of vengeance and the disposition of armed factions to pursue violent revenge at any opportunity.

A cycle of revenge was closely tied up with rhetorical appeals to the liberation movement's language of 'community'. Throughout the 1980s and 1990s, the armed factions legitimated their actions by constructing their identities as the 'defenders of the community', with the 'community' being the most important political symbol in the landscape of South African black politics. Despite the presence of other factions, each armed grouping claimed that it alone represented the community, clinging to an image of collective unity which patently does not exist. The image is of the community as male and martial, and committed to values of valor, honor and revenge. For armed youths, revenge is justified against those who compromise community unity by committing crimes of murder, theft, robbery or simply belonging to the 'wrong' political party (which may designate the PAC as well as the IFP). Indeed, one might say that the deep chasm between the ideal of community solidarity and the reality of factionalization and fragmentation fuels the violence ever further in a spiral of manic reparation.

The murder of Dennis Moerane in Sharpeville on Christmas Day 1996 illustrates the dangers of individual attempts at reconciliation in the context of fragmented community power structures, where there are no effective constraints upon violence. His death exemplifies better than any other case I encountered the contradiction between national human rights talk about reconciliation and what happens in townships where there is no retributive justice, only unhindered revenge in a context of impunity.

Dennis' story, as told by his relatives, was this: Dennis' mother Martha Moerane died in 1978 when he was seven years old and he and his sister were raised by his grandmother, Elizabeth Mofokeng. His cousin Sadie described to me his grandmother spoiled him because he had no mother and father. He was not bright at school and Sadie had to do his mathematics homework for him. His cousins said that he was 'cheeky' and 'rebellious' like his younger sister, who became pregnant at fifteen. In his teens, Dennis became involved in a gang of petty criminals. When his family tried to rein him in and punish him for his criminal acts, he left home to live in KwaMadala hostel at the ISCOR factory only a few miles away. It was March 1993 and he was 22 years old.

In KwaMadala he was recruited by the IFP which had one of its strongest bases on the Reef in the hostel. His family did not see this as politically motivated at all – they were Setswana-speakers and so had no 'cultural' connection to the ethno-nationalist party of the Zulus. KwaMadala and the IFP were a home for criminals and police informers from the townships, often regardless of any ethnic affiliation. Dennis' new home base allowed him to steal and pilfer in Sharpeville and nearby townships with impunity. The IFP presence at KwaMadala hostel became a lightning rod for those, Zulus or not, who were marginalized in the Vaal townships, including many former ANCYL members.

The authoritarianism of apartheid was mirrored in the authoritarianism of ANC comrades in 'popular courts' where members of non-ANC political parties, black policemen, councilors, business people, petty thieves, and disaffected ANCYL comrades who fell foul of a strict code of conduct were punished harshly. In the early 1990s, many were driven out of the liberation movement and sought refuge with the IFP, which was as much a party of the underclass in the townships as it was an ethnic party of Zulus.

Dennis lived in poverty in the dire conditions of KwaMadala and became increasingly desperate. He was given a firearm license by the

Sharpeville police and directed to kill the political enemies of the IFP and apartheid system. He led attacks against ANC comrades whom he had grown up with and knew well. In 1994, he was shot in the stomach during a firefight between Sharpeville SDUs and the IFP, and he spent a month in hospital. After the massive levels of violence during the transition had largely subsided in 1994, Dennis was abandoned by the IFP and he left KwaMadala to live on the streets of the neighboring white town of Vereeniging.

He moved further away from the IFP, and slowly began to approach the ANC once again. At the urging of his uncle, the Reverend 'Gift' Moerane, he made a statement in 1994 which was included in the submission from the Vaal Council of Churches to the Goldstone Commission. In his statement, Dennis explained the role of the IFP in local political violence and its collusion with the police. He went on a witness protection program and was looked after by the ANC, who put him up for a while in the YMCA in Braamfontein in 1995. He officially rejoined the ANC, but he was slowly forgotten by them. His grandmother, Elizabeth, his only real source of family stability, had died that year. With nowhere to go, he ended up desperately poor, forced to beg and sell vegetables on the streets of downtown Johannesburg.

In April 1996, Dennis started to visit his extended family in Sharpeville, going from house to house to avoid alerting the comrades. His kin fed him, but were frightened that by harboring a known IFP hit-squad member, they too would be attacked. Armed former MK members came around and warned his relatives that 'We will burn your house if Dennis returns'. His family were mostly ANC stalwarts themselves but this did not protect them from hardened MK combatants.

Dennis tried to present himself as a 'reformed character' to the SDUs. He appealed to the Germans who controlled Rooisten, the section he lived in, and received their sanction to return home. Despite commitments undertaken by the SDU, he was attacked in July 1996 by the former members of an MK unit at midnight outside his aunt Evodia Mofokeng's house. She heard men shouting, 'Die, you stupid dog! You must eat what you gave others'. Mrs Mofokeng found Dennis lying at the gate. He had terrible head wounds, having been stabbed and shot in the head. He was taken to Baragwanath hospital in Soweto and spent a month recovering. He survived miraculously and carried around two bullets in his head which doctors feared to remove.

Still, Dennis refused to flee Sharpeville again. His aunt pleaded, 'You must go away or you will be killed'. He responded, 'Well, fine. I want to die here where I was born. I have nowhere else to go'. On the morning of 25 December 1996, while walking to his aunt's house to celebrate Christmas, he was captured by former adversaries, not the 'Germans'

SDU in Rooisten with whom he had negotiated a truce, but another faction in a nearby section. They tied him to a lamppost in front of the Sharpeville public library and stabbed him repeatedly in the head: behind the ear, and in the forehead and temple. They then emptied the magazine of an AK-47 into Dennis' body. His family found eighteen bullet holes in his corpse.

Police notified Dennis' family at noon, but his body hung from the lamppost all day since his family was too afraid to move it. There he remained for all to see on Christmas Day, a symbolic testament to failed reconciliation. Finally, the hearse arrived, and his aunt and sister collected his congealed blood in the sand and placed it with his body. The IFP regional office in Vereeniging stated that Dennis was the fourth former IFP member that year to be killed attempting to return to his home in the Vaal.

According to his friends, Dennis had been killed by former MK members, some of whom were absorbed into the new post-apartheid South African Defense Force (SANDF). At the time of Dennis' death, several former MK members from Sharpeville were stationed at the 'Vaal Commando' in nearby Vanderbijlpark. They were on holiday leave since it was Christmas time, a period when political violence increases all over South Africa as migrants and enlisted men return to their homes. It appeared that their motive was less opposition to the IFP and Dennis himself than it was part of the long-standing dispute between SDUs and MK competing over territory and protection money. Former MK exiles disputed the right of the Germans to allow the return of a former IFP member into Rooisten section. If they had respected the Germans' truce, they would have been abandoning their claim to authority in the area, and they were not willing to do that.

The family expressed little surprise or regret to me regarding Dennis' violent murder. Perhaps as a white outsider asking questions about a sensitive and painful issue, this was to be expected. Yet I got the impression that they behaved in this nonchalant manner amongst themselves also. Dennis' sister looked at me with a deadpan expression and bluntly stated, 'We are relieved that he was killed, now it is all over'. An upwardly mobile cousin studying law at a prestigious Johannesburg university spoke about township revenge with a disconcerting *sang froid*, 'You know, we were happy he finally died'.

His family feared a police investigation, and his aunt Evodia Mofokeng told me, 'He's dead. He's dead and we can't do anything about it ... We knew they were going to kill him ... Dennis knew they would kill him ... We don't want a prosecution of the perpetrators. If they go to jail, then they're going to threaten us again. We are not safe and still live in fear. God will see to them.' When I asked if they had requested to be placed on a witness protection program, they replied, 'No. Those Sharpeville police are all friends with the gangsters and would just tell them and they would come for us. The killers said to us, "If the police say something to us, then we'll know that it came from you".' (Personal interview, Sharpeville, 16 January 1997)

There was only a small private funeral for Dennis on a bright Thursday morning in summer. It was held outside of Sharpeville, in contrast to conventional township funerals on Saturdays where hundreds attend the funeral and the wake at the deceased's former house. It is customary for a cow to be killed and a feast held for the multitudes. Attendance by all in the community is obligatory. No such feast was held for Dennis. The family feared that his killers would dig up his body, so they had him buried in an unmarked grave in another cemetery in the Vaal. They then returned to the house of the Reverend 'Gift' Moerane in Steel Park where the family all washed their hands together.

In the aftermath, the police did not visit the family to ask any questions. There were no witnesses to the crime. Dennis seemingly sank without a trace, becoming an invisible murder which all foresaw, and no one particularly wanted to either prevent or avenge. His murder seemed wholly legitimate, even to most of his own family. Only his mother's brother, Java Mofokeng, was visibly moved: 'When I saw his corpse it changed me. I couldn't eat for days. I couldn't think of anything else. I wanted to take revenge.' (Personal interview, Sharpeville, 16 January 1997)

On my return to Sharpeville in November 1998, there had been a breakthrough in the case. Police had apprehended a Sharpeville man in connection with another murder apparently unrelated to that of Dennis. He was a soldier in the SANDF and a former member of MK and had allegedly killed another victim after killing Dennis. Acting on a tip-off, police found that ballistic evidence linked the two murders. He was convicted of the second murder and at the time of writing he had not been charged in connection with Dennis Moerane's murder. The killer had lodged an appeal against his conviction and was seen walking around Sharpeville in early 2000, apparently out on bail. The state witness in his court case, a Sharpeville woman, is presently in hiding.

GUNSHOTS AT NIGHT

Dennis Moerane's murder was an instance where local discourses on vengeance overwhelmed religious and human rights discourses on forgiveness and reconciliation. It seems fair to say that the greater the factionalism within a locale, and the more a social context approximates a Hobbesian moral universe, the greater the resistance will be towards post-conflict human rights talk. An informalized ethic of revenge is a clear indictment of the legal system and it seems that vigilante killings, and warring between rival Special Defense Units and other armed groups, will continue as long as the state system is not perceived to be swift and just. More thoughtful ANC officials are aware of the links between a societal revenge ethic and wider questions of nation-building identified in chapter 1. For instance, when faced with a spate of rough justice incidents (namely the hanging of robbers by one community in Natal and the shotgun murder of five teenage members of the Cape Flats 'Hard Livings' gang by an irate victim)[27] during one week in September 1995, Mr A Cachalia, advisor to the Minister of Public Safety and Security, reflected during a press conference: 'Ultimately, the transformation of our conceptions of what is a just justice system is part of the process of nation-building, and cannot be divorced from the other processes intended to reinvent South African society' (*Mail and Guardian* 29 September 1995).

These ministerial reflections did not often filter down to their intended constituency. Human rights talk, nation-building and the forsaking of revenge had little impact on how many urban residents perceived justice problems. When I tentatively inquired about the national process of reconciliation, or any possible reconciling with the perpetrators, Dennis' relatives stared at me blankly, as if the question were meaningless. It was outside the realm of their experience or expectations. In Sharpeville, only an hour's drive from the TRC offices in downtown Johannesburg, the new national 'culture of human rights' and the wider requirements of inventing a new nation were the province of another country altogether.

Sharpeville remains a township dominated by an ethic of vengeance which is not embedded in any institutionalized procedures to deal with conflict. The disorganized structures of violent revenge in such townships are the most convincing evidence for ongoing legal pluralism in South Africa as it is clear that they lie beyond the reach of state law. Despite all the candidates' claiming to represent 'the community', there are no community-wide institutions to mediate and adjudicate, and no overarching political leaders who could carry the peace. The only ones who come close are religious ministers, but they cannot work in a vacuum of authority and are themselves frustrated by the ongoing violence. As the Reverend 'Gift' Moerane told me:

> There is no politics any more, all that is left are political grudges ... people are proud of the culture of impunity and intolerance, they say, 'This is the Vaal and if you don't fight with us, then we'll kill you'. We don't get mature politicians in the Vaal, only hard liners. (Personal interview, Johannesburg, 16 January 1997)

Since there was an utter lack of legitimate community-wide procedures in Sharpeville in the 1990s to arrive at and then enforce decisions, the top-down efforts of the regional ANC and state institutions such as the TRC could not reinforce the efforts of any local leadership dedicated to conflict resolution. After the TRC came and went from the Vaal there was no strengthening of local mediation procedures in Sharpeville. The TRC was unable to even begin to create a dialogue on conflict, much less to initiate talks through which disputes (such as those between ANC members in the townships and IFP members in KwaMadala hostel) could be resolved by means other than violence. The TRC never saw this as part of its remit, but it might have expected that the conditions in certain communities were not very conducive to its message and sought to create contingency plans accordingly.

The continued militarization of youth is by no means unique to Sharpeville but is documented for the whole of South Africa. Seasoned South Africa observers will be familiar with stories like that of Dennis Moerane from the press, the radio, books, and will probably hardly have raised an eyebrow during my narrative, such is the routinization of violence in the country. Yet these stories need to be told in order to inject a little more reality into debates about dealing with the violence of the apartheid and post-apartheid era, even if they take the shine off the TRC and refocus attention elsewhere. This institution is widely praised abroad and in international conferences on post-conflict reconstruction and reconciliation around the globe, while being largely peripheral to the lives of those living in townships wracked by revenge killings.

After I had closed my notebook, we had drained our coffee cups and our interview was over, the Reverend Moerane gave me a weary look and said: 'I cannot sleep in Sharpeville because of the gunshots at night. The youth are dehumanized. They are like animals, like monsters now. So the revenge continues.'

CHAPTER 7

RECONCILIATION WITH A VENGEANCE

> Punishment is good. Victims go and watch and they are happy. It prevents further crime. If a person is committing a crime, then the people can say, 'I'll take you to the *imbizo* (isiZulu for "court" or "meeting"),' and the criminal will stop ... The law is the law, and it will stay the law. Duma Joseph Motluong, Secretary, Boipatong Residents Against Crime
>
> (Personal interview, Boipatong, 30 January 1997)

> At no stage since the establishment of the colonial state has there been a single, generally accepted adjudicative and enforcement infrastructure that accommodated the needs of the indigenous population. This milieu led to a plurality of both adjudicative and policing structures and practices which developed and co-existed with varying degrees of compatibility and friction.
>
> Sandra Burman and Wilfried Schärf (1990:735)

A SHORT HISTORY OF LEGAL PLURALISM IN SOUTH AFRICA

This chapter examines the relationship between post-apartheid human rights talk and a township justice institution in Boipatong, an African township adjacent to Sharpeville (Map 3). The two townships are only separated by a stinking municipal dump, but the kinds of legal practices one finds in each are very distinct. Specifically, Boipatong has a community court which adjudicates in local disputes and this township is not marred by the wild justice prevailing in Sharpeville.

Before we go on to look at another case of how urban Africans arrive at an understanding and practice of justice different to that found at the national level, it is important to locate township courts in urban African neighborhoods within a wider historical context of legal pluralism in South Africa. A common understanding in the social history literature asserts that the continual emergence of retributive institutions is an attempt at social ordering in the context of social fragmentation and alienation caused by conditions of modernity. At least since the end of the nineteenth century, local justice institutions have been concerned with countering the destabilizing anonymity of urban life and creating a basis for association in urban communities which transcends traditional loyalties to ethnic groups and chiefs.

This persuasive explanation of 'rough justice' focuses upon the efforts of urban Africans to create new forms of social control in the context of large-scale social upheaval. The language of vengeance uses an image of justice to construct a public (albeit male) space in general, as courts dealt with many functions other than the strictly 'legal' (Hund and Kotu-Rammopo 1983:189). Local justice has for over a hundred years, in various ways, encapsulated the desire of urban Africans to impose some kind of order on township life in the context of migration, forced removals, rapidly changing employment patterns, housing problems and social processes which produce a strain on kinship and other forms of affinity, mutuality and reciprocity.

Urban courts in black areas emerged as a form of decentralized self-governance in the late nineteenth century. A court is referred to as an *imbizo* in isiZulu, or *kgotla* [plural *lekgotla*[1]] in Sesotho. Township courts of the second half of the twentieth century have their historical antecedents in new forms of social ordering which were set up in townships, mines, prisons and hostels as responses to the radically new urban social conditions created by the Witwatersrand gold rush of 1886. Those most likely to take disputes to the *imbizo* were the members of the lowest socio-economic classes: African migrants and a new class of landless wage laborers, a marginalized lumpenproletariat according to Hund and Kotu-Rammopo (1983:190).

Charles van Onselen (1982) has written lucidly about this early period of industrialization and urbanization on the Reef (around Johannesburg), and has usefully documented the 1890–99 social movement of the 'Ninevites'; predominantly Zulu bandits who combined to form a criminal army. Van Onselen stresses the importance of gangs in imposing a disciplinary code on their members through their own courts which mirrored those of the white system. Local courts in the newly urban environments of the hostels, mine compounds and prisons challenged a repressive white state, but did so within the state paradigm, with their own 'magistrates', 'judges', 'prosecutors' and 'jurymen' (1982:182). There were close associations between gangs and courts. The Ninevites created a network of local authority through courts and military structures which at one point, argues van Onselen, threatened the very existence of the white political economy, though in the end it was crushed militarily.

From this early instance onwards, we see that local or customary justice is not wholly autochthonous and the product of isolation. In contrast, it has been, at different historical junctures, constrained, repressed and even promoted by the South African state.[2] The state has attempted to bolster and dismantle forms of local justice at various moments, depending on its assessment of the threat posed by the autonomy of locally constituted legal authorities.

Out of the violent fits and starts of late nineteenth-century South African society, the state ushered in a period of routinization and regulation of local institutions. A watershed in this process was the Native Administration Act 38 of 1927 which created a dual judicial system that lasted into the 1990s.[3] On the one side of the racial divide, there were Magistrates' Courts and the Supreme Court based on Roman Dutch law for whites. For Africans, chiefs' courts upholding 'black law and custom' were set up or officially recognized, and this allowed a certain independence in dealing with matters of private law. The black legal system was not formally under the Department of Justice, but the Department of Co-operation and Development which handled a wide range of 'black affairs'.

Despite the formal judicial segregation promulgated by the 1927 Act, there were a number of lines of connection between the two systems. Above the chiefs' courts were 'Commissioners' Courts' and Courts of Appeal which did not apply customary law but instead followed the procedure governing white magistrates' courts. The two systems linked up at the top of the hierarchy, as appeals from African Appeals Courts could be taken to the Appellate Division of the Supreme Court, which had ultimate jurisdiction over all Africans.

Urbanization in the 1940s and an increase in violent crime from a new gang culture of *tsotsis* (gang members) led to a widening and deepening of popular policing and vigilantism. This was tolerated by the state due to a lack of adequate provision of formal township policing. The Civilian Protection Service in the West Rand townships, for instance, was manned by local residents but was formally sanctioned and administered by the state. It operated until 1947, when it was disbanded. In these same townships, 'Civic Guards' or *bangalalas* ('those who do not sleep') were set up and supported by the white-run Advisory Boards (Seekings 1995:12). Vigilantism was largely inter-generational and also had a class dimension: Civil Guards were more likely to be older, longer-established and better-off male residents trying to impose order on poorer, migrant *lumpenproletariat* young men (Goodhew 1993; Mayer 1971:83). 'Tradition', in this context, became just the opposite of what it claimed to be, and instead involved established urban residents stamping their authority, and occasionally their boots, on the rural migrant poor.

The introduction of the legislative cornerstones of apartheid in the early 1950s was accompanied by a crackdown on local legal autonomy and the banning of the vigilante 'Civilian Guards' in 1952. Less than ten years later, this line of policy was reversed with the Urban Bantu Councils Act (79) of 1961 which replaced Advisory Boards and delegated more legal authority to black councilors – albeit at the discretion of white officials. Urban Bantu Councils facilitated a new command structure which promoted and linked up with local dispute settlement forums and organized them around block or ward committees. In some areas, these ward committees worked in the way the state intended, and in others, they attracted hostility for being puppets of the white regime (Seekings 1995).

We get a sense here of the historical shifts of legal power between white and black administrative structures, of centralizing and pluralizing processes occurring simultaneously, to return to the arguments made earlier. There was flux over the years 1927–1994 and, although the dual legal system was controlled predominantly by white administrators, it did allow Africans certain spaces for autonomous self-governance. Blacks, through their local policing and adjudicative institutions, also claimed and widened this space through resistance and political action.

The late 1970s and early 1980s saw a proliferation of mass-based vigilantism and dispute settlement in local courts and many such courts enjoyed a widespread legitimacy: one survey in the early 1980s showed that 95 per cent of those surveyed in Mamelodi township outside of Pretoria saw the *imbizo* as the best way of achieving access to justice (Hund and Kotu-Rammopo 1983:181). Such a resounding vindication of 'African justice' was not surprising in a context where there was only one understaffed police station and the Commissioners Court served primarily to enforce apartheid legislation and had a reputation for bribery and corruption. Only two per cent of the 250,000 blacks under the Commissioners Court's jurisdiction brought their claims there (183).

The majority of township courts in the late 1970s were politically conservative and patriarchal and were concerned with enforcing intergenerational authority within the urban community. In the literature many are characterized as a form of 'parents' organization' reining in recalcitrant and usually unmarried youth who were deemed 'out of line' or 'undisciplined'. According to one female court leader in Soweto, 'The only medicine for children is *sjambok* thrashing: you must teach them the law' (Seekings 1995:12).

In the aftermath of the 1976 Soweto uprising, the apartheid state initiated limited reforms in a failed quest for legitimacy, and expanded black participation in the administration of township services. More legislation was introduced – in the Community Councils Act (No. 125) of 1977, the failed advisory boards and Urban Bantu Councils were replaced with 'Community Councils'. Greater autonomy was granted to urban black authorities on issues of law and order, justified in National Party language as 'self-responsibility' which every 'civilization' should be accorded. The Act provided for the Minister of Cooperation and Development to grant one community councilor the powers of criminal jurisdiction formerly conferred on a chief or headman under the 1927 Native Administration Act.[4] Links were reinforced with local neighborhood structures carrying out dispute-resolution functions; called 'ward committees', these had been established earlier by the Urban Bantu Councils Act. The Act also provided for the establishing of 'community guards', with the state attempting to legitimate its authority in the name of the 'community'.

In the late 1970s, there was a clear government strategy to co-opt local structures. The Community Councils would call together all the street and ward committees to dispense government orders, and they were also the adjudicative court of last appeal for Africans.[5] Therefore it is misguided to suppose that local justice institutions have always been wholly opposed to apartheid administration. Indeed, Burman and Schärf write of a close association between Community Councils and *lekgotla* ('courts') in 1978–9 in the Western Cape. It should also be pointed out that *lekgotla* in this period referred to a wide range of hybrid legal organizations from 'street committees' to 'courts', with different functions, from settling disputes to welfare counseling. Many local courts at this time were not politically radical, but were officially recognized by the police and the Minister of Justice and had close links to local Community Councils and white-run Administration Boards.

It was not until the mid-1980s that the political radicalization of local courts truly got under way, when power and authority shifted from the conservative, gerontocratic elders to young militants. Youth *lekgotla* had come out of Soweto in the early 1980s, initially working in tandem with the adult *lekgotla* (Hund and Kotu-Rammopo 1983:195). There came a point, however, when youth courts declared unilateral independence from their adult counterparts. Youth courts led by ANC comrades acted independently and challenged the power of elders. Indeed comrades put the shoe on the other generational foot and sat in judgement of their elders. If they found them guilty then they beat them. The comrades rejected backward-looking tribalism in favor of the modernizing language of the liberation struggle.

Increasingly, extra-state forms of dispute settlement and policing began to breach the gap made by the abandonment of state institutions in the townships. Political resistance to apartheid took advantage of the new spaces for local forms of regulation and discipline which were created. During 1985, people's courts were established in nearly every sizeable township in the country, mostly under the guidance of the United Democratic Front and within the structure of the 'civics' run by the South African National Civic Organization, or SANCO. Civics were ANC-aligned structures which originated in the Eastern Cape in the late 1970s as part of local resistance to apartheid, with SANCO furnishing many local government services during the struggle in the 1980s. Civics then spread across the country in the 1980s, providing an alternative (which some saw as revolutionary) to local apartheid government structures, and forming the foundational infrastructure for the United Democratic Front (UDF), launched in 1983.

Police estimated during the Moses Mayekiso Treason Trial in 1988 that there were 400 people's courts in the country.[6] Local forms of justice and regulation were harnessed to the task of reshaping society and implementing a new revolutionary strategy. Local courts became embroiled in the growing conflict in the townships, and were used by ANC comrades to enforce rent and consumer boycotts. 'Popular justice' was generating, for some rather hyperbolic commentators (admittedly with the unfair advantage of hindsight), the 'prefigurative' embryonic institutions of future people's power.[7]

These new revolutionary 'people's courts' were characterized by their delivery of instant and highly punitive redress. Their language of justice was not that of the liberal individual and of human rights, but the 'will of the people'. They showed a disregard for natural rights principles in favor of 'collective judgment', which was loudly proclaimed by a new group of young male political actors who began to operate independently of political movements and parties.[8] They became less and less accountable from 1986 onwards, depending on the region, and became more and more bent on revenge. At times they terrorized their own communities, dispensing lashings and murdering so-called 'sell-outs' by the horrific public spectacle of 'necklacing'.[9] A just war fought by unjust means reinforced the power of comrades at the local level, but over the long term undermined the legitimacy of community justice and damaged the liberation struggle.

The rise of so-called township justice led to a fierce campaign of opposition from the Ministry of Justice, which criminalized membership in people's courts, and in practice banned them. The police smashed up courts in operation and court leaders were detained, prosecuted and often jailed.[10] Urban courts were virtually wiped out by 1988; in that year the security police chief boasted 'the almost total elimination of the so-called people's courts' (*Citizen* 25 August 1988, quoted in Seekings 1995:19) Operations remained minimal until restrictions were lifted in February 1990, with the unbanning of the ANC, UDF, PAC and other liberation organizations. The UDF revived courts once again in 1990 under the auspices of civics, but this time it was more careful, and encouraged the drawing up of, and adherence to, a code of conduct for each court.

Since the 1994 multiracial elections, there has been a limited revival of township courts. The township courts of the 1990s are both different and similar to their predecessors in significant ways. Post-1994 structures combine the elder male urban traditionalism of the 1970s and certain popular court elements from the 1980s. Interestingly, only *Umkhonto we Sizwe* (MK) cadres, the most disciplined and trained element of the *amaqabane* or comrades, are often incorporated into the structures. Many MK combatants were out of the country receiving military training elsewhere in Southern Africa or Eastern Europe when the worst excesses of the 'popular courts' were committed in the mid-1980s.

Historically, local courts were conservative and patriarchal organizations which grew up as a response to the repressive and destructive political economy of apartheid, but were transformed by the liberation struggle in the 1980s. In the present environment they find themselves still responding to the blighted economy of townships and the criminality it engenders, but in a different national political context. In the years immediately after the 1994 elections, they were seen as out of step with the new 'human rights culture' and more humanistic forms of social regulation.

Yet national leaders promote the new language of human rights in an inauspicious moment, when the repressive strictures have been lifted and the country is in the grip of a massive crime wave, as is common in countries emerging from authoritarian rule. This crime occurs in the context of a creaking judicial and policing infrastructure and a lack of legitimacy. Before 1994, police and justice institutions were keen enforcers of an institutionalized bureaucratic framework of racial discrimination. Police were concerned with liquor or pass raids or suppressing dissident political activity; the judiciary largely upheld apartheid legislation and blacks were excluded from an inaccessible and expensive national criminal justice which drew upon an alien moral code.[11] This legacy cannot be swept aside easily. Magistrates' courts are still seen as the domain of institutionalized white power. In 1997, 62 per cent of judges, magistrates and state advocates were white (Stack 1997:19).

South Africa has one of the world's most liberal constitutions but also one of the highest indexes of socio-economic inequality,[12] where 50 per cent of the population is classed as living in poverty (SAIRR 1998:411). The nineteen million black poor have little access to state institutions generally and especially to the justice system, which has been structured to serve the needs of the white population for decades. As one commentator put it, South Africa has a Bill of Rights like a Mercedes-Benz with a justice machinery like a Volkswagen Beetle.[13] Access to justice for the black majority is not dramatically different from the apartheid days, mostly for want of resources and infrastructure, rather than lack of political will.

The vast majority of black defendants in criminal trials still have no legal representation even though this right is enshrined in the Bill of Rights of the 1996 Constitution.[14] The funds made available by the Treasury to the Legal Aid Board's rose by 40 per cent a year between 1994 and 1997, but demand still outstrips supply; in the 12 months up to March 1997, the Board was besieged by 125,000 applications for 'constitutional' legal aid, 115,000 of which it accepted, leading to a parliamentary justice committee inquiry. Some 29,000 people languished in prison awaiting trial in 1996, out of a total prison population of 120,000; this is in a country of a little more than 41 million. South Africa has among the highest incarceration rates in the world. One suggestion to the parliamentary justice committee from legal commentator Dennis Davis (*Mail and Guardian* 27 April 1997) was the obvious but important point that the country needs a public defender network: there were only ten public defenders in the whole country in 1997. They have an average age of 22, six months' experience and earn low salaries (*Mail and Guardian* 11 April 1997).

The justice system has been paralyzed by its own internal transformation, involving the unification of nine previously separate police agencies. The Justice and Safety and Security Ministries have encouraged a move from a confession-based to an evidence-based criminal justice system. Police are being trained more thoroughly to undertake time-consuming forensic work, rather than rely upon confessions, too many of which have been extracted under duress, and even torture.[15] While this organizational restructuring draws on huge resources, the crime figures continue to soar and South Africa is a much more violent place than it was even during the high point of political resistance to apartheid in the mid-1980s: in 1986 there were 9,913 murders but in 1997 there were 24,588 (SAIRR 1998:20).

Johannesburg and its surroundings are the epicenter of this storm. According to the Human Sciences Research Council, in 1996–7 the province of Gauteng led the country in rapes reported (12,938), thefts of motor vehicles (54,086), vehicle hijackings (that is, with the owner in the car at the time of theft – 7,612) and robbery (31,305) (SAIRR 1998:29–47). In a survey of police stations by the main daily Johannesburg paper, *The Star*, in 1997 it was reported that there were on average 14 car hijackings per day in the area, with over half occurring in Soweto (not, as many whites had assumed, in downtown Johannesburg) (*Star* 9 May 1997). Police ineffectiveness is legendary: only 50 per cent of murders were solved in 1995 (Stack 1997:7). Not surprisingly,

Gauteng showed the highest level of support for vigilante action against criminals (SAIRR 1998:38).

Public disillusionment with the criminal justice system has led to even more worrying (especially for the state) movements than urban courts. In August 1996, the violent vigilante group PAGAD (People Against Gangsterism and Drugs) based in Cape Town rose to national prominence by challenging, or, more accurately, summarily killing,[16] drug dealers in the Cape Flats.[17] The seeds of PAGAD had been sown in 1980s neighborhood watch schemes in middle-class Muslim areas, and it also had origins in a small militant Muslim organization called *Qibla*, which has close links with the Pan Africanist Congress. According to Jeppie (1999) the rise of PAGAD is linked to both local factors, such as the crisis of leadership within the Western Cape Muslim community, and national factors, such as the perception that post-apartheid governments were soft on crime (for example, with the abolition of the death penalty and promotion of 'reconciliation'). In eight months in 1996, PAGAD staged 112 marches to the homes of alleged drug dealers and in six months of 1997 it carried out 71 drive-by shootings, petrol bombings and hand-grenade attacks (SAIRR 1998:57). According to Jeppie (1999:10), during 1998, at least 225 people died as a result of 'urban terrorism' in the greater Cape Town area, much of it related to the conflict within the Muslim community between gang leaders and PAGAD.

With the rise to national prominence of vigilante groups such as PAGAD, there has been great pressure on ANC governments to find new ways of making crime-ridden communities feel more involved in issues of law and order. In formal policy-making (although police on the ground were ignoring official policy), this never extended to integrating local forms of justice. The first post-apartheid Justice Ministry under Dullah Omar maintained an ambivalent position towards local courts, generally perceiving them as undesirable, slightly embarrassing and conservative organizations. However, Justice Department officials did not have the luxury of doing without urban courts and the like in the context of a crisis of crime and policing in the townships. There have been a few experiments (in Guguletu and Alexandra townships) in bringing community courts and local policing mechanisms within the ambit of the Justice Ministry, but most still remain outside. The thinking within the ministry on what to do with popular justice institutions is revealed in a number of 'Position Papers' on the subject commissioned by the Ministry's Planning Unit in 1997. One of these, entitled *Popular Participation in the Administration of Justice*, concluded: 'Township justice structures have never felt the need to conceal the fact that the right to judge others is a manifestation of power, local political power. This clearly does not sit well with the new social contract and the Bill of Rights' (Frank et al. 1997:20)

In another paper, by Wilfried Schärf, the author argued that on balance, 'community courts' were prone to abuses and contravened section 34 of the 1996 Constitution, the clause devoted to rights and access to justice (1997:22–33). He noted that although a Ministry of Justice discussion document in 1996 on community courts recommended granting them limited criminal jurisdiction, the draft legislation for the Community Courts Act modeled them instead on small claims courts. The paper by Frank et al. (1997) actively recommended this claims court option and asserted that the incorporation of township and rural courts into the formal structure were not feasible since there were just too many of them. Integrating an extra 1,500–2,000 judicial institutions into an already creaking judicial structure would simply be too difficult, given the available resources.

Instead of finding a way of incorporating informal courts and policing structures into the formal system, the government relied upon the National Crime Prevention Strategy (NCPS). The NCPS, introduced in 1996, was an interdepartmental project including Defence, Justice Intelligence and Welfare Departments. Much was made of the NCPS's engagement with the public: its stated aims were to encourage 'popular participation', and create 'strategic partnerships between state and civil society'. Township and rural courts were largely excluded from such partnerships; the NCPS bypassed them and worked through two wholly new local channels: a lay assessors' scheme and 'Community Policing Forums'.

Lay assessors were introduced under the 1991 Magistrates' Court Amendment Act. In the apartheid past, there had only been white juries and they were abolished in 1969, meaning that in lower courts all authority rested with the magistrate. In 1994, in a pilot project in Cape Town, nine lay assessors were appointed to Cape Town's magistrates' courts and this initiative was then spread around the country.

By 1999, the lay assessors' scheme had completely broken down in many areas (especially in criminally high-achieving Johannesburg), and was only functioning in pockets of Cape Town, Nelspruit and Pretoria. Justice Ministry papers recognized the existing opposition and ambivalence felt by magistrates, who protested that the lay assessors had no training or expertise. A magistrate could be outvoted by two lay assessors, and only a few magistrates to date have ever appointed two, most of them sticking to a token one. Research by the Law, Race and Gender Unit suggests that assessors have made little impact on either the quality of justice or popular legitimacy (Frank et al. 1997:16).

Community Policing Forums were set up in 1994 by the first post-apartheid government as a way of making the police seem more accountable to the community, and to create more legitimacy for the criminal justice system and – importantly for our discussion – to eradicate township courts and vigilantes by drawing them into formal structures.[18] At Community Policing Forums, the police would meet with community members, hear their problems, explain their own efforts and come to a common understanding of how to fight crime together. Communities were to become the eyes and ears of the police, and in certain areas this has happened. Forums were also the structure which would integrate all local mechanisms for fighting crime – whether ANC Special Defense Units, ad hoc vigilantes or township courts.

At the end of his Position Paper, Schärf (1997) concluded that community courts should *not* (his emphasis) be incorporated into the state court hierarchy, but should become subcommittees of Community Policing Forums. This is the general view within the higher echelons of the Ministry of Justice and one which, as we will see, magistrates have upheld when hearing cases of abuse brought by victims of punishment meted out by a township court. Yet the Community Policing Forum strategy has met with mixed results. There has been a tendency among police officers to show 'limited commitment to substantial change' and to see community participation as an irritating waste of time, as politically-driven social work which detracts from the main aim of catching criminals (Schärf 1997:21).

In sum, we can characterize the policies of post-apartheid governments towards informal justice as centralizing. Centralizing and unifying justice institutions, and ironing out local legal systems, is a common strategy adopted by post-colonial governments in sub-Saharan Africa. Martin Chanock observes that post-colonial state elites have pursued a unitary model of the western state, not simply because they are mimicking the West, but because 'legal forms enable particular people to gain particular types of power over others, and particular sorts of economic advantage' (1998:221). Both civic nation-building and the centralization of the state administrative apparatus are vehicles for the realization of the interests of the main beneficiaries of decolonization, a new legal-bureaucratic elite.

Local justice in Boipatong

The small Vaal township of Boipatong is one of the most industrialized places on earth. It is wedged between Sharpeville, the municipal garbage dump, the massive ISCOR iron and steel works, Consolidated Wire Industries, Van Leer packaging and the Cape Gate canning factory. Off in the distance loom the cloudy smoke stacks of SASOL, the

South African State Oil company. Its population numbers (now at about 40,000) exploded in the 1960s as it became a dormitory for the industrial army laboring in the huge surrounding factories. Like other urbanized areas of Africa, it is a heterogeneous linguistic mixture, including speakers of Sesotho, Shangaan, isiZulu, Pedi, and Setswana who all manage to communicate using a township creole, although Sesotho is dominant. Further, Boipatong is a class and status conglomeration of wealthy professionals, industrial laborers, domestic workers, seasonal migrants and a large number of unemployed.

Like Sharpeville, it holds a special place in the history of violence in South Africa, as the peace talks between Nelson Mandela and F W de Klerk were broken off in June 1992 after armed Inkatha members, allegedly with police accompaniment, streamed across from KwaMadala hostel and arbitrarily slaughtered over 40 residents in Boipatong's squatter settlement called Slovo Park.[19] Boipatong is also similar to Sharpeville, in that the understanding of justice as requiring punishment is hegemonic, but it is crucially different in one major respect: there exist institutions in Boipatong which place checks on revenge and channel vengeance into a more mediated (although still violent) form of retribution. The language of vengeance is very similar in the two townships, but it is embedded in different institutional contexts. In Sharpeville, there are only weak church and political party structures which have not so far been able to restrain a cycle of violent revenge. In Boipatong, there is the kind of overarching 'legitimate community institution' to which Mr Mothibedi referred in the last chapter – a local court – which has the coercive capacity to protect former apartheid councilors and enforce a more lasting peace than is the case in surrounding townships.

It is important to distinguish between townships like Boipatong, where the neighborhood courts, or *imbizo*, have a fairly widespread legitimacy, and townships such as Sharpeville, where feuding armed gangs nominally affiliated to political parties continue to undermine the possibility of any overarching justice structure. Nevertheless, we should not romanticize or reify the concept of community, since it is the product of conditions of the present, rather than something handed down from the mists of the traditional past. Who represents the community varies according to context, history and the position of the speaker. Communities are not homogeneous, and community justice is not a stable, given concept but is reworked in the cut and thrust of local politics.

The notion of the community is, and has always been, contentious in the townships of South Africa (Seekings 1995). It became heavily politicized during the years of anti-apartheid struggle and came to represent a cornerstone in the revolutionary ideology of local ANC cadres opposed to the authoritarian state. An ability to speak and act on behalf of the community represented a key element in ANC comrades' effort to create and reinforce their structures of social control.

In the post-apartheid era, the concept of community justice is being reinvented by local residents, primarily in order to cope with a crime wave and acute problems of social order. The view that justice is best administered by 'the community', not the state, is now reinforced by the new conditions of criminality and the limited resources of the state to deal with them. By emphasizing the continued importance of retributive justice within their definition of community, residents position themselves in opposition to reconciliatory human rights talk.

Residents of Boipatong mediate and adjudicate many disputes with little reference to the national legal system or bodies such as the TRC, which was seen by local people I interviewed as weak, ineffectual and as a 'sell-out'. The low level of reparations for victims and the generous amnesties granted to perpetrators combined to strengthen the view that the TRC's version of human rights violated perceived, everyday principles of justice. Instead of appealing to human rights commissions to solve problems of social order, local adjudication occurs through the daily court referred to as the *imbizo*. This local forum mainly deals with petty crimes and domestic disputes, but its presence also has implications for the legacy of political violence.

Intriguingly, the Boipatong court has protected black councilors who participated in the apartheid local government structure – the Transvaal Provincial Administration between 1988 and 1990. In 1984 during the 'Vaal Uprising', three councilors had been burnt alive by militant crowds and attacks on local government figures continued into the 1990s. In 1992, the mayor of Lekoa Council, Esau Mahlatsi, was murdered by anti-apartheid militants. Now Boipatong is unique in the Vaal in that apartheid-era councilors can live relatively free of intimidation and this is largely the result of a local legal institution founded upon principles of retributive justice. The Boipatong court's protection of former 'apartheid collaborators' is a concrete example of the arguments made in chapters 1 and 6: that principles of punitive justice may lead to reconciliation in the long run.

In Boipatong, we see one of the many ironies of human rights talk in South Africa; where the dominant local language of vengeance is ostensibly opposed to the TRC's emphasis on forgiveness and restoration, and has more of an affinity to the punitive framework of criminal justice, local justice in practice ends up carrying out many of the objectives of the TRC and other nation-building institutions by actually mediating in cases of which originate in apartheid-era political conflict.

Justice as practiced in Boipatong provides concrete evidence, in my view, for the assertions that a retributive understanding of human rights can provide a meaningful basis for creating legitimacy for legal institutions, and that retributive justice can achieve many of the aims of peaceful co-existence sought by advocates of reconciliation and forgiveness.

LOCAL COURTS AND THE STATE: AMBIVALENT RELATIONS

> The *imbizo* was formed to bring peace, against those that thought they were above the law. We ran to the police to solve the crime, but they couldn't catch the criminals, so we took the burden from them. We used tribal law to solve the crime.
>
> Duma Joseph Motluong, Boipatong Residents Against Crime
> (Personal interview, 30 January 1997)

The Boipatong local court has always occupied an ambiguous position with regard to state legality, not quite being 'outside the law' nor wholly integrated within its formal structures. The *imbizo* was formed in 1994, after a public meeting called by the local civic association (SANCO) where residents decided they wanted a community court. Township representatives were sent to seek approval from the white-run magistrate's court in Vereeniging and the police station in Vanderbijlpark, instead of the black-run township police station at Houtkop, Sebokeng.

Imbizo officials take pride in their association with the police and show visitors a written letter of approval from Capt. Du Plessis of the Vanderbijlpark police. Written in their constitution are the aims 'to build trust between police and the community' and to 'walk hand in hand with the police'. *Imbizo* members and the police often agree a division of labor where they take over cases which have also been denounced to the police and a docket taken out. White police, with a respect for decentralization and local tradition that the British colonial administrator Lord Lugard[20] would have admired, often drop a case if it has been heard at the *imbizo* level. More often than not, *imbizo* members wait for the outcome of the police investigation, before taking up a case, if it is unresolved. There is a constant traffic of memoranda back and forth between *imbizo* and police officials.

The *imbizo* performs a bridging role between the police and former anti-apartheid activists as it is integrated into the structure of the executive committee, or civic, of Boipatong. This township civic is itself part of the national body of civic associations, SANCO. Many *imbizo* members are also members of SANCO. SANCO entered a period of confusion in the immediate post-apartheid years as the 1995 local government elections brought many ANC civic leaders into positions of authority on the newly democratic Vaal Metropolitan Council. During fieldwork, both Vaal Metropolitan Council and SANCO structures operated alongside one another, but SANCO was in steep decline. SANCO now has a limited role in conflict resolution: it used to be involved deeply in resolving local disputes, but it is no longer the final authority. After being heard at the *imbizo*, a dispute can be taken to SANCO, but higher still is the Vaal Metropolitan Council.

The immediate post-apartheid era was one of turmoil in the tiers of regulation and governance above the community, in both criminal (i.e. policing, which was going through its own radical transformations) and civil institutions. Where the division of responsibilities became unclear, this actually meant more power for township structures in the short term, as one *imbizo* member asserted: 'We are the bottom line.'

PATRIARCHY AND PROCEDURE OF THE BOIPATONG COURT

As in many other locales, the neighborhood court has a strong patriarchal character,[21] which is sanctioned by the founding myth of the Boipatong Residents Against Crime (BRAC). BRAC was set up in April 1994 as the first multi-racial elections approached. In the light of the previous chapter, it is perhaps appropriate that township mythology counterposes the social ordering functions of the Boipatong imbizo to the mayhem emanating from neighboring Sharpeville. The founding myth – which is not *wrong*, but is a partial truth with ideological overtones – involves a notorious incident in early 1994 where the Germans gang of Sharpeville (which readers will remember was the gang that 'allowed' the return of Dennis Moerane to their territory in Rooisten section) stopped a bus full of children from Lebohang High School on a field trip to Pretoria zoo. The gang members removed eleven girls from the bus and took them to Sharpeville church where they raped them until the next morning.

Boipatong Residents Against Crime came into being as a vigilante group dedicated to waging war on the Germans gang. The threat of public disorder prompted the police to arrest some of the gang members and defuse the situation. Almost all township courts share a common myth of origin where they were set up to protect young girls from young male rapists of an adjacent community. This is the mythical charter which sanctions their patriarchal nature,[22] since it creates an image of community threatened by untamed sexual violence and in dire need of patriarchal authority. Reviewing the national literature, it soon becomes apparent that the control of young men provides much of the symbolism and *raison d'être* of urban courts. In the early years the Boipatong *imbizo* regularly patrolled at night and imposed strict curfews on young men. The overall impetus of the court is inter-generational control; clamping down on recalcitrant male youth generally, and reinforcing parental and male household authority in disputes between family members. In the majority of family disputes, there was a tendency to treat the male head of household as legally responsible for enforcing court decisions on other members of the household, and especially on wives and children.

The permanent members of the court fall into two groups; older men over 45, many of whom were former convicted *com-tsotsis* or 'gangsters', and younger men between 20 and 30, most of whom were MK combatants of the armed wing of the ANC. Nearly all the men are ANC sympathizers and most are card-carrying party members. There are a few members of the Pan Africanist Congress and even former members of the National Party, but none from the IFP. The composition of the post-1994 *imbizo* is a fusion of two models of township justice: the patrimonial and gerontocratic courts of the 1970s and the popular revolutionary courts of the 1980s. The very existence of the court is due to a kind of reconciliation at the level of the township since it required a combination of two groups who were often violent political adversaries during the height of the liberation struggle in the mid-1980s: the conservative old men and the revolutionary 'young lions'.

The personal profile of the *imbizo* secretary, Mr Duma Motluong, is characteristic of many of the older men. Now a mechanic in his fifties, Mr Motluong is open, and even a little humorous, about having been a former petty criminal. He was detained in jail while awaiting trial, but received several suspended sentences between 1968 and 1974 for stealing mechanics' tools and household items. He was never taken to an *imbizo* or local court as they did not exist then. He is a devout member of the Zionist Christian Church, or ZCC, a form of 'African Christianity' popular among rural people (especially of the Northern Province) and the economically marginal urban poor. The ZCC forms an interesting counterpoint to our previous reflections on the progressive Catholic and orthodox Protestant churches of the urban black middle classes. In contrast to the anti-apartheid agitation of the progressive ecumenical alliance of the South African Council of Churches (SACC), the ZCC always preached a conservative message of compliance with apartheid political authorities. In the post-apartheid era, the national executive of the ZCC compliantly campaigned for the new project of forgiveness and reconciliation.

Yet the ZCC does not just blow with the prevailing ideological winds. As Jean Comaroff (1985) has demonstrated for other historical periods, members of Zionist sects have taken a more resistant stance to political authority. Since the early 1990s, rank and file ZCC members seem to privilege a punitive ethic which contradicts the governmental language of reconciliation. The religious dimension should not, therefore, be absent from our understanding of the local court, as the Boipatong court contains a significant number of Zionist Christian Church members. As a rule, then, we could say that the TRC's reconciliation talk appealed more to mainstream Catholics and Protestants of the urban middle class, but was further from the ethical and moral frameworks found among the rural poor and industrial classes, from whom Zionists and Pentecostals draw a large part of their constituency.

TOWNSHIP COURT PROCEDURE

Every day at 4–5pm (weekdays and weekends), disputes are brought before the 30–40 men of the *imbizo*.[23] Elder patriarchs cross-examine witnesses, led by the fearsome Chairman Adons Ramaele, an elder of 78 years from rural Lesotho with a full white beard and booming voice. At the *imbizo*, he would brandish his cane with dramatic effect while carrying out a withering line of inquisition in order to get at 'the truth'. I saw quite a few defendants collapse and confess during his persistent haranguing. The stocky Mr Ramaele is like a wrathful Old Testament patriarch, who would brook no evasions, catch all liars, excoriate all fools and punish all those deemed 'guilty' to the fullest extent of his powers.

The court hears many domestic violence cases, cases of petty theft, assault, unpaid debts, some rape cases, but not murders. The majority of cases involve assault, usually in illicit drinking houses, or *shebeens*, or on the street at weekends. Most victims and accused admitted to being under the influence of drink. In about half of the cases I heard, an assault took place between a man and woman and their proxies. The court would hear extended testimony from the applicants and witnesses, and court officials would examine reports from medical professionals to establish the extent of injuries.

Tuesdays and Thursdays are 'Ladies Days' and I was surprised (given the male-dominated nature of the *imbizo*) at how many women brought their cases to the football stadium. In 1996–7, one female ANC activist endorsed the court saying, 'If you're guilty, then they beat you and then they take you to hospital and after that I tell you, you will never do it again'. One explanation for the court's legitimacy among many women was the lack of other inexpensive alternatives for justice. The court, despite its patriarchal nature, did occasionally act against rapists and men who persistently beat wives or lovers.

Court officials on the other hand insisted that they would not hear 'love problems', adultery, and crimes of passion, for instance. They would often get round this injunction by reclassifying aspects of the crime as a non-love crime; for example in one case, a woman attacked her husband's lover and the case was heard as an offence of 'possession of a knife'. 'Love problems' were usually resolved by establishing the blame of both parties and pressuring them to sign a 'peace agreement' that they would not engage in any further acts of abuse (verbal or physical) against one another. The *imbizo* came under increasing pressure to mediate and adjudicate in 'home affairs', and it increasingly began to take on domestic cases, which, as we will see later, would precipitate its sudden (but possibly temporary) demise.

Those found guilty are subjected to two related forms of justice: restorative justice, which usually takes the form of a pledge to improve social relations, and compensation through monetary payments or free labor. This was mostly and commonly deployed in intra-family disputes where no physical harm had been done, for example, where a young male was fined his monthly wage of 800 Rand (about US$100) after he publicly insulted his grandmother.

The *imbizo* also relies to a great degree upon retributive justice, which frequently requires a public beating in the football stadium with whips, *sjamboks* (quirts, or mule whips), and golf clubs with the heads removed. The two categories of justice are interlinked, as the former is backed up with the threat of the latter. If repayments are not made, or a peace agreement is violated, then the transgressor could be whipped or, in local parlance, 'given a flander'.

Punishment is a bloody and violent public spectacle attended by victims. Those punished are meant to leave both publicly chastised and also having paid in full for their transgressions. The purpose of the penalty is to cancel out the crime and therefore beating is meant to end all grudges and animosities. The sentencing is seen as proportional to the crime and the number of lashes varies from five to about fifty: court members would object to the idea that proportionality was not applied and that they were just engaged in cruelty – as regularly occurs in Sharpeville – for its own sake. In terms of ideology at least, punishment is the physical and proportional enactment of a desire for vengeance (i.e., it is characterized as retribution, not revenge) which has as its main aims deterrence and the canceling of crimes, rather than more 'modern' notions of correction, rehabilitation or moral reform.

Those beaten must sign a consent form, as a number of township courts around the country have been prosecuted in magistrates' courts. Beatings can be quite severe and those beaten often require hospital treatment. There is a car standing by to take them to the local hospital.

Despite this, the 'guilty' often consent to a public flogging by members of their own township rather than face being handed over to the white-run Vanderbijlpark police station and face possible torture, police-cell beatings and a jail sentence from the white magistrate. Many consent to the beating as they see it as the more desirable of a set of undesirable options. One *imbizo* member explained it to me thus,

> Many ask for the punishment. They say, 'I don't want to be prosecuted because then I'll be in danger'. It's better to have it out and have sore buttocks ... People feel satisfied, because jail is a long time and they prefer to be beaten and then go back to work.

The punitive nature of the Boipatong *imbizo* drew attention from the national press in 1995, when a man hanged himself after receiving a summons from the court regarding his marital problems. Boipatong was pilloried in Johannesburg's quality press as having a 'kangaroo court' administering 'jungle justice' (*Weekend Star* 8 April 1995), but the *imbizo* nevertheless received the full blessings of SANCO civic association chair David Mthimkulu and Vaal South African Police Service (SAPS) spokesman Lt-Colonel Piet van Deventer. The media lost this first round of hostilities in 1995, but would return to deal a more severe blow to the urban court in 1998.

TRIBAL LAW?

The *imbizo* draws its legitimacy from the claim that it is an expression of traditional authority and customary law. Its members assert that it is 'tribal law' and in so doing they draw an oppositional boundary against all forms of extra-community justice, including both the criminal courts and international human rights. Tribalism is the ideology of community sovereignty which jealously guards the right to punish.

The claim to be following tribal law is based upon distinctive procedures and the *imbizo*'s approach to 'truth'. Members are proud of the fact that there is no escape for suspects through bail until they have been formally tried. Bail has been a highly politicized issue during the post-1994 crime wave, with populist politicians both inside and outside the ANC calling for a toughening up on existing legislation. There is strong support for haranguing and even physically mistreating the accused first in order to establish their innocence or guilt and opposition to the idea that the accused have rights (for example, to protection, to silence) as promulgated by human rights organizations. As one of the Ministry of Justice Position Papers on community courts suggested, 'the legal subject is thus not the atomized individual, protected by the state as epitomized by the Bill of Rights, but one embedded in "the community", narrowly constructed' (Schärf 1997:19). In Boipatong, and even among those who were uncomfortable with the *imbizo,* everyone I interviewed supported the suspension of the rights of accused individuals in favor of 'community' interests.

Unlike a magistrate's court, however, individual leaders like Chairman Ramaele do not sentence those found guilty – responsibility is passed to the collective. As Duma Motluong put it to me: 'We don't decide. We ask the people at the stadium and they decide, or their family decides' (personal interview, 30 January 1997). *Imbizo* men take turns carrying out the beatings, with each administering only a few of the lashes, so that it cannot be said that only one man is responsible, or that he was just doing it to settle a personal score. In this sense, the punishment meted out fulfils some of Nozick's criteria of retribution rather than revenge, as does the claim by members I interviewed that they experience no pleasure in beating offenders.

Unlike the national criminal justice system, sentencing by the *imbizo* avoids incarceration. Yet there are areas of overlap: both magistrates' courts and the township court focus on punishment in their pursuit of redress. And the systems attribute different meanings to the act of punishment, since beatings are a substitute for material compensation, as one *imbizo* member told me: 'Before if you committed a crime, the chief would make you pay cattle. Now people don't have livestock so they must be *sjambokked.*'

The *imbizo* and the TRC uphold markedly different views of the relationship between truth and punishment. The *imbizo* mimics the practice of the police who have relied predominantly on confessions, and in the Vaal, there have been many cases where confessions were beaten, or tortured, out of suspects. Mr Motluong describes to me how the *imbizo* members deal with a criminal who they think has a gun: 'We must hunt him down and catch him and ask where the gun is. If he doesn't say then we will give him lashes. Without punishment he will never talk.' (Personal interview, 30 January 1997)

With this perspective, the *imbizo* members heap disdain upon the amnesty process of the TRC, as they cannot see how it can provide the truth since applicants are never likely to be physically punished. Only through physical duress is the truth likely to emerge, they maintain. In contrast to anonymous encounters between strangers at human rights commissions, *imbizo* members hold that cross-examination from members of the same community always finds out the guilty, and achieves justice through vengeful punishment, rather than 'reconciliation' and amnesty.

Township residents use notions of community and tribe to establish and uphold a discontinuity with national and international law.

They create an image of their own alterity as traditional rural, tribal, pre-modern peoples. Apart from the venerable Chairman Ramaele, however, few have ever seen a rural African farm, and most live a thoroughly urbanized existence with all the accoutrements of modern life. Many of my middle-aged contacts had cars and worked in offices; they carried cell phones, and their children hankered after designer clothes and played their Janet Jackson CDs on impressive hi-fi systems. In the context of a well-established place in modernity, tribalism becomes the ideology of an idealized African community which no longer exists (and probably never did), but which provides the moral authority for local rules and processes. This idealization is contested by different social actors: whereas elite Africans on the Constitutional Court see the 'African community' as a site of forgiveness and benign generosity, township residents see the African community as punitive and unyielding.

The Copperbelt studies in Zambia by the late Bill Epstein are still instructive for understanding urban tribalism in South Africa. Epstein stated that 'the term "tribe" did not carry the same meaning in the towns as it did in the rural areas: "tribalism" in urban and rural contexts related to phenomena of quite different order' (1978:10). The difference was, according to Epstein, the existence of *the state*. He also recognized that all the ambiguities and inconsistencies in the urban social process were expressed in Africans' approach to their tribal identity. In Boipatong, many ambiguities are apparent at first glance, such as the distinctions and similarities between the township court and the criminal justice system. The introduction of human rights discourse as never before into the South African context from the 1990s onwards created new inconsistencies and tensions in the struggle over jurisdictional boundaries between the community and state.

RECONCILIATION VERSUS THE RIGHT TO PUNISH

> In the realm of due process, the state's judicial authorities tend, at least officially, to deplore procedures which flout their own complex rules ... those in authority express hostility to 'rough justice'.
>
> Ray Abrahams (1996:50)

There is a longstanding and implacable enmity towards township courts from the media,[24] the Ministry of Justice and the TRC. Hostile commentators incite a moral panic by characterizing informal courts as overrun by the murderous violence of the lynch mob, which is actually more prevalent in places such as Sharpeville, where there is no township court. In the new political order, township courts are seen as outmoded institutions of the struggle which undermine the rule of law. Moreover, they are an obstruction to the creation of a new democratic order and a culture of rights.

In contrast to the political parties of the ANC and PAC, in the 1980s most politically progressive religious and human rights organizations condemned the punishment ethic of popular courts and their use of the whip and burning tyre 'necklace'. Liberal religious institutions such as the South African Council of Churches denounced township justice as far back as 1977 in statements such as: 'these so-called "courts" have often resulted in barbaric public floggings ... the ghastly actions of these "courts" cannot be condoned in our civilized societies' (*Rand Daily Mail*, 13 April 1977, cited in Hund and Kotu-Rammopo 1983:205). Opposition to local courts was regularly expressed by liberals, for example by MP Helen Suzman, during the debate on the Community Councils Bill in 1977. Because human rights has been seen by politicized Africans as at odds with the punishment of alleged apartheid collaborators,[25] human rights are equated with weakness on issues of social order, as soft on criminals and apartheid-era murderers, and as pro-bail and pro-amnesty for perpetrators.

There are deeper distinctions between popular courts and human rights commissions at the level of value-orientations. Whereas human rights activists look forward to a future of rehabilitation, redemption and reconciliation, retributionists in the townships look back at the past and still feel the burden of a crime that has not been canceled by punishment. There are therefore two very different approaches to history, with the advocates of punishment more likely to adhere to a continuity with the past. This is dangerous to the new and fragile nation-building project: the new historicity of a reconciling political elite. The urban courts and human rights organizations take a different approach to the place of suffering in their construction of justice. In the township court, *lex talionis* rules. Like must be repaid for like, and physical suffering can only be repaid with commensurate physical suffering, or with symbolic suffering in the form of a monetary compensation which stands for physical suffering. Finally, there are differences in their respective approaches to equality: equality of rights and moral worth is a key tenet of Christianity and human rights doctrines, but this principle is fundamentally rejected in *imbizo* procedures, where certain men assume the right denied to others (women, young unmarried men) to apprehend, try, sentence and punish.

Boipatong's own recent history of political violence in the 1990s did not provide fertile ground for the new culture of human rights. In 1992, IFP members streamed across from Kwamadala hostel and arbitrarily slaughtered over 40 Boipatong residents in a massacre which rocked the country and temporarily derailed the peace process. There was strong evidence from dozens of witnesses that the police and South African Defense Force escorted the vigilante killers in armed personnel carriers, but the report by British criminologist Peter Waddington (1992) found no evidence of police or army involvement or complicity in the massacre. The Waddington Commission did not visit the township (partly due to the precarious conditions at the time) and took no testimonies from eyewitnesses, but instead relied solely on the local police force for its evidence. This experience is one of the main reasons why human rights commissions carry a poor reputation in the township; they failed to reveal 'the truth' and to uphold the prosecution of wrongdoers.

PUNISHMENT AND SUFFERING: COMPARING INFORMAL AND OFFICIAL STATE COURTS

> Rather than reject the state, vigilantism commonly thrives on the idea that the state's legitimacy at any point in time depends on its ability to provide citizens with the levels of law and order they demand. Its emergence is often a vote of no confidence in state efficiency rather than in the concept of the state itself ... Vigilantism has been part of [citizens'] efforts to make sense of their lives and maintain some sort of order in the world.
>
> Ray Abrahams, writing on *Sungusungu* vigilantes in Tanzania. (1996:42)

The centrality of retribution in township courts calls for greater attention to 'justice' as understood and practiced by many urban South Africans. A focus on vengeance draws out both the contrasts between human rights talk and local justice, as well as the parallels between the *imbizo* and criminal institutions, which we will turn to now.

The place of 'suffering' in the application of justice highlights the differences and similarities between community justice, criminal law and human rights as reconciliation. The importance granted to suffering as a form of redress in magistrates' decisions resonates with local courts' judgments. Sentencing in common law recognizes retribution but seeks to subdue the 'collective will', and rationalize inchoate passions of hatred and vengeance.[26] Due to their shared valuing of punishment, there are a number of links between local courts and the police. The Boipatong community court is officially recognized by the local magistrate and police station, and the court sends certain types of cases it cannot resolve (e.g. murder and rape) to higher levels of adjudication. It assists the police in apprehending suspects, and hands over those who will not consent to beatings. This connection between systems is not a new development. During the apartheid years, the state at various historical junctures enhanced the integration of a dual system of justice, and at times promoted the setting up of customary courts in rural areas and community courts in the townships.[27]

The centrality of punishment in both formal and informal justice institutions points towards how the relational discontinuities between the two systems might be bridged, and in particular how human rights talk might be made more meaningful for the majority of South Africans. If human rights talk emphasized how justice could be achieved through fair procedure and due process and requiring an appropriate and proportional punishment, then this could have provided a more successful way of linking local understandings of justice to the national transformation of the criminal justice system. Although there are discontinuities between the systems, they are relational and characterized by points of contact and mutual influence. As we have seen, there are certain connections between magistrates' courts and informal township courts and relations between the former white and African sectors have improved since the end of apartheid. Africans are, as we will see later in this chapter, increasingly taking cases to magistrates' courts and arguing them in the language of human rights, but with fair punishment of offenders as their aim. By focussing on the popular appeal of 'just desserts' for offenders as the basis of human rights talk, the post-apartheid state could have found more success in connecting with local values, creating greater legitimacy for middle-level courts and shifting legal practices in the townships further along the continuum from revenge to retribution.

UNINTENDED CONSEQUENCES OF POPULAR JUSTICE

The *imbizo* went beyond just punishing petty crimes and mediating in domestic disputes, to have an impact upon the legacy of political violence. In the post-1994 era, the *imbizo* has acted as a conservative force in clamping down on militant political activities. It has stopped acts of politicized public violence even as it drew expressions of violent justice into its own structures. For instance, *imbizo* members called for curfews which replaced the restrictions set by the ANC comrades. They dismantled barricades and urged youth to stop fighting the police. They came out on the streets and calmed youths who still wanted to *toyi-toyi* (a defiant dance popular in the 1980s) outside the houses of those deemed political 'sell-outs', and threaten to burn them down.

Perhaps most importantly, the urban court in Boipatong has dealt quite successfully with outstanding questions of the political conflicts of the past. It is no coincidence that two former National Party members and councilors from 1988–90 have remained in their homes in the township, whereas other 'apartheid collaborators' have been killed or chased away in other Vaal townships.[28]

During interviews, the former councilors in Boipatong reported that since 1994, they are no longer verbally or physically assaulted and feel protected by the neighborhood court which, they say, is prepared to act punitively against anyone who threatens them. This contrasts strongly with the situation in neighboring townships without local courts such as Sharpeville, where no councilors have returned to their original homes, but are banished to shantytowns or special barbed-wire enclosed camps constructed by the police. The existence of an overarching justice institution in Boipatong, which can negotiate political compromises and enforce retribution, has paradoxically created an environment less conducive to revenge killings.

The unintended consequences of 'popular justice' are worth exploring further. Despite the opposition in Boipatong to the TRC, the local court realizes many of the objectives of human rights institutions around conflict mediation. I hesitate to use the word 'reconciliation' since no one in Boipatong thought that it accurately described the process of co-existence with former 'apartheid collaborators', locally referred to as *mdlwembe*, or 'sell-outs'. Yet it is ironic that a neighborhood court, which portrays itself as a punitive 'tribal' authority and which rejects the TRC's humanitarian view of human rights for a more retributive view of justice, in the end facilitates the kinds of solutions extolled by the TRC. It does so not through notions of reconciliation and redemption derived from Christian ethics, but through patriarchal institutions imbued with an ethic of vengeance which do not shirk physical retaliation against any who flout its decisions.

This evidence seems to both vindicate and challenge the arguments of Alison Renteln (1990), who asserts that the only brake to a cycle of revenge is the likelihood of revenge itself. Similar ideas of vengeance do seem extraordinarily widespread, and have been documented not only in Africa but also among white working-class Americans (Merry 1990). Perhaps we can accept Renteln's insights in this case, without accepting the rest of her argument that *lex talionis* is the only effective basis for a universal theory of human rights. I would not accept, in particular, the decontextualized nature of her arguments: revenge in Sharpeville only begets more revenge since political violence is highly territorialized and fragmented, whereas retributive sentiments in Boipatong are channeled through a single institution which, for all its limitations, at least makes vengeance more predictable and routinized. Renteln's attempt to ground human rights in reciprocal revenge would be more acceptable if she replaced 'revenge' with 'institutionalized retribution'.

JUSTICE AND THE TRC

The history of legal pluralism in South Africa has resulted in a pattern of resistance to state legality external to 'the community'. Local forms of social ordering were constructed in opposition to state forms, and an attitude of wariness prevails. This is not wholly a relationship of resistance, however, and bridges are built on local justice's terms as well, when its own norms and procedures are reinforced and vindicated. When official state ideology has such little bearing upon local formulations of revenge and retributive justice, as occurred with the TRC, then they are rejected and ignored. That historical legacy has not yet been transformed enough in the 'new South Africa' to generate the basis for a different set of relationships between local, national and transnational rule systems, which are still characterized by relational discontinuities.

Reviewing the history of township justice helps us to understand how urban Africans perceive and react to human rights talk and the TRC. The TRC was often blind to these historical factors, and in its urge not to assert a rupture with the apartheid past, acted as if it were in an historical vacuum, and as if all previous forms of ordering and retributive understandings of justice could be swept aside in order to create a new utopia of 'the culture of human rights'. In the TRC's formulation, township courts were part of the violent past and had no place in the new constitutional order. The recommendations in the 1998 TRC Report sought to eradicate informal justice institutions and to dissolve them in favor of the formal criminal justice system.

The *Report* recommended that the Ministry of Justice eradicate physical punishment in chiefs' courts: 'Despite the fact that such courts do not have criminal jurisdiction, the *de facto* position is that, in many areas, this right has been assumed and corporal punishment and illegal sanctions are routinely imposed. This practice must be ended as a matter of urgency' (p. 327). The TRC also urged the state to suppress township courts when it recommended that 'steps be taken to inhibit the reappearance of the "people's court" phenomenon'.

In the light of these recommendations, as argued throughout this book, the TRC should be seen as part of a continuous history of state efforts to centralize and reduce legal pluralism and to transform local notions of justice. For those committed to community justice, however, the TRC was just one more state institution with little legitimacy. The language of vengeance prevalent among urban Africans undermines national attempts to centralize justice using moral injunctions to reconcile and forgive. We can only understand that clash by examining the historical regulatory actions of the state. The largely negative response by those who actually *adjudicate* in townships to the well-meaning reconcilers of the TRC only starts to make sense when we see the TRC as part of a longer struggle between the community and the state over administrative power and judicial autonomy.

These arguments can be applied more widely to other African contexts. In post-conflict situations, states often impose forms of conflict-resolution in a top-down manner and in so doing, usually fail to appeal to local moralities and institutions to create the conditions for peace. This is also the conclusion of Jan Abbink's (1998) paper on the post-conflict EPRF government's efforts at reconciliation in southern Ethiopia, which bypassed local cultural expectations. Government officials would not participate in local rites of reconciliation, involving killing an ox, hanging the fat around the necks of participants, smearing bodies with blood and making speeches upon the hide. These local rituals would end with a collective washing of hands in the ox's stomach contents and the shooting of guns into the earth, but like in South Africa, they occurred outside the national reconciliation project.

Overall, the TRC missed innumerable opportunities to engage with local justice structures, however difficult that may have been. Nevertheless it was vital to have tried, since local courts (as we saw in Boipatong) mediate the conflicts of the apartheid era and therefore facilitate a situation where adversaries do not gun each other down in the street in broad daylight (as happens in neighboring Sharpeville). There is still ongoing political violence from the apartheid era in the Vaal and the rest of South Africa (and especially Kwazulu-Natal). It is not as intense as it was, but it is still a reality in certain areas. There is a range of disjointed peace initiatives which vary from locale to locale. Yet my impression of the TRC was that it was disconnected from most of them. It was certainly irrelevant in mediation between the IFP and ANC in the Vaal, and did nothing to resolve the ongoing tragedy that is Sharpeville.

Most Vaal townships, perhaps with the exception of Sharpeville, are in a slow transition from an ethic of revenge to one of retribution; that is, to a context where conflicts are routinized (even if punishment for transgression remains violent) and the rule of law might actually become meaningful. Local justice cannot be seen for ever as the expression of an absence of a rights culture, but instead should be included in the national project to make it happen. Of course, to just blame the TRC for everything that is wrong with South African justice would be misguided and unfair. The TRC must be seen in the wider context of state unification and centralization, the reform of criminal justice and the rise of new human rights institutions such as the Constitutional Court and Human Rights Commission.

A CODA TO BOIPATONG: HUMAN RIGHTS, LOCAL JUSTICE AND GENDER

Just weeks before I returned to South Africa in November 1998 to catch the fall-out from the publication of the TRC's *Report*, there was upheaval in the Boipatong *imbizo*. Two of its leading officials, Adons Ramaele and William Ubane had been found guilty of indecent assault and grievous bodily harm and sentenced in the Vanderbijlpark District Court. Their defense argued that they were acting on behalf of the community, but this time the magistrate was not allowing this timeworn rhetoric of 'community' justice. The Afrikaans-speaking magistrate J A van Staden called them 'bullies and liars' of the first order and ordered them to spend a year in jail or pay a fine of 2,000 Rand each. Ramaele paid up, but William Ubane was languishing in jail when I arrived to interview Boipatong residents about the case.

The story behind the District Court case was a fascinating one. As we saw earlier, the Boipatong *imbizo* had been taking on more domestic cases (often involving women 'neglecting' their domestic duties) and 'love problems' (mostly adultery cases) throughout 1997, under pressure from both men and women. It had also become increasingly punitive in these cases, especially towards women found guilty of adultery or minor domestic 'crimes', and had beaten half a dozen women (including, in one case, a girl of 15) during 1997. On a few of these occasions *imbizo* members had stripped (allegedly adulterous) women naked, paraded them through the township and then beaten them in the football stadium in front of cheering crowds. Perhaps it is needless to say that this type of public humiliation would never have been heaped upon an adulterous man.

Matters came to a head on 5 June 1997, when 38-year-old Elizabeth Mahlangu was brought to the *imbizo* by her own mother, who accused her of having abused an infant in her household. The indomitable Chairman Ramaele presided over the case and having found her guilty with apparently little right of reply, the court sentenced her to lashes with a *sjambok*. William Ubane fetched her from her house when she was sentenced (*in absentia*) by the *imbizo* and he participated in the beating. The two sides disputed in court the number of lashes given, the *imbizo* members maintaining that no more than five lashes were given and Ms Mahlangu's counsel claiming that 50 was more like the right figure. Ms Mahlangu clearly suffered a horrible beating, and she was hospitalized for nearly two weeks, and photos of the extensive injuries to her buttocks and legs were shown in court.

Ms Mahlangu then received support to take her case to the police and then to the District Court from a number of disaffected groups. She was encouraged by other women of the township, such as one ANC

Women's League activist, and local chairperson of 'Women Against Violence Against Women' who had herself been beaten in 1997 by the *imbizo* for having an affair with a married man. Women's resentment was supported by the ANC Youth League, whose members had also chafed at the bit of elder patriarchal control. In the 1980s, the 'popular courts' run by ANC comrades had generated a large part of its constituency from women who were unhappy with gerontocratic township courts, and this political axis realigned itself in the late 1990s.

Crucially, Elizabeth Mahlangu's case was sustained by the local *Vaal Vision* newspaper, which paid her relatively handsomely for her story, called in the national press and the South African Broadcasting Company (SABC), and supported her throughout her legal case; one ANC *imbizo* member claimed that this was because the *Vaal Vision* editor, Peter Mabuye, was 'out to get the *imbizo*'. Mabuye is widely seen as a PAC sympathizer who is antagonistic towards ANC structures. So there were many different ingredients in the stew over 'tribal law': gender, male generational conflict and party political hostility.

The magistrate referred to the *imbizo* officials' actions as like 'jungle justice in the Wild West' (*Vaal Vision* 23 October 1998). Ubane was labeled a bully who went out of his way to find women 'culprits' in their homes so as to bring them to the *imbizo* for a beating. What was especially interesting was how the magistrate invoked human rights in his decision, saying that Mr Ramaele was a stubborn belligerent old man who had no respect for other people's human rights (quoted in *Vaal Vision* 23 October 1998). Human rights discourse would in all likelihood not have been invoked in a case like this before 1994 – indeed the whole case would probably have never come to the District Court at all but would have been referred to a separate part of the black administrative system.

Local residents sought to invoke human rights also, but did so in an uninformed and haphazard manner. At the risk of sounding pedantic, no one in Boipatong could tell me which of Ms Mahlangu's human rights had been violated – not even she herself. No one could refer to which right enshrined in the Bill of Rights in the South African Constitution had been violated either. Perhaps I expected too much knowledge of the law and Constitution, but these were politicized middle-level ANC members and many held office jobs.

When I questioned an ANC Woman's League activist from Boipatong which of Ms Mahlangu's rights had been violated she replied, 'She was abused'. When I persisted and requested clarification on which right *exactly* was at issue, she repeated, 'She ought not to have been abused' and then began talking about how the *imbizo* was a valid and even valuable institution, but should not overstep the boundaries of appropriate punishment, especially with regard to women, whom it was originally dedicated to protecting. Men should treat women with respect according to 'the rules of the culture', she argued. It was all right for the court to beat young men caught thieving, but it should not transgress into women's domestic terrain and start throwing its weight around.

All this tells us something more interesting than just that there is a lack of awareness of the details of human rights codes. It demonstrates that residents were wrapping their own local moral discourses within human rights talk without any real worries about how the two interact. The moral language of the 1970s and 1980s – of customary morality rather than written legal rules, of separate men and women's worlds, of men respecting and protecting women and even doing so through a punitive township court – was still relatively intact, but had now been swept into the path of the new national language of justice: human rights. Long-standing tensions around social regulation and inequality in the townships are now dressed in the language of human rights. This allegiance is quite superficial, and is little more than a new idiom for a much older language of justice and morality.

So what looked like a triumph of gender equality over inequality, and the rule of law over arbitrary justice, in fact pointed to a much more contradictory situation: that rights talk is vague enough to cloak a variety of claims and entitlements which may not be rights-derived at all. In this case, human rights did on occasion provide a bridge between two justice systems, but only when motivated by a desire for punishment and integrated into an institutionalized structure of retribution. It is worth pointing out that the beaten women did not want to reconcile with the old men of the *imbizo*, they wanted a higher legal body to punish the men appropriately. In this formulation, human rights provided the idiom for Africans to enter an old-style Afrikaner magistrate's court, which many had boycotted as a symbol of apartheid only five years earlier. Again, we have evidence from Boipatong that 'human rights' became more meaningful for local actors when associated with deeply held, common law notions of retributive justice.

Human rights talk once again served in a centralizing capacity, drawing local ideas and institutions of justice into the state, and pushing out all that did not fit. Ms Mahlangu's case was supported by the members of the Boipatong Community Policing Forum, and the Vanderbijlpark magistrate in his sentencing judgment instructed the *imbizo* members to 'stop their nonsense and join the Community Policing Forum instead' (quoted in *Vaal Vision* 23 October 1998). In Boipatong, the CPF and the *imbizo* were functioning side by side and, although there was some animosity, there was also co-operation and overlapping membership. But the deep structural circumstances of criminal justice reform in South Africa in the late 1990s meant that such co-existence was unstable and the state has acted in a number of ways to centralize and unify and so extend its authority. Human rights talk is a vital part of this project of state centralization, being one of the main channels through which state discourse on justice is transmitted to 'the masses'. It is one of the main state discourses which legitimates the incorporation of semi-autonomous institutions of spheres of social action, and the exclusion of those it cannot tame.

It can be rather unsettling to have one's object of study disappear even before the study is complete, but also rather instructive. The zealous protection of women's sexuality by men was part of the origins of the *imbizo* and the over-zealous control of women's sexuality was at the heart of its downfall. When I left the Vaal in late 1998, the Boipatong *imbizo* was in a parlous condition: two leading members were sentenced, one was in jail, and many men, such as the secretary Duma Motluong, had resigned; shaking his head, Motluong told me in his mechanic's shop, 'I told them they must not get involved in family affairs. They were wrong and the magistrate was right to punish them' (Personal interview, 17 November 1998). Whereas before I had been welcomed to the daily court sessions, without the accompaniment of Duma Motluong I was excluded from the few *imbizo* meetings still being held, as were all other 'outsiders'. The local press was overtly ostracized. The *imbizo* still limped along, its authority and independence in tatters. It was holding only a few meetings a week, and wisely refusing any domestic cases, confined its hearings to theft, and it had (at least temporarily) stopped beating those (mostly youth, as usual) found guilty. Officials were now more prone just to hand over suspects to the police without trying or sentencing them and the urban court was therefore even more integrated into the state criminal justice system than ever before.

We could conclude this section with the assertion that human rights and the rule of law were triumphant in Boipatong, with the end of township courts and vigilante justice in sight, but history is seldom that straightforward. Urban courts have shown a remarkable durability and resilience to state efforts to dismantle them over the last hundred years. Although the centralizing tendencies are now hegemonic, a situation of tangled, knotty and contradictory legal pluralism is likely to continue for some time.

LEGAL PLURALISM REVISITED

In this final section I return and address the theoretical problems raised in the introduction of chapter 5, in the light of the intervening ethnographic material. Until the early 1960s, 'Legal Pluralism I' held sway in the field of legal anthropology. It proposed an equivalence between all types of legal rules and social norms, and operated with a static and isolated view of customary law which too readily assumed the existence of different systems. Over time, it moved from codifying customary rules to advocating a processual approach which portrayed local law as characterized by open and seemingly limitless individual negotiation and choice-making.

Legal Pluralism I was the dominant intellectual paradigm in decades of writings on 'the Tswana', in what is now South Africa and Botswana. From Schapera (1938) in the early part of the century, to Comaroff and Roberts (1981), to more recent writers such as Gulbrandsen (1996), studies of legal practices and discourses among Setswana-speaking peoples largely accepted the dualistic colonial and apartheid legal system at face value and ignored how state law transformed local adjudicative institutions. This paradigm may have resulted from the actual historical experiences of Setswana-speaking peoples, but is in my view more likely to have been the result of an entrenched analytical frame which reproduced assumptions of isolation and autonomy. Certainly those people forcibly categorized as 'Tswana' in the former South African 'homeland' of Bophuthatswana, run by the despotic Lucas Mangope, had an intimate knowledge and experience of legal coercion from a violent state.

'Legal Pluralism II' emerged in the early 1970s from within 'critical legal studies' and the cross-disciplinary 'law-and-society' movement. The focus of studies of legal pluralism soon became the dialectical relationship between state institutions and local normative orders and the relations of dominance and resistance between them. Marxist legal anthropologists such as Snyder (1981) argued, rightly, that the processual approach treated dispute processes as too self-contained and thus tended to ignore the wider political context. Local moralities and norms were in a subordinate but resistant relationship to state law, demanding recognition on their own terms (Merry 1990:181). Studies in this tradition then began to look at the politics of judicial processes, drawing from Gramscian notions of hegemony where law is an ideology which expresses and maintains structures of inequality. Michel Foucault's writings influenced many who came to see law as a disciplinary apparatus and a site of struggle and contestation between dominant and resistant discourses of power (Humphreys 1985; Hunt and Wickham 1994).

Legal Pluralism II is adequate in many ways for understanding the uniquely polarized history of apartheid legality. It is particularly well-suited to analyzing the dualistic legal system administered by a white-run political and legal bureaucracy and resisted by local political actors who carved out a sphere of 'popular justice' in the 1980s. Yet Legal Pluralism II, with its narrative of dominance and resistance is predisposed to ignore the real connections between local and state law, and the ways in which especially elite Africans (in chiefs' courts and 'Bantustan' bureaucracies) have participated in, and acquiesced to, state policies. Relations between formal and informal justice institutions in the initial post-apartheid context are even more volatile and contradictory than before, and they present a socio-legal environment that prior formulations of legal pluralism or centralism cannot fully encompass.

A revised legal pluralism would have to preserve from Legal Pluralism II the idea that many states engage in centralizing efforts to resolve their hegemonic crises, but it could not accept that there is always an inherent asymmetry between centralizing and pluralizing processes. Instead of the stark polarity of dominance and resistance which reduces the complexities of a historically produced political-legal context, we must turn our attention to shifting patterns of dominance, resistance and acquiescence, which occur simultaneously. As we have seen in Vaal townships, local courts both connect up with policing structures and bypass them in order to exercise a certain degree of autonomy to judge and punish. The Boipatong *imbizo* was simultaneously working with the Vanderbijlpark police, while being prosecuted and sentenced by the magistrate who told them, in the name of human rights, to cease their activities and join the Community Policing Forum. Religious moralities and institutions, on the other hand, encourage a more favorable disposition towards a reconciliatory vision of human rights. What I have termed adductive affinities and relational discontinuities allow us to move away from generalizations about law and society and offer more concrete ways of theorizing the uneven reception of human rights talk in a locale. Such specific terms which arise out of ethnographic research also allow us to transcend the either/or logic of the universalism/relativism debate where one is forced to opt either for rights as conceived universally or for local practices, narrowly con-ceived. Instead, as we have seen throughout this book, there are all kinds of concrete connections between local, national and transnational institutions.

In this multivalent context, the degree of plurality of legal fields is often a matter of the strategic perspectives of social actors. The legal system may appear quite pluralistic from the Olympian vantage of the Justice Ministry, which surveys hundreds of unregulated armed units and local courts across the country, each dispensing a different version of 'justice' over which it has only a tentative control. However, from the perspective of a petty criminal apprehended by Boipatong *kgotla* members and handed over to the police in Vanderbijlpark, the institutions of justice look relatively unified and integrated.

There are multiple connections between state institutions, religious organizations and local courts, to the extent that we see a splintering of the unified fields of state and society, and an eradicating of their hard boundaries. Diverse social fields in African countries are too complex and emergent to be constrained by any explanation which sees law and society as *a priori* structural categories to be understood by a single explanatory framework. Instead of two coherent unified systems which are locked in a structurally determined struggle, we see combinations of actors and collective groups who are involved in the production of norms and who create new historical experiences and experiences of history.

The direction of social change in post-apartheid South Africa, what Touraine refers to as 'historicity', is the product of the social action of individuals and collective actors (political parties, local courts, religious organizations and such) engaged in the reflexive self-production of society.[29] Society is no longer an overbearing system handed down from the past, but is actively created by social actors using new types of knowledge and cultural orientations. In Touraine's formulation, society can no longer be defined according to an organic and unitary model as during the high point of industrialism and modernity. This is one reason why the appeals of moral leaders and national politicians to a single vision of South African society (captured in the phrases 'rainbow nation' and 'culture of human rights') are bound to meet with acceptance, avoidance and resistance, since there are other important social actors with different agendas and cultural orientations. As Touraine writes:

> Society can no longer be defined as a set of institutions, or as the effect of a sovereign will ... It is a field of conflicts, negotiations and mediations ... Human beings make their own history, but they do so through social conflicts, and on the basis of cultural choices. (1995:358)

Just as civil society implies too much common purpose among non-state actors towards state versions of human rights, neither is the state itself unified and coherent in its policies. The diversity in human rights practices within the South African state can be well demonstrated by juxtaposing the activities of different arms of the state in the Vaal in 1995–96. Only months before the TRC was taking statements from victims, arranging its one week hearing in the Vaal townships and carrying out public education on human rights in the area, policemen in the Murder and Robbery Unit at the nearby Vanderbijlpark police station were routinely torturing criminal suspects using methods honed during years of defending successive National Party regimes (1948–1994). Due to successful litigation by human rights lawyers,[30] four Vaal policemen were suspended in late 1995 for torturing thirty prisoners. The presiding judge struck down prisoners' confessions exacted through torture, and recommended an internal police investigation. When I re-interviewed a staff member at the Vaal Legal Aid Center in 1998 and asked if the situation had improved, he replied, 'Yes. Prisoners awaiting trial are no longer being tortured. They are only being assaulted'.

Since 1994, post-apartheid South African governments have engaged in an agonizing process of state reformation and democratization. ANC ministers are unifying, consolidating infrastructure, and desperately trying to transform institutions such as the police, prisons and magistrates' courts, which were historically tainted by their involvement in administering apartheid. The project of state centralization and national unification is the most important thing to realize about the first post-apartheid regime. It found itself opposed to legal pluralism and a dual system of justice and administration for blacks and whites, which it set about dismantling. Yet this shift from one type of governance to another – from separate development and racial and cultural difference to equality and universal human rights – created a legitimacy crisis. Despite a clear state project and a strong mandate from the electorate, the ANC found itself in an unsatisfactory power-sharing arrangement with former apartheid rulers and up against a legacy of orchestrated difference, dramatic inequality, and entrenched division.

Human rights talk is a key component in the new language of government in the 'New South Africa', and the last four chapters have traced some of the ways in which state officials combine human rights with religious notions of redemption and forgiveness. As we have seen, state formulations of human rights either resonate with local perspectives (adductive affinities), circumvent local perspectives altogether (pragmatic proceduralism), or are repulsed by them (relational discontinuities). The social processes described work in different directions simultaneously, both reinforcing and obstructing the introduction of human rights values into a context of semi-autonomous legal and moral fields. If revised, then legal pluralism remains one useful category which allows us to move beyond stark formulations of state and society, to chart the concrete consequences of competition between social actors over the direction of social and historical change in the area of justice and reconciliation.

CHAPTER 8

CONCLUSIONS: HUMAN RIGHTS, RECONCILIATION AND RETRIBUTION

The South African Truth and Reconciliation Commission came at a remarkable juncture in global politics and this is one reason for the international fascination with it. Around the world, governments and non-governmental organizations championed human rights institutions in post-apartheid South Africa as they desperately wanted to see a success story at the end of a truly horrific twentieth century. The century had begun with the unprecedented industrial annihilation of millions in a conventional war in Europe, culminated mid-century with a fascist genocide and ended with an upsurge in violent ethno-nationalist conflicts in Rwanda and the former Yugoslavia. In the dying embers of the twentieth century, South Africa represented a positive scenario, where a white supremacist regime gave way to non-racial constitutionalism in the absence (it seemed) of widespread retaliation and revenge. Out of the ashes of ruined Afrikaner nationalism, a new human rights commission led by a figure of unquestioned moral authority, former Archbishop Desmond Tutu, was explicitly dedicated to building a culture of human rights and an inclusive 'rainbow nation'.

South Africa's transition became yet another example of the triumph of liberalism as it also coincided with the end of the Cold War, the subsequent demise of socialist ideologies and the rise of laissez-faire economics. Since global conditions were much less conducive to the defiant third world nationalism prevalent during the decades of decolonization, national elites in democratizing countries turned to human rights talk as the hallmark of a new democratic order. The incorporation of international human rights laws into a national constitution was seen as coterminous with democracy, freedom and the creation of a new social contract with citizens.

The globalization of human rights talk meant that human rights dominated political and economic life more than at any other point in history. Globalization in the 1990s also meant an expansion in the range of claims made within the language of human rights. For many political leaders, human rights talk seemingly had the ability to create a fully-blown moral-ethical code, to forge a moral unity and to legitimate the new democratic order. The difficulties experienced in the implementation of these new formulations of rights derive in part from the success of the idea of rights. The constant expansion of the functions of human rights institutions had at some point to reach an upper limit, beyond which it becomes apparent that the capacities of rights have been overreached.

This book has taken the view that human rights are best conceptualized as narrow legal instruments which protect frail individuals from powerful state and societal institutions.[1] During the transformation from an authoritarian regime, human rights can play a vital role in establishing accountability and the rule of law. It is misguided to fetishize rights and treat them as a full-blown political and ethical philosophy, as only the most anemic moral system could be constructed from a list of rights. Human rights are important preconditions of liberty and freedom but they are too narrow to define liberty itself. They are instruments for realizing common goods such as legal and political accountability, but they cannot entirely define the common good and may even impede certain visions of it which emphasize socio-economic redistribution. Understanding the limits of what the instituting of rights can achieve is the only way to understand why the reformulations of human rights by South African political and religious leaders did not gain rapid legitimacy.

We must therefore be more cautious about what human rights discourses and institutions in democratizing countries can accomplish, and give greater attention to a realist investigation of what social actors and institutions actually do with rights, and what level of legitimacy their actions have. This critical attitude requires us to look closely at the motivations of governmental elites establishing new human rights commissions and at the sociological consequences of attempts to build a 'culture of human rights'. Governments do not exalt the language of rights solely because it contains fine liberal principles, but also because it allows them to pursue nation-building and to centralize state authority in a legally plural context.

Throughout this book, we have seen that the societal consequences of human rights talk are ambiguous and paradoxical. On the one hand, human rights ideals are progressively modernizing and encourage a critical reflection on authority, tradition and patriarchal notions of community. Human rights commissions create a space which did not exist before where narratives of suffering could emerge and become incorporated into the official version on the past. Public recognition of formerly repressed narratives allowed greater mutual understanding between the sections of South African society separated by the racialized boundaries of apartheid. This made possible a greater 'fusion of horizons', a base line of understanding, and it defined the parameters of discussion of the past. No one can now claim that apartheid was a well-intended policy of good neighborliness that somehow went wrong. Nor can they deny that tens of thousands were killed by the operatives of an abhorrent political system. The range of permissible lies is now much narrower because of the work of the TRC.

At the same time, human rights are an intrinsic part of the legality of the modern state apparatus and as such they constitute an element in the onward march of legal domination identified by the sociologist Max Weber in the late nineteenth century. They subordinate the lifeworld[2] of social agents to the systemic imperatives of nation-building and the centralization of the legal and bureaucratic apparatus. Rights transform political problems into technical ones and thereby remove them from the reach of parliamentary legislation.[3] The combination of scientism, legal positivism and human rights seeks to create the conditions for greater legitimacy by raising truth out of the realm of political struggle and negotiation into the rarefied ether of scientific objectivity.

Human rights are entwined with a project of modernist rationalization, and this book has explored some of the consequences of rationalization for the production of an official version of the past.[4] Human rights place normative restrictions upon citizens' subjectivities, narrowing them and squeezing into the allowable categories of legal positivism. Human rights forms of investigation and documentation are too legalistic for adequately recording and reflecting upon past violations. The instrumental rationality of law and rights systematically transforms the lifeworld, rather than being a sensitive device for listening to subjectivity on its own terms. By extending legal domination into ever more areas of social life, human rights institutions can close down the space for popular forms of understanding the past. We saw how the South Africa TRC restricted both the narrative form and the content (especially, excluding revenge) of deponents in a process of legal colonization of the realms of personal experience.

Although human rights are part of the iron cage of rationalization, not all truth commissions are inherently doomed from the start. Instead, the question is more how to strike the right balance between legal-forensic investigations and historical approaches to truth. Those truth commissions which have been more successful in my view are those which have abandoned the trappings of law, allowed the courts to administer amnesty provisions, and concentrated more on truth-finding. They are designed more as a history project, rather than a court of law.

Some Latin American commissions have used a more reflexive and historical approach to truth in order to produce a more coherent account of the past which could be used as a charter for future reforms of the state and society. The Guatemalan Historical Clarification Commission (CEH),[5] which delivered its report *Guatemala: Memoria del Silencio* on 25 February 1999, had no amnesty functions and was precluded from 'individualizing responsibility'. Its revelations could not have any legal consequences and it could not name perpetrators. This clearly had unfavorable implications with regard to the wall of impunity surrounding the security forces, but the Guatemalan commission turned necessity into virtue and produced a bold and persuasive historical account of the country's violent past. Freed of the need to make legal findings, it could subordinate statistics to a sophisticated explanatory account of the past. *Guatemala: Memoria del Silencio* went much further than the South African report in identifying the structural causes of violence, beginning with colonial history and the creation of a racist and authoritarian post-independence state, the exclusionary nature of the economic model of development chosen, the militarization of the state, the rise of a Doctrine of National Security and the consequences of US intervention in the twentieth century.[6]

There is a general point here which might be borne in mind by those setting up human rights commissions in other parts of the world, and that is that different institutions must carry out clear and distinct tasks which they are designed to carry out. Truth commissions do not function well if they are overloaded, as the South African TRC was, with a variety of tasks including holding public hearings, writing a report on the past, recommending reparations policy and granting amnesty. Many South African human rights activists have realized that human rights talk has spun out of control and the editorial of a Human Rights Committee publication in April 2000 stated: 'the situation facing us is an unwelcome cocktail. The blend of a great number of rights institutions together with wide mandates may instead of providing for an effective and efficient system of promoting rights ... actually result in a flailing around ... We have the suspicion that too many institutions are trying to be too much to too many with the result that they are doing too little for too few' (Human Rights Committee of SA 2000:2).

Turning now to consider efforts by the TRC to create national reconciliation, we can see that this undertaking shared many of the characteristics of the truth-writing project. Reconciliation talk sought to transform the lifeworld according to systemic imperatives in order to displace revenge, retribution and physical punishment in popular views on the 'just desserts' of human rights offenders. Reconciliation talk had as its aim the centralization of justice and the augmentation of the state's monopoly on the means of coercion. The post-apartheid program of state-building involved drawing adjudication institutions from their many multiple sites (local township courts, armed gangs,

Special Defense Units) into those institutions sanctioned by the state. The establishment of the TRC and a number of human rights institutions was therefore only intelligible in terms of the hegemony-building project of the new state in the area of justice.

The TRC's objectives of centralization, state-building and reducing legal pluralism were only partially fulfilled. For all their media coverage, TRC hearings were often little more than a symbolic and ritualized performance with a weak impact on vengeance in urban townships. The transfer of values from an elite to the masses was uneven and equivocal. In the same way that the rationalization of truth production created a dissonance between bureaucratic and popular understandings of the past, the rationalization of justice created new relational discontinuities between institutional and informal justice. These discontinuities centered around widespread practices of revenge which were demonized by the human rights constituency as dangerous to the well-being of the new rainbow nation.

There was an acute lack in the TRC of concrete mechanisms to pursue conflict resolution and it interacted with local communities primarily through progressive mainstream church networks. Churches represent a significant urban black constituency, but there was no attempt to connect up with the punitive structures at the local level – warring party political branches, township courts or Special Defense Units. Although the use of physical punishment by neighborhood courts was an unpalatable reality for Commissioners, human rights institutions ignore popular conceptualizations of justice at their own peril. Nor was there any attempt to facilitate victim–offender mediation between individuals, either by the TRC itself, or through the many conflict resolution non-governmental organizations available.

The TRC was not particularly effective in creating a new culture of human rights or greater respect for the rule of law. As long as human rights institutions function as a substitute for criminal prosecutions, they will be resisted by some victims and denounced as a 'sell-out' by informal justice institutions. There are other more important state institutions to consider here, namely the criminal justice system itself, which has only received a fraction of the international interest shown in the TRC. In this context, the TRC deflected attention from the more serious project of the transformation of the legal system in order to make it more representative, quick and fair.

We should not just blame the TRC for not achieving what it never had the capacity or political backing to achieve single-handedly: a shift from an ethic of revenge to an ethic of retributive justice and the legitimation of justice institutions. Our disapprobation is also allayed by placing the TRC within a wider context of the legacy of apartheid and a long-standing legal pluralism which meant that any new language of justice, such as human rights, could not have a uniform impact. By taking into account these systematic constraints, we can have a more balanced view of what truth commissions can and cannot achieve. What they can achieve well, if carefully designed, is a sophisticated historical account of a violent past which integrates a structural analysis with the consciousness of those who lived through it. The rest should either be left to justice institutions, or to non-governmental organizations of civil society with expertise in mediation.

The most damaging outcome of truth commissions is a result of their equating of human rights with reconciliation and amnesty. This delegitimizes them enormously in relation to popular understandings of justice and can lead to greater criminal activity in society. There is growing evidence from Eastern Europe and elsewhere that it is necessary for democratizing regimes to challenge directly the impunity created during the authoritarian order, if they are going to avoid an upsurge in criminality and a lack of respect for state institutions. John Borneman's study of the countries of post-communist Eastern Europe contended that 'a successful reckoning with the criminal past obligates the state to seek retributive justice and that a failure to pursue retributive justice will likely lead to cycles of retributive violence' (1997:6).

In applying this argument to South Africa, there is evidence enough in the crime statistics and the wild justice in places like Sharpeville to assert that criminality has been exacerbated by the lack of full accountability for human rights offenders.

This view is backed up by a salient interpretation of international human rights treaties, which holds that those responsible for gross human rights violations must be brought before a court of law and held accountable.[7] The justice advanced by some statutes contained in international human rights conventions refers to retributive justice – punishment for offenders and just compensation for victims. However, in countries emerging from authoritarian rule, human rights talk often comes to undermine accountability in favor of nation-building, and thus to signify the reverse of the requirements of many international human rights treaties. It means (individual or blanket) amnesty for perpetrators, selective prosecutions of others who do not submit to the established process, and a limited truth finding operation as a parallel compromise solution.

Human rights talk has become the language of pragmatic political compromise rather than the language of principle and accountability. This is the main obstacle to popular acceptance of human rights as the new ideology of constitutional states.

Constitutionalism purports to be the foremost political system to defend the rights of citizens and principles of justice, whereas human rights talk in South Africa or Chile or Argentina has come to be about political deals where everything is negotiable, where cut-off dates (for example, for amnesty) are always extended and seemingly resolved issues (again, amnesty) keep being placed back on the negotiating table. The perception that human rights is more about compromise than justice for offenders was reinforced time and time again. For instance, the Chair of the Human Rights Commission, Dr Barney Pityana, stated in 1999 that all further apartheid-era prosecutions should be halted: 'We [the Human Rights Commission] counsel against such a course of action [prosecutions]. The simplest solution is to say that those who have escaped the net of the [Truth and Reconciliation] Commission must receive the forgiveness of the nation (*Sunday Independent*, 26 July 1999).

If human rights are associated instead with a principled position of accountability of key human rights offenders,[8] then this would bring human rights into greater alliance (both discursively and in practice) with that majoritarian constituency which views justice as proportional punishment for wrongdoing. This would also connect national scenarios to a progressive trend in international human rights law, which is increasingly taking the view that there are no conditions under which a torturer or a mass murderer should go free. In the light of the establishment of the International Criminal Court, and extradition proceedings against General Augusto Pinochet in Britain in 1999, which established that heads of state do not enjoy immunity from prosecution for human rights violations such as torture, the stage seems set even more than before for international human rights law to transcend national legal systems and to prosecute those involved in gross human rights violations with greater vigor. In April 2000, the right-hand man to Radovan Karadzic and most senior Bosnian Serb to be arrested for suspected war crimes, Momcilo Krajisnik, was seized in a dawn raid at his Pale home by French troops who then sent him to The Hague to the UN International Criminal Tribunal for the former Yugoslavia (*Guardian* 4 April 2000). Only a month earlier, the same UN tribunal sentenced a former commander of Croat forces in Bosnia, General Tihomir Blaskic, to 45 years in jail on 20 counts, including breaches of the Geneva Conventions and crimes against humanity (*Guardian* 4 March 2000).

Despite the protestations of some post-authoritarian elites, these international prosecutions are seen as wholly just by many of those who lived through periods of violence, terror and authoritarianism. In an international context where the jurisdiction of human rights institutions is intensifying and broadening, it is misguided to delegitimize human rights at the national level by detaching them from a retributive understanding of justice and attaching them to a religious notion of reconciliation-forgiveness, a regrettable amnesty law and an elite project of nation-building. Democratizing regimes should not seek legitimacy through nation-building, efforts to forge a moral unity and communitarian discourses, but on the basis of accountability and justice defined as proportional retribution and procedural fairness. The role of human rights and the rule of law in all of this is to create the bedrock of accountability upon which democratic legitimacy is built.

The many writers in law, politics and philosophy who applauded the South African TRC hoped that enlarging the definitions of human rights and the functions of human rights institutions might expand a culture of human rights. This view is well-meaning, but erroneous. We should recognize that human rights are most effective when conceived of as narrow legal instruments designed to defend individuals from political institutions and to hold accountable those responsible for violations. This formulation is simple, efficacious, and commands a great deal of legitimacy because it is usually reinforced by popular conceptions of justice. This could be the basis for establishing the rule of law in a democratizing context, rather than amnesties and reconciliation which only perpetuate impunity. Turning human rights talk into a moral-theological treatise which extols forgiveness and reconciliation in an effort to forge a new moral vision of the nation in the end destroys the most important promise of human rights; that is, its possible contribution to a thoroughgoing transformation of an authoritarian criminal justice system and the construction of real and lasting democratic legitimacy.

NOTES

PREFACE

1 Charles Taylor (1995:186–187) describes as 'procedural' the kind of liberalism which became popular in the English-speaking world and democratizing countries. This political ideology sees society as an association of equal individuals with inalienable rights, which is not founded upon any notion of the common good, 'The ethic central to a liberal society is an ethic of the right rather than the good' (p. 186).

2 The writings of Huntington (1991), Tucker (1999), and Zalaquett (1990; 1991) are paradigmatic of this genre, which has been adopted by some South Africa observers such as Jung and Shapiro (1995).

3 The exact number of truth commissions depends upon how one defines them – I am using Hayner's (1994) wide definition, and adding Guatemala and South Africa to her list of 15 commissions. Other readings from the ever-expanding literature on truth commissions include Aguilar et al. (2001), Barahona de Brito (1997), Cassell (1993), Cohen (1995), Diamond (1994), Ensalaco (1994), Hayner (2000), Krog (1998), Lyons (1997), Mamdani (1996), Minow (1998), Nuttall and Coetze (1998) Popkin and Roht-Arriaza (1995), Werle (1996) and Wilson (2000).

4 Although Jeffery (1999) excoriates the TRC for not being legalistic enough in its investigations and testing and treatment of evidence. I am, however, talking about a different function, namely the history-writing mandate of the TRC.

1 HUMAN RIGHTS AND NATION-BUILDING

1 Jan-Erik Lane defines constitutionalism succinctly as, 'the political doctrine that claims that political authority should be bound by institutions that restrict the exercise of power. Such institutions offer rules that bind both the persons in authority as well as the organs or bodies that exercise political power. Human rights are one central component of constitutionalism; another essential element is the separation of powers in government' (1996:19).

2 On transitional justice in Eastern Europe after 1990, see Borneman (1997), Ellis (1997), Garton Ash (1997a), Offe (1992; 1993; 1996) and Rosenberg (1995).

3 See also Habermas (1994) on the politics of recognition in constitutional states.

4 See Adam (1994); Degenaar (1990; 1993; 1994); Pampallis (1995); Rhoodie and Liebenberg (1994); Rietzes (1995); and Simpson (1993).

5 See Inkatha Freedom Party adviser Marinus Wiechers (1994).

6 Cf. Irina Filatova: 'Few examples would support the idea of successful nation-building unless the process unfolds naturally' (1994:55).

7 African National Congress (ANC): Formed in 1912, the ANC is South Africa's oldest political party. It is a broad church which includes political positions from the far left (the South African Communist Party), to the center-right. It is South Africa's most popular political party, having won massive majorities in the 1994 and 1999 elections. See McKinley (1997) for a critical history; more recently, Dubow (2000) provides a short, accessible history of the party.

8 On the positivism inherent in apartheid jurisprudence, the slain Namibian human rights campaigner Anton Lubowski wrote: 'For many years the prevailing view in ruling class South African jurisprudence was a notion of the legal system as a neutral, value-free forum for the settlement of disputes by the application of principles' (1988:14).

9 For a discussion of how Constitutional Court decisions are shaped by values, attitudes and ideologies of judges, see van Huyssteen (1996).

10 For an unabridged discussion of human rights in this period see Wilson (2001).

11 The National Party (NP) was founded by General J B M Hertzog in 1914 in an effort to unify Afrikaners politically. It ruled between 1948 and 1994 and its party leaders built apartheid through racist legislation such as the Population Registration Act (1950), the Group Areas Act (1950), the Bantu Authorities Act (1951), Bantu Education Act (1953), Natives' Resettlement Act (1953) and the Preservation of Coloured Areas Act (1961).

12 Landsberg notes that in 1989, the USA warned State President F W de Klerk that he had only year to end the state of emergency, release political prisoners and lift the ban on the liberation movement (1994:280).

13 For a discussion of constitutionalism as a binding force between political actors in South Africa, see chapter 4 by Atkinson in Friedman and Atkinson (1994), Mureinik (1994), van Huyssteen (1996) and Wilson (1996). On constitutional theory more generally, Lane (1996) provides a useful guide.

14 The Record of Understanding was a settlement signed between President de Klerk and Nelson Mandela, agreeing on conditions for restarting talks. The ANC had walked out of talks after the Boipatong massacre of 17 June and intensified its mass action campaign. For most commentators, September 1992 represented the critical moment when the balance of power in the transition shifted away from the NP to the ANC, which then began to set the agenda.

15 Since T H Marshall (1950), many have noted that there is a deep contradiction between the principles of rights and the politics of class.

16 The 1993 Interim Constitution was written in the constitutional assembly talks and revised after the 1994 elections, leading to the final version ratified in 1996.

17 For a discussion of the ANC's shift away from Stalinism, see chapter 4 in Adam and Moodley (1992).

18 There is a social democratic current in the ANC, perhaps strongest among members of the ANC in exile and coalescing around Thabo Mbeki, which is more sympathetic to rights talk. See Nolutshungu (1991) for a history of human rights within the ANC.

19 Section 79.4 states that each Bill passed by parliament must be referred to the Constitutional Court for a decision on its constitutionality. See Dyzenhaus (1998a:32–33) for a useful discussion of the South African constitutional structure.

20 During CODESA I, F W de Klerk angered Nelson Mandela with a statement on amnesty. The issue was then left aside until after the formal political negotiations were concluded. For a discussion of amnesty in the negotiations, see Wilson (2001).

21 The Indemnity Act 35 of 1990 and Further Indemnity Act 151 of 1992 enabled the return of anti-apartheid exiles and the release of political prisoners.

22 The usual pattern was for the main negotiators to make an agreement in principle, to be worked out in detail by the technical committee which was made up of lawyers.

23 The electoral successes of the ANC does not countenance the view that victims therefore supported the amnesty provisions — it is not clear what percentage of victims voted for the ANC, nor what priorities motivated their voting behavior and finally, counterfactually, the ANC might have received even more votes had it opposed amnesty.

24 See also Tutu (1999) for his account of the TRC and further exposition of his ideas on restorative justice and *ubuntu*.

25 Restorative justice generally eschews criminal prosecution of offenders in favor of material and symbolic reparations for victims and the establishing of a forum for victims to tell their stories. It is generally seen as 'victim-centered' rather than oriented towards the offender, as is the case with common law. Its stated aims are the restoration of social bonds, the reaffirmation of the dignity of victims, and the rehabilitation of offenders within the community rather than punishment for offenders.

26 For a legal commentary on *ubuntu* in *S v Makwanyane*, see R English (1997).

27 The association between human rights and restorative justice is also found in Latin America, see Benomar (1993), Minow (1998) and Roht-Arriaza (1995).

28 A *Sunday Times* poll (11 June 1995, p. 5) reported that more than 80 per cent of whites and 50 per cent of blacks in urban areas of South Africa (support is usually higher in rural areas) were in favor of the death penalty.

29 See also Wilson (1995).

30 Paraphrased from Tutu's press release on his appointment to the TRC on 30 November 1995, where he stated that the Commission's work involved 'opening wounds to cleanse them ... [to] stop them from festering'.

31 Tina Rosenberg writes of the need for official acknowledgement, 'If the whole nation is suffering from post-traumatic stress disorder, this process would be appropriate for the whole nation' (1995:24).

32 Demjanjuk's conviction was overturned by the Israeli Supreme Court on the grounds that the 50-year-old memories of victims were too unreliable.
33 See, for example, *Guatemala: Memoria del Silencio* http://hrdata.aaas.org/ceh/; *Report of the Chilean National Commission on Truth and Reconciliation.* 1993. *From Madness to Hope: the Twelve Year War in El Salvador*, UN Security Council, UN Doc. S/25500,1993, *Nunca Mas: A Report by Argentina's National Commission on Disappeared People.* 1986.
34 As Fred Hendricks has affirmed, '... while there have been some crucial institutional changes in South Africa in relation to human rights – the establishment of the Constitutional Court and the Bill of Rights – the judiciary itself has not changed in any fundamental way since 1994' (1999:6).
35 Source: Legal Aid Board 1998.
36 The main work of the TRC ended in 1998, but the Amnesty Committee carried on into 2001.
37 Note that Ngoepe uses 'political' instead of 'legal' immunity, seeking to distance the law from the amnesty process.
38 The TRC's approach to evidence has been criticized by Jeffery (1999) and Hendricks who writes, 'The decisions of the [amnesty] committee do not involve a great deal of detailed evidence at all – certainly not of the sort that usually accompanies criminal prosecution in a court of law' (1999:9).
39 Some 161 amnesty applications had been withdrawn and 21 partly refused/partly granted.
40 Former Defense Minister General Magnus Malan and ten other high-ranking former military and intelligence officials were tried in connection with a massacre of 13 people in KwaZulu-Natal in 1987. The seven-month trial centered upon whether the massacre in KwaMakutha township, by agents of the IFP, was on the direct orders of Malan and top military officials. In October 1996, the judge accepted that Inkatha agents undertook the killings after having been trained and armed with AK-47s by the SADF, but found no evidence to connect the material authors to the military top brass. The case against Malan demonstrated all the weaknesses of the judicial system and the state prosecution was a procedural nightmare. It called unreliable state witnesses but neglected to call other witnesses who could have corroborated the state's case. It was incapable of producing evidence through sophisticated forensic work and then arguing it cogently in the court. This prosecutorial incompetence was the legacy of apartheid legality.
41 De Kock confirmed that a key member of the covert 'Third Force' violence in the early 1990s was IFP leader Themba Khoza, Youth Leader of the IFP in the Transvaal. Khoza was arrested in September 1990 at a roadblock in Vanderbijlpark with his car boot full of AK-47s, on a day of violent armed confrontations in the Vaal which had left 15 dead. Charges were later dropped.
42 The survey had a minimum sample of 1,237.
43 For instance, both advocates and opponents of national amnesties refer to different sections of the Geneva Conventions of 1949. Article 6.5 of Protocol

II to the Geneva Convention of 12 August 1949 recommends that the 'broadest possible amnesty' be granted to participants in internal (that is, non-international) armed conflicts. See Roht-Arriaza and Gibson (1998).

44 I understand retributive justice to refer to the prosecution of alleged criminal acts in a court of law according to standard procedures and rules of legal evidence and, if guilt is established, then sentencing (as punishment) proportional to the gravity of the harm and the degree of responsibility of the wrongdoer. My understanding follows that of Robert Nozick, who advocates a 'non-teleological retributivism' (1981:363–397) that does not have as its aim the moral improvement of the offender. Instead, Nozick asserts that retributive punishment is both a right and a good in itself, since it reconnects the wrongdoer to correct values. See also chapters 6 and 7 of this book.

45 Desmond Tutu writes: 'Social harmony is for us [Africans] the *summum bonum* – the greatest good. Anything that subverts or undermines this sought-after good is to be avoided like the plague. Anger, resentment, lust for revenge, even success through aggressive competitiveness, are corrosive of this good' (1999:35). Here, a collective good – social harmony – is prioritized over the individual's right to justice.

46 See Roht-Arriaza (1995) and Roht-Arriaza and Gibson (1998) for a comparative review of amnesty arrangements in many countries.

47 On justice in transition in Latin America, and particularly amnesty, see Aguilar et al. (2001), Barahona de Brito (1997), Popkin (1999), Roht-Arriaza and Gibson (1998), Sieder and Wilson (1997) and Weschler (1990).

2 TECHNOLOGIES OF TRUTH

1 This chapter aims to complement research done by others such as Lars Buur, who, in writing about the activities of the Investigative Unit, notes that 'there is literally no information about everyday aspects of the Commission' (1999:1).

2 Unless, in extreme cases, the Commissioners decide to include specific cases under the rubric of 'severe ill treatment'.

3 See Dyzenhaus (1998b) for a thorough and critical evaluation of the TRC's legal hearings.

4 Quotes and the summary in this section are drawn from 'Few escape the taint of apartheid era crimes against humanity', Alex Duval Smith and David Beresford, *Guardian* 30 October 1998.

5 See note 3, above.

6 This view is not 'owned' by interpretative social science, but is also recognized within legal philosophy, by those who argue that law must be understood in relation to the subjective meanings of individuals within a legal order.

7 Positivism was not confined to the South African TRC – other post-authoritarian commissions, such as the Commissions of Vindication/Rehabilitation in the former East Germany, were forced to act as positivist juridical bodies (Borneman 1997:127).

8 Strategic Communication (STRATCOM) was set up in 1985 by the State Security Council as part of an emerging 'total strategy' of counter-insurgency.
9 According to the *Report* (1:159).
10 The twelve investigators in Johannesburg were swamped, having to cover events in four large provinces over a 34-year period. Deponents' statements were subjected to a 'low level corroboration', which in practice meant obtaining newspaper reports, police dockets, death certificates, and inquest reports. There was no forensic work done and little primary investigation. Statements were generally not used for in-depth investigations. Victims were often promised at HRV hearings that their case would be properly investigated but there was no internal mechanism to pass on cases from hearings to the IU.
11 See Cotterrell (1992:8–15) for a useful comparative discussion of positivism in both sociology and in law.
12 This is also illustrated in Lars Buur's (1999) account of an interview of a dead victim's family by investigators. As the interview wore on, both sides became more and more impatient with one another, as the family considered that the questions investigators asked were not important, and investigators felt that the family were hopelessly unable to provide any information that could be valuable in corroboration.
13 In the revised protocol, after the personal details of the deponent came three main sections: 1 *Acts* according to 4 categories mentioned in the mandate – torture, killings, disappearances and detentions, but not, for some reason, severe ill-treatment; 2 *Details of persons* perpetrators, victims and witnesses; 3 *Consequences* for victims of acts. At the very end came 8 lines for 'anything else'. The form allowed little room for deviation and was constrained in terms of the space allotted for answers.
14 It is important to distinguish, as Habermas does, between science generally and a more narrow scientism. Not all branches of science lapse into scientism. Some scientific traditions can and do acknowledge human subjectivity and perspective.
15 Hermeneutic interpretation, of course, does this also, but at least it is more reflexive about the relationship between the historian or ethnographer and his/her subject matter.
16 See Habermas' critique of the scientization of politics in modernity, where a technocratic consciousness transforms political questions into technical ones (1986:111).
17 This was partly the consequence of a reputed aversion to statistics on the part of the Research Unit director, Charles Villa-Vicencio, but also of the way the information system was constructed, as discussed earlier in this chapter.
18 TRC policy was that all individual gross human rights violations were morally equivalent, but that apartheid was an evil system. This meant that a just war was fought against apartheid but unjust means were sometimes used by the liberation movement. Many in the ANC (from grassroots activists to leading figures such as Matthews Phosa) believed that the end justified the means, and that the whole distinction was a form of bourgeois moralizing.

19 A phrase used by Jonathan Allen (1999) and attributed to Carlos Forment.

20 For instance, the right to legal representation, which is still not enjoyed by all criminal defendants. What is being created here is a hierarchy of rights, with human rights at the top and other rights further down the list.

21 See Slaughter (1997) for a discussion of how human rights narratives construct a universal individual subjectivity.

3 THE POLITICS OF TRUTH AND HUMAN RIGHTS

1 In its 1996 submission to the TRC, the ANC alleged that in the 1990s 'The violence was a calculated campaign with the objective of creating conditions which would assist the regime in weakening the hand of the liberation movement at the negotiations table, thereby manipulating the constitutional negotiations process to its advantage on various levels – in other words, an attempt to "manage" the transition to the advantage of the state' (p.42).

2 Peace Action, the Human Rights Committee and the Independent Board of Inquiry, for example.

3 Another earlier version asserted that the Third Force wanted to derail the negotiations completely so as to leave the National Party in power, but this version lost support as multiracial elections became inevitable.

4 The South West African People's Organization. The destabilization strategy, detailed in a National Intelligence Service document in 1988, reduced the vote of SWAPO from an estimated 80 per cent to 60 per cent, meaning that the liberation movement party did not have the majority necessary to rewrite the new constitution. For a discussion of the importance of the Namibian settlement on the South African peace process, see Landsberg 1994.

5 This line of rhetoric, of course, ignored the fact that the conflict in Natal (which had claimed 14,000 lives in 13 years of war) was between the same Zulus of different political affiliations, and that the ANC was founded by a Zulu and includes a preponderance of non-Xhosas at all levels of the party.

6 See Rian Malan and Dennis Beckett, 'On the Inside Looking Out', *Sunday Star* 28 June 1992. For a more recent statement by Malan, see 'Boipatong's Third Force myth', *Mail and Guardian* 2 June 1999.

7 Kane-Berman also wrote the introduction to Anthea Jeffery's (1999) book, where this argument is reiterated.

8 Formally called the 'Commission of Inquiry into Certain Alleged Murders' chaired by the Hon. L T C Harms, its report was submitted in September 1990. Several witnesses who appeared before the Harms Commission subsequently told the TRC that they were instructed to lie by the police.

9 The 'Commission of Inquiry Regarding the Prevention of Public Violence and Intimidation' was headed by Judge Richard Goldstone. It was established in 1992 and made its final report in October 1994.

10 It should be pointed out that Waddington never investigated charges of police involvement and did not reject the allegation, but said that he found no evidence to support it. The issue of police involvement in Boipatong has therefore never been properly investigated by an independent enquiry.

11 The author of the section was Vanessa Barolsky who joined Peace Action as a monitor in the Vaal some months after the massacre. The Commission admitted that it had carried out no further investigation or forensic work into the incident.

12 The 15 IFP members convicted of the Boipatong massacre in the criminal trial applied successfully to the TRC for amnesty. Another former IFP member, A Nosenga (who was convicted of drive-by shootings in 1992, not in relation to Boipatong), claimed that white policemen were involved in the execution of the massacre. The AC rejected Nosenga's evidence and amnesty application. The decision to grant amnesty contradicted the TRC *Report*'s assertion that white police were involved in the attack, since this was denied by most IFP amnesty applicants.

13 In 1999, a group including former Law and Order Minister Adriaan Vlok, former Commissioner of Police van der Merwe and former C Unit Commander Eugene de Kock were given amnesty for their involvement in the bombing of Khotso House in 1988. Amnesty was granted on 5 August in respect of public violence, malicious damage to property, unlawful possession of arms and defeating the ends of justice.

14 Apart from Law and Order Minister Adriaan Vlok's application for amnesty in relation to the bombing of Khotso House.

15 Although one NEC member reported to me that the NEC had been split, with nearly half against any court action arguing that it would make the ANC look like de Klerk. Reportedly, Thabo Mbeki made the casting vote in favor of legal action.

16 See 'Mangosuthu Buthelezi' in 'The A–Z of South African Politics, 1999'. Johannesburg: *Mail and Guardian.*

17 The TRC's mandate had run out when Botha's subpoena had been issued.

18 Buthelezi was a member of the ANC until Inkatha broke ties with the organization in 1979.

19 'Thabo Mbeki's First Cabinet', Mungo Soggot, *Mail and Guardian* (http://www.mg.co.za/mg/za/news/99jun/cabinet/buthelezi.html)

20 I thank Piers Pigou for this insight. See Piers Pigou's 'Uncovering the real conspiracy of Boipatong', *Mail and Guardian* 24 May 1999.

21 TREWITS was the Afrikaans acronym (Teen Revolusionere Inligtings Taakspan).

22 The Coordinating Intelligence Committee, or KIK, developed profiles on 'state enemies' such as the ANC and the PAC from 1990. It reported to the President and State Security Council.

23 Code name, 'Operation Marion'.

24 Later the National Co-ordinating Mechanism, which carried out the same functions.

25 Ellis (1998) provides an excellent account of the increasing criminalization of the security forces post-1992.

26 Represented primarily by the Concerned South Africans Group (COSAG).

27 This led to a variety of confrontations at the national and regional levels. For instance, Eastern Cape Commissioner Bongani Finca excoriated NP secretary-general Roelf Meyer for his party's failure to accept an 'iota of

responsibility for the 1992 Bisho massacre'. 'Bisho: Roelf rapped by Truth body', *Citizen* 19 November 1996.

28 PWV-Pretoria-Witwatersrand-Vereeniging area.

29 Sentenced to 212 years on 31 October 1996, on 89 charges, including six counts of murder.

30 See also on De Kock's criminal pursuits Ellis (1998); and in the TRC final *Report* see especially Volume 2, chapter 7.

31 We might assume that they would not have killed one of their own supporters for beating his wife.

32 See Chapter 4, section 20, 3.

33 That is, the relationship between the act and the stated objective.

34 According to the terms of the NURA, the Amnesty Committee had to deal first with the applications of those serving prison sentences.

35 All text from TRC hearings comes directly from the transcripts on the official TRC Website CDROM, November 1998.

36 Price (1997:170) points out that the ANC, since it was prevented from doing so by the Constitution, did not introduce a single piece of legislation requiring the use of racial criteria in the allocation of resources or for affirmative action. However, the Employment of Equity Act of 1998 broke with this non-racialism with its references to racial categories in its 'designated groups': for instance Chapter 1 at 1 defines 'black people' as a 'generic term which means African, Coloureds and Indians'.

37 See, for a start, Leiman (1993); Malik (1996); Donald and Rattansi (1992); Emile Boonzaier 'Race and the Race Paradigm' in Boonzaier and Sharp (1988); Gilroy (1987); Rex (1970); Rex and Mason (1986); Solomos (1989).

38 See the introductory chapter of Dubow (1995) for a discussion of the literature on the lived experience of racism.

39 Wanton Matshoba and Sazise Cyprion Qheliso.

40 Brigadier Mofokeng of APLA, at a TRC hearing, justified treating all whites as targets thus, 'The pillars of apartheid protecting white South Africa from the black danger, were the military and the process of arming of the entire white South African society. This militarization, therefore, of necessity made every white citizen a member of the security establishment'. (TRC *Report* 2:6)

4 RECONCILIATION THROUGH TRUTH?

1 Chapter 2, Section 3:1(a–d) 'Objectives of Commission'.

2 Section 11(g).

3 *Baas* is Afrikaans for 'boss' or 'master'.

4 See 'TRC tension not just an issue of race', and 'Who constitutes the "white liberal clique"?', Robert Brand, *Star* 30 January 1997.

5 There is a voluminous literature on the 'just war' tradition within moral philosophy. One might usefully start with Richard Norman (1995).

6 Omar argued (*Financial Mail* 29 March 1996) that there is no moral equivalence between fighting against and defending apartheid since apartheid was a crime against humanity.

7 When the final *Report* was released in 1998, after the TRC hearings process was over, the TRC formally accepted that apartheid was a crime against humanity and that a just war was waged against it. However, it argued, unjust means were adopted at times in fighting this just war, leading to human rights violations.
8 TRC Executive Secretary Paul van Zyl, once an ardent NGO advocate of victim-oriented reconciliation, told me, 'Reconciliation cannot work on an individual level. Perhaps it could only be the end product of the TRC process'.
9 An abstract historical reading was also supported by Alex Boraine, manager of the TRC. In *The Healing of a Nation?* Boraine took a broad politician's perspective on national reconciliation, writing: 'It is when South Africa begins to take its past seriously that there will be new possibilities for renewal.' (1995:xv),
10 TRC workshop on reconciliation February, 1997.
11 Many individuals giving testimony that I interviewed were persuaded by former Archbishop Desmond Tutu, or at least so overawed that they dared not resist his views. The moral authority of charismatic figures such as Tutu was crucial in the process of impressing the ideals of the Commission upon the individuals that came before it.
12 Tutu writes, 'Forgiving means abandoning your right to pay back the perpetrator in his own coin, but it is a loss which liberates the victim' (1999:219).

5 RECONCILIATION IN SOCIETY

1 For a discussion of legal pluralism in legal philosophy and sociology, see Santos (1995, Part II), and Teubner (1997, Part I).
2 Despite Malinowski's functionalist assumptions about organic stability and stasis. This point has been extended by Marilyn Strathern (1985).
3 See D. Guillet (1998) for a thorough discussion of new developments in legal pluralism in relation to law-and-economics studies.
4 Such as Schapera (1938), for example.
5 See also Dembour (1990).
6 A point recognized by historians Mann and Roberts (1991:9). See the watershed work of Chanock (1985).
7 This can also be done within a state-discourse-centered approach, such as Fitzpatrick (1987) who analyzes how law operates, without having to adopt an approach 'outside' of state law. My thanks to Marie-Bénédicte Dembour for this observation.
8 As they are in Foucault's writings and postmodern legal theory, such as Davies (1996) and Santos (1995).
9 See Hunt (1993:42–43) on the place of Weber in the 'law as social control' tradition.
10 See also Charles van Onselen's superb work (1982) on vigilantes on the Witwatersrand at the turn of the twentieth century.

11 An approach found also within the postmodernist legal theory of Santos (1995:116).
12 See Tom Lodge and Bill Nasson (1992).
13 On the limitations of human rights in Latin American democratization processes, see Panizza (1995).
14 For instance, Miriam Molete appealed to both the Vaal Council of Churches and the TRC to pay for the special educational needs of her handicapped daughter, Mitah, who received a serious head wound during the Boipatong massacre.
15 The second being Magouws Motau, a fieldworker of the Catholic Church's Justice and Peace office in Johannesburg. Her view of reconciliation was as follows: 'It is good to forgive. If you do not, then something remains inside and hurts you.'
16 Moerane was, at the time of writing, Coordinator of the Gauteng Council of Churches.
17 The five former policemen being J Cronje, J Hechter, P van Vuuren, R Venter and W Mentz.
18 Thibedi was at the time of the amnesty hearings a professional ANC politician and Speaker of the Northwest Provincial Legislature.
19 At the time of amnesty hearings, Reverend Mkhatshwa was the Deputy Minister for Education.
20 Testimony at hearings was not published in the final *Report*, but was available on the Commissions's website, and later on CDRom (TRC website November, 1998, Copyright Steve Crawford and the TRC, 1998).
21 See note 20, above.
22 See the return to the question in Abercrombie, Hill and Turner (1990) *Dominant Ideologies.*
23 See van der Merwe (1998) for more information on the TRC in Duduza.

6 VENGEANCE, REVENGE AND RETRIBUTION

1 There is an extensive literature on informal justice in South Africa, but one could start with Burman and Schärf (1990), Rycroft et al. (1987), Seekings (1995), and van Onselen (1982).
2 For a useful summary of a vast literature, see Matthew Pauley (1994).
3 See particularly Nietzsche's disdainful treatment of religion in *Beyond Good and Evil.* It must be recognised however that Kant and Hegel in their own ways endorsed a retributive perspective on justice and, for instance, supported the use of the death penalty.
4 See W Connelly (1999) on *ressentiment* and capital punishment.
5 Central Statistical Service 30/9/98 *Report: Crimes: Prosecutions and convictions with regard to certain offences* http://www.css.gov.za/reports/prosecut/
6 For a fruitful use of Nozick to counter the claims of Tutu and others in South Africa, see Crocker (2000).
7 See also Jon Elster (1990) and Susan Jacoby (1983).
8 See TRC final *Report*, Volume 2, Chapter 6, on the Mandela United Football Club special investigation.

9 *Azanian Peoples Organisation (AZAPO) and others v the President of the Republic of South Africa and others* 1996 (4) SA671 (CC). The decision was published on 25 July 1996, Case CCT 17/96.
10 The 'necklace' was a gruesome means of killing prevalent in the 1980s which involved placing a burning tyre filled with petrol around the neck of suspected police informers.
11 Which became in the South Africa Constitution of 1996, Chapter 2 Bill of Rights No. 34. 'Access to courts: Everyone has the right to have any dispute that can be resolved by the application of law decided in a fair public hearing in a court or, where appropriate, another independent and impartial forum.'
12 Article 50 of the first Geneva Convention, article 51 of the second Geneva Convention, article 130 of the third Geneva Convention and article 147 of the fourth Geneva Convention.
13 CCT 17/96 at 19.
14 Ibid. at 18.
15 Ibid. at 26–27.
16 South African lawyer John Dugard (1997), for instance, accepts that amnesty is not incompatible with international human rights law.
17 CCT 17/96 at 30.
18 9 December 1948, 78 UNTS 277.
19 'Truth Commission not losing credibility, says Tutu', SAPA news, 11 April 1996. www.struth.org.za/index.pl?&file=sapa/1996-04/S960411C.HTM
20 'Truth Commission opponents aiding apartheid offenders: ANC', SAPA news, 11 April 1996. www.struth.org.za/index.pl?&file=sapa/1996-04/S960411E.HTM
21 Ibid.
22 On the Sharpeville Six legal case, see Prakash Diar (1990) and Parker and Mokhesi-Parker (1998).
23 For a useful overview of gangs in twentieth-century South Africa, see Kynoch (1999). On gangs and school politics in Soweto, see Glaser (1998).
24 The IFP in turn created its own armed vigilante structures called Self-Protection Units, or SPUs.
25 The TRC Report included findings on the Vaal conflicts between MK-ANCYL and MK-NUMSA (Volume 3, pp.691–692).
26 Cf. Paul Thulare (1997) on the incorporation of SDUs into the SAPS on the East Rand.
27 In September 1995 in Sizanenjana in the province of Natal, two alleged criminals Mthembu and Sithole were apprehended while allegedly attempting to rob a homestead, tried in a 'popular court' hearing, convicted and then sentenced to hang themselves in the presence of 'the community'. In Meadowlands in Soweto, a member of an SDU, Montsheng Sekatane (former MK soldier and bodyguard to Winnie Mandela) tracked down and shot dead, in the back while he was running away, an 18-year-old robbery suspect, Linda Dladla. Sekatane, expressing his contempt for formal legal processes, showed little remorse: 'I won't stop in my duty of protecting the community against criminals.' The final publicised incident during the

same week occurred in the Delft neighborhood of Cape Flats, when Desmain Joshua was robbed at home of her husband's weekly wage at knife point. Her husband, Harry Joshua, then took a shotgun and confronted the 'Hard Livings' gang sitting across the street from the Joshua home. He demanded the money back and, when refused, he went on a killing spree which left five youths (all under the age of 17) dead, and two wounded.

7 RECONCILIATION WITH A VENGEANCE

1 On local courts and 'popular justice' see Burman and Schärf (1990), Goodhew (1993), Pavlich (1992), Scheper-Hughes (1995), and Schärf and Ngcokoto (1990).
2 See also Klug (1995).
3 For a thorough historical overview, see T W Bennett (1985).
4 See Burman and Schärf (1990:700).
5 This was especially the case in the Western Cape. See Burman and Schärf (1990).
6 A figure which, given the highly political circumstances in which it was delivered, must be treated with caution.
7 See Allison (1990).
8 See Schärf and Ngcokoto (1990:346).
9 For a discussion of violent redress in the 1986 period see Burman and Schärf (1990). For a more apologetic view, which asks whether criticism of necklacing is a form of disguised white racism, see Scheper-Hughes (1995).
10 For instance, in the famous case of the *State vs Mayekiso and others 1988.*
11 See Richard Abel (1995). This last point is nowhere better illustrated than in the case of a man condemned to death for killing a fellow hostel-dweller who he believed to be a malignant being sent through witchcraft (see Wulf Sachs 1996 *Black Hamlet*).
12 South Africa has a Gini coefficient of 0.61.
13 University of Cape Town Public Law Professor, Hugh Corder, cited in Stack (1997:5).
14 The 1996 Constitution says citizens have the right 'to have a legal aid practitioner assigned to the accused by the state, and at state expense, if substantial injustice would otherwise result, and to be informed of this right'. In April 1997, the Johannesburg High Court freed a hijacker sentenced to 10 years in jail because he was refused state-backed legal representation.
15 The lawyer Peter Jordi, who has carried out numerous successful cases against the police for torture, estimates that between 1 and 2 per cent of people in custody are tortured (Atkins 1998:36). In 1997, police reporting officer for Gauteng Jan Munnick submitted a report to the commissioner of police detailing 19 cases of torture.
16 The first drug dealer killed, named Rashaad, was burned on a bonfire in August 1996. His brother Rashied was boss of the infamous Cape Flats Hard Livings gang (Jeppie 1999:9).

17 For an idea of the level and tone of early press reporting on Pagad, see 'Pagad Targets Omar', *Mail and Guardian* 6 December 1996; 'Crowd ignores plea to disperse – then bullets fly', *Cape Argus* 17 December 1996; 'The Battle of Bellville', *Cape Argus* 17 December 1996; 'Pagad has become just another gang', *Cape Times* 18 December 1996; 'Armour-piercing bullets used against police', *Cape Times* 18 December 1996.

18 See Frank et al. (1997) for an evaluation of lay assessors and CPFs.

19 There are differences in the numbers reported killed. The Waddington Commission declared 42 dead, whereas the TRC asserted that 46 were murdered.

20 See Lugard's 'The Dual Mandate in British Tropical Africa: Methods of Ruling Native Races' (reprinted 1997).

21 See Burman and Schärf (1990) for a discussion of the conservative and patriarchal nature of street committees in the Cape.

22 Likewise the Ward Four *imbizo* of Mamelodi township near Pretoria claimed its origins in 1977 with an assault on a young woman by a young man who was not pursued by the police (Hund and Kotu-Rammopo 1983:185).

23 For comparative material on the operation of township courts in the Western Cape, see also Burman and Schärf (1990), Scheper-Hughes (1995), Schärf and Ngcokoto (1990).

24 A small sample of the voluminous press coverage of this topic could include: in the local press; '"Courts" Haunting Townships', *Sunday Times* 24 October 1993; 'Return of the Kangaroo Court', *Mail and Guardian* 16 September 1994; '50 Die, 62 hurt in "people's court" action', *Argus* 1 September 1995; 'Tougher Sentences for Kangaroo Court Five', *Argus* 12 December 1994; 'Crime-busters to Criminals', *Star* 10 November 1998; and finally in the international press: 'We Fight Crime the African Way', *Guardian* 12 May 1999.

25 See Scheper-Hughes (1995:157) for an interview with a township youth that demonstrates this discursive opposition.

26 In his characteristic rebuttal of religious and human rights values, Friedrich Nietzsche in *Thus Spoke Zarathustra* speaks of how law attempts to dignify itself through the notion of proportional retribution, all the while keeping its spoon in the pot of hatred (1969:162).

27 The creation of the modern dual legal system is usually traced back to the 1927 Native Administration Act.

28 Vaal residents are very hostile to local government councilors from the apartheid era, and all remember the homicidal gangs who rampaged on 3 September 1984 and set the region on fire. They protested against the new tier of apartheid-controlled local government, the Lekoa Town Council, which was perceived as an agent of the white-controlled Orange-Vaal Development Board. Matters came to a head when the Council demanded a 5.90 Rand per month increase in service charges (Lodge and Nasson 1992). Almost every shop in the Vaal was burned and all the homes of Lekoa councilors were reduced to ashes; four councilors did not escape the protestors and were burned alive (Kuzwayo Jacob Dlamini of Sharpeville, Jacob Chakane and Cesar Motleane of Sebokeng and Philemon Diphoko of

Evaton). Attacks on councilors then spread to townships around the country, especially in the (then) Transvaal and Eastern Cape.

29 These observations are more generally applicable to narratives on history in Latin America and Eastern Europe. On the latter, see Garton Ash (1997a), Moeller (1996) and Rosenberg (1995).

30 Such as Tony Richards and Peter Jordi, then of the Vaal Legal Aid Clinic and Law Clinic at the University of the Witwatersrand, respectively. Richards has since been elevated to a high-ranking position on the state Legal Aid Board.

8 CONCLUSIONS

1 See Bryan Turner's (1993) discussion of frailty as the basis for his outline of a theory of human rights.

2 Lifeworld in the Habermasian sense of a culturally transmitted set of linguistically organized patterns used to interpret meaning. See Habermas (1987:124).

3 Here I would remind the reader that the South African Constitutional Court can strike down any piece of legislation which it deems contradicts an article of the Bill of Rights.

4 Rationalization does not only bring negative effects and both Marx and Weber recognised the possible progressive consequences of the rationalization of the lifeworld (e.g., in secular education) which generates values (equality, individualism) which can then turn back on the system and transform it.

5 Comisión para el Esclarecimiento Histórico de las Violaciones a los Derechos Humanos y los Hechos de Violencia que han Causado Sufrimiento a la Población Guatemalteca.

6 It created an understanding of the past which integrated over 7,000 oral testimonials into a singular historical perspective. Injustice and violence were apprehended in terms of hundreds of years of social exclusion, poverty and racial discrimination against the indigenous majority. Between September 1997 and May 1998, CEH investigators visited about 2,000 communities, some as many as ten times, and collected 500 collective testimonies and 7,338 testimonies in all. The CEH interacted directly with more than 20,000 people who provided information.

7 The Convention on the Prevention and Punishment of the Crime of Genocide and the Convention Against Torture and other Cruel, Inhuman or Degrading Treatment or Punishment both stipulate that signatory governments must punish violators. The Universal Declaration of Human Rights (especially Article 8) and the International Convenant on Civil and Political Rights (ICCPR) both recognize the rights of victims of crimes to recourse to 'effective remedy'. See Orentlicher (1991).

8 And, in the context of amnesty, those who do not qualify for amnesty.

BIBLIOGRAPHY

Abbink, Jan 1998. 'Violence and the crisis of conciliation: Suma, Dizi and the state in Southwest Ethiopia'. Paper presented at the 5th Biannual EASA Conference, Frankfurt, 4–7 September.

Abel, Richard 1995. *Politics by Other Means: Law in the struggle against apartheid, 1980–1994.* London: Routledge.

Abercrombie, N., S. Hill and B. S. Turner 1980. *The Dominant Ideology Thesis.* London: Allen & Unwin.

—— (eds) 1990. *Dominant Ideologies.* London: Unwin Hyman.

Abrahams, Ray 1996. 'Vigilantism: Order and disorder on the frontiers of the state'. In Olivia Harris (ed.) *Inside and Outside the Law: Anthropological studies of authority and ambiguity.* London: Routledge.

Adam, Heribert 1979. 'The Failure of Political Liberalism in South Africa'. In H. Adam and H. Giliomee (eds). *The Rise of Afrikaner Power.* Cape Town: David Philip.

—— 1994. 'Ethnic versus Civic Nationalism: South Africa's Non-Racialism in Comparative Perspective'. *SA Sociological Review* 7(1):15–31.

Adam, H. and K. Moodley 1992. 'Political violence, "Tribalism" and Inkatha'. *Journal of Modern African Studies* 30, 3.

—— 1993. *The Opening of the Apartheid Mind: Options for a New South Africa.* Berkeley: University of California Press.

African National Congress 1996. Statement to the Truth and Reconciliation Commission. Johannesburg: ANC Department of Information and Publicity.

Aguilar, P. A. Barahona de Brito and C. Gonzalez (eds) 2001. *The Politics of Memory.* Oxford: Oxford University Press.

Allen, Jonathan 1999. 'Balancing Justice and Social Unity: Political theory and the idea of a Truth and Reconciliation Commission'. *University of Toronto Law Journal* 49, 3, pp. 315–353.

Anderson, Benedict 1991. *Imagined Communities: Reflections on the Origins and Spread of Nationalism,* second edition. London: Verso.

Antze, Paul and Michael Lambek (eds) 1996. *Tense Past: Cultural essays in trauma and memory.* London: Routledge.

Asmal, Kadar, Louise Asmal and Ronald S. Roberts 1997. *Reconciliation Through Truth: A reckoning of apartheid's criminal governance,* second edition. Cape Town: David Philip.

Atkins, Ros 1998. 'Breaking the Cycle'. In *The Right Thing: Two perspectives on public order and human rights in South Africa's emerging democracy.* Centre for Policy Studies, research report no. 64.

Atkinson, D. and S. Friedman 1994. *The Small Miracle: South Africa's negotiated settlement.* South African Review 7. Johannesburg: Ravan Press.

Ball, Patrick 1996. 'Evaluation of the TRCSA information flow and database, with recommendations'. 8 September 1996. Internal TRC document.

Barahona de Brito, Alexandra 1997. *Human Rights and Democratization in Latin America: Uruguay and Chile.* Oxford: Oxford University Press.

Bayart, Jean-François 1993. *The State in Africa: The politics of the belly.* New York: Longman.

Bennett, T. W. 1985. *Application of Customary Law in South Africa.* Kenwyn: Juta and Co.

—— 1994. 'Customary Law and the Gender Equality'. *South African Journal of Human Rights* 10, 1, pp. 122–130.

Bennett, T. W. and J. W. Roos 1992. 'The 1991 Land Reform Acts and the Future of African Customary Law'. *South African Law Journal* 109, 447.

Bennun, Mervyn 1995. 'Understanding the Nightmare: Politics and violence in South Africa.'. In Bennun, M. and M. Newitt (eds) *Negotiating Justice: A new constitution for South Africa,* pp. 26–61. Exeter: University of Exeter Press.

Bennun, Mervyn and Malyn Newitt (eds) 1995. *Negotiating Justice: A new constitution for South Africa.* Exeter: University of Exeter Press.

Benomar, Jamal 1993. 'Confronting the Past: Justice after transitions. *Journal of Democracy* 4(1), January, pp. 3–14.

Berryman, Phillip E., trans. 1993. *Report of the Chilean National Commission on Truth and Reconciliation.*

Bettelheim, Bruno 1952. *Surviving and Other Essays.* New York: Vintage.

Bhaskar, Roy 1978. *A Realist Theory of Science.* Brighton: Harvester Press.

—— 1979. *The Possibility of Naturalism: A philosophical critique of the contemporary human sciences.* Brighton: Harvester Press.

Bohannon, P. 1957. *Justice and Judgment Among the Tiv.* London: Oxford University Press.

—— 1967. *Law and Welfare: Studies in the anthropology of conflict.* New York: Natural History Press.

Boonzaier, Emile and John Sharp (eds) 1988. *South African Keywords: The uses and abuses of political concepts.* Cape Town: David Philip.

Boraine, Alex 1995. *The Healing of a Nation?.* Cape Town: Justice in Transition.

—— 2001. *A Country Unmasked.* Oxford: Oxford University Press.

Borneman, John 1997. *Settling Accounts: Violence, justice and accountability in postsocialist Europe.* Princeton: Princeton University Press.

Boschi, Renato 1990. 'Social Movements, Party systems and Democratic Consolidation: Brazil, Uruguay and Argentina'. In Diane Ethier (ed.) *Democratic Transition and Consolidation in Southern Europe and Latin America and Southeast Asia.* London: Macmillan.

Bourdieu, Pierre 1991. *Language and Symbolic Power.* Cambridge: Polity Press.

Bowman, Glenn 1998. 'Constitutive Violence and Rhetorics of Identity: a Comparative Study of Nationalist Movements in the Israeli-Occupied Territories and Former Yugoslavia'. In Bruce Kapferer (ed.) *Nationalism and Violence.* Oxford: Berg Press.

Bozzoli, Belinda 1998. 'Public Ritual and Private Transition: The Truth Commission in Alexandra township, South Africa 1996'. *African Studies* 57, 2, pp. 167–195.

Breytenbach, Willie 1994. 'Comment on Heribert Adam specifically in the African Context'. In Rhoodie, Nic and Ian Liebenberg (eds) *Democratic Nation-Building in South Africa.* Pretoria: HSRC Publishers.

Bronkhorst, D. 1995. *Truth and Reconciliation: Obstacles and opportunities for human rights.* Amsterdam: Amnesty International.

Brysk, Alison 1994. 'The Politics of Measurement: The contested count of the disappeared in Argentina'. *Human Rights Quarterly* 16:676–692.

Burman, Sandra and W. Schärf 1990. 'Creating People's Justice: Street committees and people's courts in a South African city'. *Law and Society Review* 24:693–745

Butler, Jeffrey, Richard Elphick and David Welsh 1987. *Democratic Liberalism in South Africa: Its history and prospect.* Middletown, Conn.: Wesleyan University Press.

Buur, Lars 1999. 'Monumental History: Visibility and invisibility: the work of the South African Truth and Reconciliation Commission'. Paper presented at the conference 'The TRC: Commissioning the Past', 11–14 June 1999, University of the Witwatersrand.

Cassell, D. 1993. 'International Truth Commissions and Justice'. *Aspen Institute Quarterly* 5 (3) Summer, pp. 69–90.

Catholic Institute of International Relations (CIIR) 1996. *South Africa: Breaking new ground.* August 1996. London: CIIR.

Chanock, Martin 1985. *Law, Custom and Social Order: The colonial experience in Malawi and Zambia.* Cambridge: Cambridge University Press.

—— 1991. 'Paradigms, Policies and Property: A review of the customary law of land tenure'. In Mann, K. and R. Roberts (eds) *Law in Colonial Africa.* London: James Currey.

—— 1998. *Law, Custom and Social Order: The colonial experience in Malawi and Zambia.* Portsmouth, NH: Heinemann. (1985).

Citizen. 'Bisho: Roelf rapped by Truth Body', 19 November 1996.

Cockrell, Alfred 1996. 'Rainbow Jurisprudence'. *South African Journal on Human Rights* 12(I): 1–38.

Cohen, A. P. 1985. *The Symbolic Construction of Community.* London: Routledge.

Cohen, Stanley 1995. 'State Crimes of Previous Regimes: Knowledge, accountability, and the policing of the past'. *Law and Social Inquiry* March 20:7–50.

Collier, Jane 1975. 'Legal Processes'. *Annual Review of Anthropology* 4:121–144.

Comaroff, Jean 1985. *Body of Power, Spirit of Resistance: The culture and history of a South African people.* Chicago: University of Chicago Press.

Comaroff, John and Simon Roberts 1981. *Rules and Processes: The cultural logic of dispute in an African context.* Chicago: University of Chicago Press.

Conley, John M. and W. O'Barr 1990. *Rules Versus Relationships: The ethnography of legal discourse.* Chicago: University of Chicago Press.

Connelly, William. 1999. 'The Will, Capital Punishment and the Cultural War'. In A. Sarat (ed.) *Killing State: Capital punishment in law, politics and culture.* Oxford: Oxford University Press.

Cotterrell, Roger 1992. *The Sociology of Law: An introduction*, second edition. London: Butterworths.

Crocker, David A. 2000. 'Retribution and Reconciliation'. Paper presented at the Munk Centre for International Relations, University of Toronto, February.

Das, Veena 1987. 'The Anthropology of Violence and the Speech of Victims'. *Anthropology Today* 3(4):11–13.

—— (ed.) 1994. *Mirrors of Violence: Communities, riots and survivors in South Asia*. Delhi: Oxford University Press.

Davies, Margaret 1996. *Delimiting the Law: Postmodernism and the politics of law*. London: Pluto Press.

Davis, Dennis 1998. 'Democracy and Integrity: making sense of the Constitution'. *South African Journal on Human Rights* 14, pp. 127–145.

Degenaar, Johan J. 1990. 'Nations and nationalism: The myth of the South African nation'. Occasional Paper No. 40, IDASA, Mowbray.

—— 1993. 'No Sizwe: The myth of the nation'. *Indicator South Africa* 10, 3, Winter, pp. 11–16.

—— 1994. 'Beware Nation-Building Discourse'. In Rhoodie, Nic and Ian Liebenberg (eds) *Democratic Nation-Building in South Africa*. Pretoria: HSRC Publishers.

Dembour, Marie-Bénédicte 1990. 'Le pluralisme juridique: une démarche parmi d'autres, et non plus innocente'. In *Revue interdisciplinaire d'études juridiques* 24:43–59.

Diamond, L. 1994. 'Toward Democratic Consolidation'. *Journal of Democracy*. July 5(3):4–17.

Diar, Prakash 1990. *The Sharpeville Six*. Toronto, London: McClelland and Stewart.

Donald J. and Ali Rattansi (eds) 1992. *Race, Culture & Difference*. London: Sage in association with the Open University.

Douglas, Lawrence 2000. *The Memory of Judgment: Making law and history in the trials of the Holocaust*. New Haven: Yale University Press.

Du Toit, André 1999a. 'The Product and the Process: On the impact of the TRC Report'. Paper presented at conference 'The TRC: Commissioning the Past'. 11–14 June 1999, University of the Witwatersrand.

—— 1999b. 'Perpetrator findings as artificial even-handedness? The TRC's contested judgements of moral and political accountability for gross human rights violations'. Paper presented at conference 'The TRC: Commissioning the Past'. 11–14 June 1999, University of the Witwatersrand.

Dubow, Saul 1995. *Scientific Racism in Modern South Africa*. Cambridge: Cambridge University Press.

—— 2000. *The African National Congress*. Johannesburg: Jonathan Ball.

Dugard, John 1978. *Human Rights and the South African Legal Order*. Princeton: Princeton University Press.

—— 1984. *The Denationalization of Black South Africans in Pursuance of Apartheid*. Johannesburg: University of the Witwatersrand Press.

—— 1997. 'Retrospective Justice: International law and the South African model'. In McAdams, A. J. (ed.) *Transitional Justice and the Rule of Law in New Democracies*. Notre Dame: Notre Dame University Press.

Durkheim, Emile 1915. *The Elementary Forms of the Religious Life.* London: George Allen & Unwin.

Durkheim, Emile 1965. *The Elementary Forms of the Religious Life.* New York: The Free Press.

Dworkin, Ronald 1977. *Taking Rights Seriously.* London: Duckworth.

Dyzenhaus, David 1998a. 'Law as Justification: Etienne Mureinik's conception of legal culture'. *South African Journal on Human Rights.* 14, pp. 11–37.

—— 1998b. *Judging the Judges, Judging Ourselves.* Oxford: Hart.

Ellis, Mark S. 1997. 'Purging the Past: The current state of lustration laws in the former Communist Bloc'. *Law and Contemporary Problems* 59(4):82–196.

Ellis, Stephen 1998. 'Historical Significance of South Africa's Third Force'. *Journal of Southern African Studies* 24(2):261–299.

Elster, Jon 1990. 'Norms of Revenge'. *Ethics* 100:862–885.

English, Rosalind 1997. 'Cases and Comments: *Ubuntu*: the quest for an indigenous jurisprudence'. *South African Journal on Human Rights* 13(4): 641–648.

Ensalaco, Mark 1994. 'Truth Commissions for Chile and El Salvador: A report and assessment'. *Human Rights Quarterly* 16:656–675.

Epstein A.L. 1978. *Ethos and Identity: three studies in ethnicity.* London: Tavistock.

Fagan, Anton 1995. 'In Defence of the Obvious: Ordinary language and the identification of constitutional rules'. *South African Journal on Human Rights* 11, pp. 545–570.

Filatova, Irina 1994. 'Comment on Heribert Adam'. In Rhoodie, Nic and Ian Liebenberg (eds) *Democratic Nation-Building in South Africa.* Pretoria: HSRC Publishers.

Fitzpatrick, Peter 1987. 'Racism and the Innocence of Law'. *Journal of Law and Society* 14, 1, pp. 119–132.

Foucault, Michel 1979. *Discipline and Punish: The birth of the prison.* Harmondsworth: Peregrine Books.

Foweraker, Joe 1995. *Theorising Social Movements.* London: Pluto Press.

Frank, Cheryl et al. 1997. *Popular Participation in the Administration of Justice.* Position Paper, commissioned by the Planning Unit, S. A. Ministry of Justice, Pretoria.

From Madness to Hope: The Twelve Year War in El Salvador. Report of the Truth Commission, 1993, UN Security Council, UN Doc. S/25500.

Friedman, Steven 1993. *The Long Journey: South Africa's quest for a negotiated settlement.* Johannesburg: Ravan Press.

Friedman, Steven and Doreen Atkinson 1994. *South African Review 7. The Small Miracle: South Africa's Negotiated Settlement.* Johannesburg: Ravan Press.

Fromm, Eric 1984. *The Anatomy of Human Destructiveness.* London: Penguin.

Frost, B. 1998. *Struggling to Forgive: Nelson Mandela and South Africa's search for reconciliation.* London: Harper Collins.

Garton Ash, Timothy 1997a. *The File: A personal history.* London: Harper Collins.

—— 1997b. 'True Confessions'. *New York Review of Books* 17 July 1997, pp. 33–38.

Geertz, Clifford 1983. 'Fact and Law in Comparative Perspective'. In *Local Knowledge: Further essays in interpretative anthropology.* New York: Basic Books.

Gellner, Ernest 1988. *Plough, Sword and Book: The structure of human history.* London: Collins Harvill.

Gerth, H. H. and C. Wright Mills (eds) 1991. *From Max Weber: Essays in sociology.* London: Routledge.

Gibson, James L. and Amanda Gouws 1998. 'Truth and Reconciliation in South Africa: Attributions of blame and the struggle over apartheid'. Paper presented at the 1998 meeting of the American Political Science Association, Boston, 3–6 Sept.

Gills B., J. Rocamora and R. Wilson (eds) 1993. *Low Intensity Democracy: Political power in the new world order.* London: Pluto Press.

Giliomee, H. and L. Schlemmer (eds) 1989. *From Apartheid to Nation-Building.* Cape Town: Oxford University Press.

Gilroy, Paul 1987. *There Aint no Black in the Union Jack.* London: Routledge.

Glaser, Clive 1998. 'We must infiltrate the Tsotsis': School Politics and Youth Gangs in Soweto, 1968–1976'. *Journal of Southern African Studies* 24(2): 301–328.

Gluckman, Max 1967 *The Judicial Process among the Barotse of Northern Rhodesia.* Manchester: Manchester University Press.

—— (ed.) 1969 *Ideas and Procedures in African Customary Law.* London: Oxford University Press.

Goodhew, David 1993. 'The People's Police Force: Communal policing initiatives in the western areas of Johannesburg, circa 1930–1962'. *Journal of Southern African Studies* 19, 3 (Sept).

Grandin, Greg n.d. 'Chronicle of a Death Foretold, or Repetition Taken for Fate: The Guatemalan Historical Commission's *Memoria del Silencio*'.

Guardian. 'Police "liar" admits to hitting Biko'. 31 March 1998.

—— 'Zulu Chief Tied to Abuses'. 30 October 1998.

—— 'Apartheid Victims Reject Handouts'. 3 January 2000.

—— 'UN Tribunal jails Croatian war criminal for 45 years'. 4 March 2000.

—— 'Top Serb Seized in Nato Raid'. 4 April 2000.

Guatemalan Commission for Historical Clarification 1999. *Memoria del Silencio.* http://www.hrdata.aaas.org/ceh

Guatemala: Nunca Mas. 1998. Informe Proyecto Interdiocesano de Recuperación de la Memoria. Vols. I–IV. Guatemala: Oficina de Derechos Humanos del Arzobispado de Guatemala.

Guillet, D. 1998. 'Rethinking Legal Pluralism: Local law and state law in the evolution of water property rights in northwestern Spain'. *Comparative Studies in Society and History* 40(1):42–70.

Gulbrandsen, Ørnulf 1996. 'Living their Lives in Courts: The counter-hegemonic force of the Tswana kgotla in a colonial context'. In O. Harris (ed.) *Inside and Outside the Law: Anthropological studies in authority and ambiguity.* London: Routledge.

Habermas, Jürgen 1986. *Knowledge and Human Interests.* Cambridge: Polity Press.

—— 1987. *The Theory of Communicative Action: Volume 2,* trans. Thomas McCarthy. Cambridge: Polity.

—— 1992. 'Citizenship and national identity: Some reflections on the future of Europe'. *Praxis International* 12(2):1–19.

—— 1994. 'Struggles for Recognition in the Democratic Constitutional State'. In Taylor, C., Amy Gutman et al. (eds) *Multiculturalism: Examining the politics of recognition.* Princeton, NJ: Princeton University Press.

Hamber, Brandon 1995. 'Do Sleeping Dogs Lie? The psychological implications of the Truth and Reconciliation Commission in South Africa'. Seminar Paper No.5 Johannesburg: Centre for the Study of Violence & Reconciliation.

—— 1997. 'Living with the Legacy of Impunity: Lessons for South Africa about truth, justice and crime in Brazil'. Unisa Latin American Report, 13(2):4–16, July–December. Pretoria: Unisa Centre for Latin American Studies, University of South Africa.

—— (ed.) 1998a. *Past Imperfect: Dealing with the past in Northern Ireland and societies in transition.* Derry/Londonderry: University of Ulster/INCORE.

—— 1998b. 'Repairing the Irreparable: Dealing with double-binds of making reparations for crimes of the past'. Paper presented to the African Studies Association of the UK, London, 14–16 September.

Hamber, Brandon and Steve Kibble 1999. *From Truth to Transformation: South Africa's Truth and Reconciliation Commission.* Briefing paper. London: Catholic Institute for International Relations.

Hamber, Brandon and Richard A. Wilson 2001. 'Trauma, Liminality and Symbolic Closure: The legacy of political violence in South Africa'. In Cairns, Edward and M. Roe (eds) *Memories in Conflict.* Proceedings of the American Psychological Association. London: Macmillan.

Hart, H. L. A. 1958. 'Positivism and the separation of law and morals'. *Harvard Law Review.* 71(4):593–629.

—— 1961. *The Concept of Law.* Oxford: Oxford University Press.

Hayes, G. 1998. 'We Suffer our Memories: Thinking about the past, healing and reconciliation'. *American Imago.* 55, 1, Spring, pp. 29–50.

Hayner, Priscilla B. 1994. 'Fifteen Truth Commissions – 1974 to 1994: A comparative study'. *Human Rights Quarterly* Vol. 16:597–655.

—— 2000. *Unspeakable Truths: Confronting state terror and atrocity.* London: Routledge.

Hendricks, Fred 1999. 'Amnesty and Justice in Post-Apartheid South Africa. How not to construct a democratic normative framework'. Paper presented at conference 'The TRC: Commissioning the Past', 11–14 June 1999, History Workshop, University of the Witwatersrand.

Higley, John and Richard Gunther (eds) 1992. *Elites and Democratic Consolidation in Latin America and Southern Europe.* Cambridge: Cambridge University Press.

Hill, Stephen 1990. 'Britain: The dominant ideology thesis after a decade'. In Abercrombie, N., S. Hill and B. S. Turner (eds) 1990. *Dominant Ideologies.* London: Unwin Hyman.

Hobbes, Thomas 1985. *Leviathan.* C. B. MacPherson (ed.) London: Penguin.

Hobsbawm, Eric 1992. 'Ethnicity and Nationalism in Europe Today'. *Anthropology Today* 8, 1., February.

Holmes, Oliver Wendell 1909. *The Common Law.* Boston MA.: Little, Brown.

Howarth, David R. and Aletta J. Norval (eds) 1998. *South Africa in Transition: New theoretical perspectives.* London: Macmillan.

Human Rights Committee of South Africa (HRC) 2000. *Access: quarterly publication of the New Institutions Project.* Braamfontein, Johannesburg: HRC.

Humphreys, Sally 1985. 'Law as Discourse'. *History and Anthropology* (1): 241–264.

Hund, John and Malebo Kotu-Rammopo 1983. 'Justice in a South African township: the sociology of *makgotla. Comparative and International Law Journal of Southern Africa.* 16:179–208.

Hunt, Alan 1993. *Explorations in Law and Society: Towards a constitutive theory of law.* London: Routledge.

Hunt, Alan and Gary Wickham 1994. *Foucault and Law.* London: Pluto Press.

Huntington, Samuel 1991. *The Third Wave: Democratization in the late twentieth century.* Norman: University of Oklahoma Press.

Huyse, Luc 1995. 'Justice After Transition: On the choices successor elites make in dealing with the past'. *Law and Social Enquiry* (1):51–78.

Ignatieff, Michael 1993. *Blood and Belonging: Journeys into the new nationalism.* London: Chatto and Windus/BBC Books.

—— 1998. *The Warrior's Honor: Ethnic war and the modern conscience.* London: Chatto & Windus.

Jacoby, Susan 1983. *Wild Justice: The evolution of revenge.* New York: Harper and Row.

Janoff-Bulman, R. 1985. 'The Aftermath of Victimisation: Rebuilding shattered assumptions'. In Figley, C. R. (ed.), *Trauma and its Wake.* New York: Brunner Mazel.

Jeffery, Anthea 1999. *The Truth About the Truth Commission.* Spotlight Series. Johannesburg: South African Institute of Race Relations.

Jelin, Elizabeth 1998. 'The Minefields of Memory', *NACLA Report on the Americas.* Report on Memory. Vol. XXXII, No. 2, September/October.

Jeppie, Shamil 1999. 'Islam, Narcotics and Defiance in the Western Cape, South Africa'. Paper presented at the African Studies Conference, May 1999, Centre for African Studies, University of Edinburgh.

Jung, Courtney and Ian Shapiro 1995. 'South Africa's Negotiated Transition: Democracy, opposition, and the new constitutional order'. *Politics and Society* 23(3):269–308.

Kane-Berman, John 1993. *Political Violence in South Africa.* Johannesburg: South African Institute of Race Relations.

Kentridge, Matthew 1990. *An Unofficial War: Inside the conflict in Pietermaritzburg.* Cape Town: David Philip.

Kleinman, Arthur et al. (eds) 1996. Issue on Social Suffering. *Daedelus* Winter issue. 125(1).

Klug, Heinz 1995. 'Defining the Property Rights of Others: Political power, indigenous tenure and the construction of customary law'. Center for Applied Legal Studies, University of the Witwatersrand: Working Paper 23.

Kristeva, Julia 1993. *Nation Without Nationalism,* trans. Leon S. Roudiez. New York: Columbia University Press.

Krog, Antjie 1998. *Country of My Skull.* Johannesburg: Random House.

Kynoch, Gary 1999. 'From the Ninevites to the Hard Livings Gang: Township gangsters and urban violence in twentieth century South Africa'. *African Studies.* 58, 1, pp. 55–85.

Landsberg, Chris 1994. 'Directing From the Stalls? International community and the South African negotiating forum'. In Atkinson, D. and S. Friedman (eds) *The Small Miracle: South Africa's negotiated settlement.* South African Review 7. Johannesburg: Ravan Press, pp. 276–300.

Lane, Jan-Erik 1996. *Constitutions and Political Theory.* Manchester: Manchester University Press.

Lapsley, Michael 1997. 'Healing the Memory: Cutting the cord between victim and perpetrator: Interview with Father Michael Lapsley by Hannes Siebert'. *Track Two.* 6, 3 & 4, December.

Leiman, Melvyn 1993. *The Political Economy of Racism.* London: Pluto Press.

Liebenberg, I. 1994. 'Reply to Degenaar and Alexander'. In Rhoodie, Nic and Ian Liebenberg (eds) *Democratic Nation-Building in South Africa.* Pretoria: HSRC Publishers.

Llewellen, Karl and E. Adamson Hoebel 1941. *The Cheyenne Way: Conflict and case law in primitive jurisprudence.* Norman: University of Oklahoma Press.

Locke, John 1988. *Two Treatises on Government.* P. Laslett (ed.) Cambridge: Cambridge University Press.

Lodge, Tom and Bill Nasson 1992. *All, Here, and Now: Black politics in South Africa in the 1980s.* London: Hurst.

Lubowski, Anton 1988. 'Democracy and the Judiciary'. In Corder, Hugh *Democracy and the Judiciary.* Cape Town: Institute for a Democratic Alternative for South Africa.

Lugard, Frederick 1997. 'The Dual Mandate in British Tropical Africa: Methods of Ruling Native Races', reprinted in Grinker, R. and C. Steiner (eds) *Perspectives on Africa.* Oxford: Blackwell, pp. 574–84.

Lyons, B. S. 1997. 'Between Nuremberg and Amnesia: The TRC in South Africa', *Monthly Review* 19(4):5–22.

Mail and Guardian. 'Generals Avoid Justice as System Struggles to Cope'. 29 September 1995.

—— 'Profile doing the Arch'. 17 March 1996.

—— 'Constitutional Court Judgment not Thorough'. 20 September 1996.

—— Review of 'Prime Evil' SABC. 18–24 October 1996.

—— '"Let the Law be a Moral Arena". Sergeant at the Bar'. 8 November 1996.

—— 'Justice at the Bottom of the Pile'. 11 April 1997.

—— 'Omar Seeks to Plug Legal Pay-outs'. 27 April 1997.

—— 'Winnie's Week of Reckoning'. 28 November 1997.

—— 'The Truth as it was Told'. 23 December 1997.

—— 'FW's Ironic Blank Space'. 2 October 1998.

—— 'Buthelezi: The BOSS Connection'. 27 November–3 December 1998.

—— 'Thabo Mbeki's First Cabinet'. 17 June 1999.

Mainwaring, Scott et al. (eds) 1992. *Issues in Democratic Consolidation: The new South American democracies in comparative perspective.* South Bend, IN: University of Notre Dame Press.

Malik, Kenan 1996. *The Meaning of Race: race, history and culture in Western society.* Basingstoke: Macmillan.

Malin, Andrea 1994. 'Mother(s) Who Won't Disappear'. *Human Rights Quarterly* 16(1) February: 187–213.

Malinowski, Bronislav 1926. *Crime and Custom in Savage Society.* London: Routledge and Kegan Paul.

Mamdani, Mahmood 1996. 'Reconciliation Without Justice'. *South African Review of Books* Vol. 46. November/December. [http://www.uni-ulm.de/~rturrell/antho3html/Mamdani.html].

Manby, Bronwen 1992. 'South Africa: The Impact of Sanctions'. *Journal of International Affairs* 46, 1, Summer, 193–217.

Mann, Kristin and Richard Roberts (eds) 1991. *Law in Colonial Africa.* London: James Currey.

Marks, Monique 1993. *Identity and Violence amongst Activist Diepkloof Youth, 1984–1993.* MA thesis. University of the Witwatersrand.

Marshall, T. H. 1950. *Citizenship and Social Class and Other Essays.* Cambridge: Cambridge University Press.

Marx, Anthony 1992. *Lessons of the Struggle: South African internal opposition, 1960–1990.* Oxford, New York: Oxford University Press.

Mauss, Marcel 1988. *The Gift: Forms and functions of exchange in archaic societies.* London: Routledge.

Mayer, Phillip 1971. *Townsmen or Tribesmen? Conservatism and the process of urbanisation in a South African City*, second edition. Cape Town: Oxford University Press

McKenzie, Penny 1996. 'Political Pawns or Social Agents: A look at militarized youth in South Africa'. *Imbizo* 3:27–34. Community Peace Foundation.

McKinley, Dale T. 1997. *The ANC and the Liberation Struggle: A critical political biography.* London: Pluto Press.

Merry, Sally Engle 1988. 'Legal Pluralism'. *Law and Society Review* 22(5): 869–901.

—— 1990. *Getting Justice and Getting Even: Legal consciousness among working class Americans.* Chicago: University of Chicago Press.

Mignone, Emílio, Estlund, Cynthia C., and Issacharoff, Samuel 1984. 'Dictatorship on Trial: Prosecution of Human Rights Violations in Argentina'. *Yale Journal of International Law* 10(1):118–149.

Minow, Martha 1998. *Between Vengeance and Forgiveness: Facing history after genocide and mass violence.* Boston MA.: Beacon Press.

Moeller, Robert G. 1996. 'War Stories: The search for a usable past in the Federal Republic of Germany'. *American Historical Review* (October) Vol. 1008.

Moore, Sally Falk 1978. *Law as Process: An anthropological approach.* London: Routledge.

—— 1986. *Social Facts and Fabrications: 'Customary law on Kilimanjaro, 1880–1980'.* Cambridge: Cambridge University Press.

—— 1991. 'From Giving and Lending to Selling: Property transactions reflecting historical changes on Kilimanjaro'. In Mann, K. and R. Roberts (eds) *Law in Colonial Africa.* London: James Currey.

Morris, Brian 1987. *Anthropological Studies of Religion: An introductory text.* Cambridge: Cambridge University Press.

Mureinik, E. 1994. 'A bridge to where? Introducing the interim Bill of Rights'. *South African Journal on Human Rights* 10:31–48.

Neal, A. G. 1998. *National Trauma and Collective Memory: Major events in the American century.* New York and London: M. E. Sharpe.

Neier, Aryeh 1994. 'Establishing and Upholding the Rule of Law'. In Boraine, A. *Dealing with the Past.* Cape Town: Justice in Transition.

Newitt, Malyn D. D. 1995. 'Introduction' in M. Bennun and M. Newitt (eds) *Negotiating Justice: A new constitution for South Africa.* Exeter: University of Exeter Press.

Nietzsche, Friedrich 1969. *Thus Spoke Zarathustra,* trans. R. J.Hollingdale. London: Harmondsworth.

—— 1990. *Beyond Good and Evil.* London: Penguin.

Nino, Santiago Carlos 1985. 'The Human Rights Policy of the Argentine Constitutional Government: A Reply to Mignone, Estlund and Issacharoff'. *Yale Journal of International Law* 11: 217–230.

—— 1991. 'The Duty to Punish Past Abuses of Human Rights Put into Context: The case of Argentina'. *Yale Law Journal* 100. June, pp. 2619–2640.

Nolotshungu, Sam C. 1991. 'The constitutional question in South Africa'. In Shivji, I. G. (ed.) *State and Constitutionalism: An African debate.* Harare: Southern African Political Economy Series Trust.

Norman, Richard 1995. *Ethics, Killing and War.* Cambridge: Cambridge University Press.

Nozick, R. 1981. *Philosophical Explanations.* Cambridge, MA.: Harvard University Press

Nuttall, S. and C. Coetze 1998. *Negotiating the Past.* Cape Town: Oxford University Press.

Observer Review. 'Black Mischief'. 23 November 1997.

O'Donnell, G., and P. Schmitter (eds) 1986. *Transitions from Authoritarian Rule (Vol. 4): Tentative conclusions about uncertain democracies.* Baltimore: Johns Hopkins University Press.

Offe, Claus 1992. 'Coming to Terms with Past Injustices'. *Archives Européennes de Sociologie* 33(1):195–201.

—— 1993. 'Disqualification, Retribution, Restitution: Dilemmas of justice in post-Communist transitions'. *The Journal of Political Philosophy* 1(1):17–44.

—— 1996. *Varieties of Transition: The East European and East German experience.* Cambridge, MA.: Massachusetts: MIT Press.

O'Malley, Kieran 1994. 'A neglected dimension of nation-building in South Africa: The ethnic factor'. In Rhoodie, Nic and Ian Liebenberg (eds) *Democratic Nation-Building in South Africa.* Pretoria: HSRC Publishers.

Orentlicher, Diane 1991. 'Settling Accounts: The duty to prosecute human rights violations of a prior regime'. *Yale Law Journal* 100:2539–2615.

Osiel, Mark 1997. *Mass Atrocity, Collective Memory, and the Law.* New Brunswick and London: Transaction.

Outhwaite, William 1987. *New Philosophies of Social Science: Realism, hermeneutics and critical theory.* London: Macmillan.

Pampallis, John 1995. 'Building a Nation'. *Indicator South Africa* 12(3):23–28.

Panizza, Francisco 1995. 'Human Rights in the Processes of Transition and Consolidation of Democracy in Latin America'. *Political Studies* 43:168–188.

Parker, Peter 1996. 'The Politics of Indemnities, Truth Telling and Reconciliation in South Africa: ending apartheid without forgetting'. *Human Rights Law Journal* Vol. 17(1–2):1–13.

Parker, Peter and Joyce Mokhesi-Parker 1998. *In the Shadow of Sharpeville: Apartheid and criminal justice.* London: MacMillan.

Pashukanis, E. B. 1978. *Law and Marxism: A general theory*, trans. B. Einhorn. London: Ink Links.

Pauley, Matthew A. 1994. 'The Jurisprudence of Crime and Punishment from Plato to Hegel'. *American Journal of Jurisprudence* (39):97–152.

Pauw, B. A. 1990. 'Widows and Ritual Danger in Sotho and Tswana Communities'. *African Studies* 49(2): pp. 75–99.

Pavlich, George 1992. 'People's Courts, Postmodern Difference and Socialist Justice in South Africa'. *Social Justice* 19, 3.

Pearce, Jenny 1996. 'How Useful is Civil Society as a Conceptualisation of the Process of Democratisation with Reference to Latin America?' In Broadhead, Lee-Ann (ed.) *Issues in Peace Studies.* Bradford: Bradford University Peace Studies.

Poniatowska, Elena 1984. *La Noche de Tlatelolco.* Mexico City: Era.

Popkin, Margaret 1999. 'Latin American Amnesties in Comparative Perspective.' *Ethics and International Affairs.* 13:99–122.

Popkin, Margaret and Naomi Roht-Arriaza 1995. 'Truth as Justice: Investigatory commissions in Latin America'. *Law and Social Inquiry* 20(1):79–116.

Posel, Deborah 1999. 'The TRC Report: What kind of history? What kind of truth?' Paper presented at conference 'The TRC: Commissioning the Past' 11–14 June 1999, University of the Witwatersrand.

Price, Robert 1991. *The Apartheid State in Crisis: Political transformation in South Africa, 1975–1990.* Oxford, New York: Oxford University Press.

—— 1997. 'Race and Reconciliation in the New South Africa'. *Politics and Society* 25(2):149–178.

Promotion of National Unity and Reconciliation Act, Act No.34. 26 July, 1995. Cape Town: Republic of South Africa Government Gazette.

Ramphele, Mamphela 1996. 'Political Widowhood in South Africa: The embodiment of ambiguity'. *Daedalus* 125(1):99–117.

Recovery of the Historical Memory Project (REMHI) 1999. *Guatemala: Never Again!* London: Catholic Institute of International Relations and Latin America Bureau.

Renteln, Alison 1990. *International Human Rights: Universalism versus relativism.* London: Sage.

Report of the Chilean National Commission on Truth and Reconciliation. 1993. trans. Phillip E. Berryman.

Report of the Truth Commission, 1993. From Madness to Hope: The Twelve Year War in El Salvador, UN Security Council, UN Doc. S/25500.

Rex, J. and D. Mason (eds) 1986. *Theories of Race and Ethnic Relations.* Cambridge: Cambridge University Press.

Rhoodie, N. and J. Liebenberg (eds) 1994. *Democratic Nation-Building in South Africa.* Pretoria: HSRC Publications.

Rietzes, Maxine 1995. 'Insiders and Outsiders: The reconstruction of citizenship in South Africa'. Johannesburg: Centre for Policy Studies. Vol. 8, No. 1.

Roberts, Simon 1991. 'Tswana Government and Law in the Time of Seepapitso, 1910–1916'. In Mann, K. and R. Roberts (eds) *Law in Colonial Africa.* London, James Currey.

Roht-Arriaza, Naomi 1995. *Impunity and Human Rights in International Law and Practice.* Oxford: Oxford University Press.

Roht-Arriaza, Naomi and Lauren Gibson 1998. 'The Developing Jurisprudence on Amnesty'. *Human Rights Quarterly* 20(4):843–885.

Rorty, Richard 1993. 'Human Rights, Rationality and Sentimentality'. In Shute, Stephen and Susan Hurley (eds) *On Human Rights.* New York: Basic Books.

—— 1998. *Truth and Progress: Philosophical papers.* Cambridge: Cambridge University Press.

Rosenberg, Tina 1995. *The Haunted Land: Facing Europe's ghosts after communism.* New York: Vintage.

Ross, Fiona C. 1997. 'Blood-feuds and Childbirth: Reflections on the Truth and Reconciliation Commission'. *Track Two* Vol. 6 (3–4):7–10. Reproduced on the Internet at www.truth.org.za/tracktwo/.

Roth, Philip 1993. *Operation Shylock: A confession.* London: Simon and Schuster.

Rushdie, Salman 1994. 'Bosnia on my Mind'. *Index on Censorship* 1(2):16–20.

Rycroft, A. J., L. J. Boulle, M. K. Robertson and P. R. Spiller 1987. *Race and the Law in South Africa.* Cape Town: Juta.

Sachs, Wulf 1996. *Black Hamlet.* Baltimore: Johns Hopkins Press.

Santner, Eric 1992. 'History Beyond the Pleasure Principle'. In Friedlander, Saul (ed.) *Probing the Limits of Representation: Nazism and the Final Solution.* Cambridge, MA.: Harvard University Press.

Santos, Boaventura da Sousa 1995. *Toward a New Common Sense: Law, science and politics in the paradigmatic transition.* Routledge: New York.

Sarat, Austin 1997. 'Vengeance, Victims and the Identities of Law'. *Social and Legal Studies* 6(2):163–189.

Sarkin, Jeremy 1998. 'The Development of a Human Rights Culture in South Africa'. *Human Rights Quarterly* 20(3), August.

Scarry, Elaine 1985. *The Body in Pain: The making and unmaking of the world.* New York: Oxford University Press.

Schapera, Isaac 1938. *A Handbook of Tswana Law and Custom.* London: Oxford University Press.

Schärf, Wilfried 1997. *Specialist Courts and Community Courts.* Position Paper commissioned by the Planning Unit, S. A. Ministry of Justice, Pretoria.

Schärf, Wilfried and Baba Ngcokoto 1990. 'Images of Punishment in the People's Courts of Cape Town 1985–87'. In Manganyi, C. and A. Du Toit (eds) *Political Violence and the Struggle in South Africa.* London: Macmillan.

Scheper-Hughes, Nancy 1995. 'Who's the Killer? Popular Justice and Human Rights in a South African Squatter Camp'. *Social Justice* 22, 3, pp. 143–164.

Schirmer, Jennifer 1997. 'Universal and Sustainable Rights? Special tribunals in Guatemala'. In Wilson, Richard A. (ed.) *Human Rights, Culture and Context: Anthropological perspectives.* London: Pluto Press.

Scott, Alan 1991. 'Action, Movement and Intervention: Reflections on the sociology of Alain Touraine'. In *Canadian Review of Sociology and Anthropology* 1991 2(8):30–45.

Seekings, Jeremy 1995. 'Social Ordering and Control in South Africa's Black Townships: An historical overview of extra-state initiatives from the 1940s to the 1990s'. Paper presented at the South African Sociological Association, Rhodes University, 2–5 July.

Sharf, Michael 1999. 'The Amnesty Exception to the Jurisdiction of the International Criminal Court'. *Cornell International Law Journal* 32(3): 507–527.

Shaw, Mark 1993. 'Crying Peace Where There is None? The functioning and future of local peace committees under the National Peace Accord'. Transition Series: Report No. 31. Johannesburg: Centre for Policy Studies.

—— 1994. 'The Bloody Backdrop: Negotiating violence'. In Atkinson, D. and S. Friedman (eds) *The Small Miracle: South Africa's negotiated settlement.* South African Review 7. Johannesburg: Ravan Press, pp. 182–203.

Shivji, Issa G. 1991. *State and Constitutionalism: An African debate on democracy.* Harare: Southern African Political Economy Series Trust.

Shklar, Judith 1990. *The Faces of Injustice.* New Haven: Yale University Press.

Shubane, K. and P. Madiba 1992. 'The Struggle Continues? Civic associations in the transition'. Research Report No. 25, Johannesburg: Centre for Policy Studies.

Shubane, Khela and Mark Shaw 1993. 'Tomorrow's Foundations? Forums as the second level of a negotiated transition in South Africa'. Research Report No. 33, Johannesburg: Centre for Policy Studies.

Sieder, Rachel and Richard Wilson (eds) 1997. 'Negotiating Rights: The Guatemalan peace process'. *Accord: An International Review of Peace Initiatives* Issue 2. London: Conciliation Resources, published in Spanish translation in the journal *Cuadernos de Debate*, Dec. 1997, Facultad Latino Americano de Ciencias Sociales, Guatemala.

Simpson, Graham and J. Rauch. 1991. 'Review of Violence 1991'. Project of the study of violence. Psychology Department, University of the Witwatersrand, Johannesburg.

Simpson, Mark 1993. 'Nation-Building: A post-apartheid superglue?' *Indicator South Africa* 10(3):17–20.

Sisk, Timothy 1991. 'Constitutional Principles: Playing by the rules'. *Indicator South Africa* 9(1), Summer, 11–14.

Slaughter, Joseph 1997. 'A Question of Narration: The voice in international human rights law'. *Human Rights Quarterly* 19:406–430.

Smith, Nicholas 1995. 'Affirmative Action Under the New Constitution'. In *South African Journal on Human Rights* II(1):84–101.

Snyder, Francis 1981. 'Colonialism and Legal Form: the creation of "customary law" in Senegal'. *Journal of Legal Pluralism.* Vol. 19, pp. 49–90.

Solomos, John 1993. *Race and Racism in Contemporary Britain.* Basingstoke: Macmillan.

South African Institute of Race Relations 1998. *South Africa Survey.* SAIRR: Johannesburg.

Sowetan. 'Ribeiros' Son Wants Murderers to Hang'. 25 October 1997.

—— 'Priest Faces his Persecutors'. 30 October 1996.

Sparks, Allister 1996. *Tomorrow is Another Country: The inside story of South Africa's negotiated revolution.* London: Mandarin.

Stack, Louise 1997.. 'Courting Disaster? Justice and South Africa's New Democracy'. Transition Series. Johannesburg: Centre for Policy Studies.

Star. 'Vlakplaas Unit Armed and Trained IFP, says de Kock'. 16 September 1996.

—— 'De Kock's Chilling Who's Who'. 18 September 1996.

—— 'Mothers Want Son's Killer Executed'. 4 November 1996.

—— 'ANC, Tutu Resolve Amnesty Dispute'. 11 November 1996.

—— 'Shoe Thrown at Showing of Video at TRC'. 28 November 1996.

Stones, Rob 1996. *Sociological Reasoning: Towards a past-modern sociology.* London: Macmillan.

Strathern, Marilyn 1985. 'Discovering "Social Control"'. *Journal of Law and Society* 12(2):111–134.

Stuckless, N. and R. Goranson 1994. 'A selected bibliography of literature on revenge'. *Psychological Reports* Vol. 75, pp. 803–811.

Suarez-Orozco, Marcelo 1991. 'The heritage of enduring a "Dirty war": Psychosocial aspects of terror in Argentina, 1976–1988'. *Journal of Psychohistory* 18(4), Spring, pp. 469–505.

Sunday Independent. 'An Unholy Conference of Buffoons'. 5 January 1997.

—— 'Call to Stop Apartheid Prosecutions'. 26 July 1999.

Sunday Times. 'Vlok is Named On Secret Dirty Tricks Tape'. 5 March 1995.

Tamanaha, Brian Z. 1993. 'The Folly of the "Social Scientific" Concept of Legal Pluralism'. *Journal of Law and Society* 20(2):192–217.

—— 1997. *Realistic Social-Legal Theory: Pragmatism and a social theory of law.* New York: Oxford University Press.

Taussig, Michael 1987. *Shamanism, Colonialism and the Wild Man: A study in terror and healing.* Chicago: University of Chicago Press.

Taylor, Charles 1990. 'Rorty in the Epistemological Tradition'. In Alan Malachowski (ed.) *Reading Rorty.* Oxford: Blackwell.

—— 1995. *Philosophical Arguments.* Cambridge, Mass: Harvard University Press.

Taylor, Rupert 1991. 'The myth of ethnic division: Township conflict on the Reef'. *Race and Class* Vol. 33, No. 2.

Taylor, Rupert and Mark Shaw 1998. 'The Dying Days of Apartheid'. In Howarth, David R. and Aletta J. Norval (eds) *South Africa in Transition: New theoretical perspectives.* London: Macmillan.

Teubner, G. (ed.) 1997. *Global Law without a State.* Aldershot, UK: Dartmouth.

Thornton, Robert 1990. 'The Shooting at Uitenhage, South Africa, 1985: The context and interpretation of violence'. *American Ethnologist* 17:2: 217–236 May.

Thulare, Paul 1997. *Uniform Solution? The attempted assimilation of community defence units into the South African Police Service.* Transition Series. Vol. 10, No. 6. Centre for Policy Studies: Johannesburg

Touraine, Alain 1971. *The Post-Industrial Society. Tomorrow's social history: class, conflict and culture in programmed society*, trans. Leonard Fox Mayhew. New York: Random House.

—— 1995. *Critique of Modernity.* Oxford: Blackwell.

Truth and Reconciliation Commission South Africa, *Report.* Vols 1–5. 1998. Cape Town: Juta and Co. Also on Internet site http://www.struth.org.za/

Tucker, Aviezer 1999. 'Paranoids May be Prosecuted: Post-Totalitarian Retroactive Justice', *Archives Europeénes de Sociologie*, 40(1):56–112.

Turner, Bryan S. 1993. 'Outline of a Theory of Human Rights,' *Sociology* Vol. 27, No. 3, 489–512.

Turner, Victor. 1967 *The Forest of Symbols: Aspects of Ndembu ritual.* Ithaca NY: Cornell University Press.

Tutu, Desmond 1999. *No Future Without Forgiveness.* London: Rider Books.

Vaal Vision. 'Two Mbizo Members Sentenced'. 23 October 1998.

Van der Merwe, Hugo 1998. *The Truth and Reconciliation Commission and Community Reconciliation: An analysis of competing strategies and conceptualizations.* PhD dissertation, George Mason University, USA.

Van Gennep, Arnold 1960 (1908). *The Rites of Passage.* Chicago: University of Chicago Press.

Van Huyssteen, Elsa 1996. 'The South African Constitutional Court and the Death Penalty: Whose values?' *International Journal of the Sociology of Law* 24:291–311.

Van Onselen, Charles 1982. *Studies in the Social and Economic History of the Witwatersrand Vol. 2, New Nineveh.* Johannesburg: Ravan Press.

Vincent, Joan 1990. *Anthropology and Politics: Visions, traditions and trends.* Tucson: University of Arizona Press.

Waddington, P. A. J. 1992. 'The Police Response to, and Investigation of, Events in Boipatong on 17 June 1992'. Submission to the Commission of Inquiry Regarding the Prevention of Public Violence and Intimidation, the Hon. Mr Justice R. J. Goldstone, Chairman.

Walzer, Michael 1997. 'Judgment Days'. *New Republic* 15 December, pp. 13–14.

Weber, Max 1949. *The Methodology of the Social Sciences.* Shils, E. A. and H. A. Finch (eds) Glencoe: Free Press.

—— 1965. *The Sociology of Religion*, trans. E. Fischoff. London: Methuen.

—— 1976. *The Protestant Ethic and the Spirit of Capitalism*, trans. Talcott Parsons. London: George Allen and Unwin.

Weekend Star. 'Township in Grip of Kangaroo Court'. 8 April 1995.

Werle, Gerhard 1996. 'Without Truth no Reconciliation: The South African Rechsstaat and the Apartheid past'. *Law and Politics in Africa, Asia and Latin America* 29(1).

Weschler, Laurence 1990. *A Miracle, a Universe: Settling accounts with torturers.* New York: Pantheon.

—— 1992. 'The Velvet Purge: The trials of Jan Kavan'. *New Yorker* 19 October, pp. 66–96.

Wiechers, Marinus 1994. 'National Reconcilation through Legitimate State Institutions'. In Rhoodie, Nic and Ian Liebenberg (eds) *Democratic Nation-Building in South Africa.* Pretoria: HSRC Publishers.

Wilson, Richard A. 1995. 'Manufacturing Legitimacy: The Truth and Reconciliation Commission and the rule of law'. In *Indicator South Africa* December, pp. 41–46.

—— 1996. 'The *Sizwe* Will Not Go Away: The Truth and Reconciliation Commission, human rights and nation-building in South Africa'. *African Studies* 55(2):1–20, December.

—— (ed.) 1997a. *Human Rights, Culture and Context: Anthropological approaches.* London, Chicago: Pluto Press.

—— 1997b. *The People's Conscience? Civil groups, peace and justice in the South African and Guatemalan transitions.* London: Catholic Institute of International Relations.

—— 1997c. 'Comment on Charles R. Hale, "Consciousness, Violence and the Politics of Memory in Guatemala"'. *Current Anthropology* 38, 5, December pp. 817–838.

—— 2000. 'Reconciliation and Revenge in Post-Apartheid South Africa: Rethinking legal pluralism and human rights'. *Current Anthropology* 41, 1, February, pp. 75–98.

—— 2001. 'Justice and Legitimacy in the South African Transition'. In Aguilar, Paloma, Alexandra Barahona de Brito and Carmen Gonzalez (eds) *The Politics of Memory: Three Decades of Transitional Truth and Justice.* Oxford: Oxford University Press.

Zalaquett, José 1990. 'International Human Rights Symposium: Confronting Human Rights Violations Committed by Previous Regimes', *Hamline Law Review,* 13(3):623–660.

—— 1991. *The Ethics of Responsibility. Human Rights: Truth and Reconciliation in Chile.* Issues on Human Rights Paper 2. Washington DC: WOLA.

INDEX